THE GREAT PYRAMID

2590 BC onwards

COVER IMAGE: The south-eastern corner of the
Great Pyramid. *(Franck Monnier)*

First published in February 2019

A catalogue record for this book is available from the British Library.

ISBN 978 1 78521 216 1

Library of Congress control no. 2018938908

Published by Haynes Publishing,
Sparkford, Yeovil,
Somerset BA22 7JJ, UK.
Tel: 01963 440635
Int. tel: +44 1963 440635
Website: www.haynes.com

Haynes North America Inc.,
859 Lawrence Drive, Newbury Park,
California 91320, USA.

Printed in Malaysia.

Acknowledgements

The authors are extremely grateful to the
following people for help producing the
Great Pyramid Manual. For facilitating the
Haynes project: David Woods and Steve
Rendle. For editing and proofreading the
manuscript: Sandra Rosendahl, Lindsay
Lightbody and Tassie Geoffrey John. For
illustrations: AERA, Valery Androsov, Jon
Bodsworth, Patrick Chapuis, the Czech
Institute of Egyptology at Prague, Glen
Dash, Bruno Deslandes, Paolo Di Pasquale,
Sylvie Favre-Briant, Paul Francois, Rita
Freed, James Harrell, the IFAO, Yukinori
Kawae, Audran Labrousse, Michel Michel,
Michel Sancho, Procuratoria di San Marco
and Pierre Tallet.

THE GREAT PYRAMID

2590 BC onwards

Owners' Workshop Manual

An insight into the construction, meaning and exploration of the Great Pyramid of Giza

Franck Monnier and David Lightbody

Contents

7 Author profiles

7 Terminology and conventions

8 Introduction

10 Before the Great Pyramid

Neolithic origins	12
Predynastic culture	15
Political concepts of the early state	18
Administration and economy	22
Elevating the pharaoh's status through monumental architecture	23
Chronology of Khufu's reign	23
The development of the first pyramids	29
Snefru's great pyramids	36
Symbolic meanings	50

60 Description of the Great Pyramid

The mortuary temple	64
The causeway, the valley temple and the platform	65
The boat pits	68
The subsidiary pyramids	69
Cemeteries	76
The 'trial passages'	77
Was the great Sphinx and its temple a part of Khufu's tomb complex?	79
The Great Pyramid	81
Were changes made to the planned project during construction?	114

118 Building the Great Pyramid

Who built the Great Pyramid?	120
Raw material sources	123
Raw material processing	126
Transport by waterway	131
Overland transport	135
Elevation of the building elements	140
Mathematics	150
Astronomy	154
Engineering	159

162 Exploring the Great Pyramid

The first archaeologists	164
Legends and exploration in the Middle Ages	168
The Renaissance and the first scientific investigations	173
Early modern period	175
The archaeological era	178
Post-war and the high-tech era	184

196 Appendices

1 Chronology of Egyptian history	196
2 Language and script of the pyramid builders	198

199 Bibliography

200 Index

OPPOSITE Steep eastern face of the Great Pyramid, now devoid of the Tura casing stones that would have formed a continuous inclined surface.
(Franck Monnier)

Author profiles

In total, the authors have studied the architecture, archaeology and artwork of ancient Egypt for over 40 years. They are co-editors of the *Journal of Ancient Egyptian Architecture*.

Franck Monnier is an engineer based in France and is currently associate researcher at the CNRS, University of Paris I, Nanterre. He specialises in the study of ancient Egyptian architecture, including ancient Egyptian construction techniques. He is the author of several books and dozens of articles in this subject area. His main research fields are funerary and military architecture.

David Ian Lightbody holds a PhD in archaeology from the University of Glasgow in Scotland and a degree in engineering. He taught Egyptian history and a survey course on Egyptian temples at undergraduate level at the University of Glasgow. He has published several archaeological reports and academic articles relating to the architecture, technical systems and iconography used in the ancient world. He is currently based in Vermont in the USA.

TERMINOLOGY AND CONVENTIONS

The acronyms BC and AD are used throughout this work. Some writers have adopted the terms BCE and CE as an alternative nomenclature that attempts to be less Christian-centric; however, the alternative system is more complex to use and lacks some degree of clarity. The simpler and more common system is retained here.

Measurements are provided using the international metric system throughout, except when quoting from publications that used other systems, such as imperial feet and inches, or when it is likely that a structure being studied was built using multiples of ancient Egyptian cubits.

> 1 cubit = 7 palms = 28 digits
> 1 cubit = 0.5237 m = 20.62 inches
> with some margin of error dependent on the period and the application.
> 1 in = 2.54 cm.

There are often issues encountered when using English definitions to refer to ancient Egyptian people, and with translations of other words from the ancient Egyptian language. Before hieroglyphs were once again deciphered, names used by the ancient Greeks were widely adopted in English language publications. This is why the owner of the Great Pyramid is often referred to as *Cheops* in older publications. In this book, the more up-to-date translation *Khufu* is used throughout. This word is based on a translation of his name directly from the ancient Egyptian hieroglyphs.

The word pharaoh is used extensively in this book to refer to the ruler of Upper and Lower Egypt, as well as the term king. In fact, the term pharaoh was not used during the Old Kingdom. Similarly, the term king is a word from the English language that was never used in ancient Egypt, and the nature of the ancient Egyptian pharaonic system was significantly different to later systems of kingship. The English word pharaoh is specific to Egyptian dynastic rulers, and it invokes some of the peculiarities of that special political and religious ruling system.

OPPOSITE The authors. David Ian Lightbody (left) and Franck Monnier (right). Background image: A grove of date-palm trees by the Nile.
(Franck Monnier)

Introduction

BELOW The basalt pavement of Khufu's mortuary temple on the east side of the Great Pyramid. *(David Ian Lightbody)*

The Great Pyramid of Giza near Cairo in Egypt is one of the greatest iconic works of human culture. It was the world's tallest monument for nearly 4,000 years, and it remains one of mankind's greatest architectural achievements. As ancient as Stonehenge and the ziggurats of Mesopotamia, it dwarfs them with its mountain of stone. Until the 19th century, it was also the heaviest structure ever built, at nearly five million tons. The levels of precision used to construct it were no less impressive. It was not until the 19th century that scientists devised equipment able to measure how precise the ancient engineering accomplishments really were, and it remains a challenge to determine the full capabilities of those who built it. Its amazing characteristics have inspired a range of scientific theories, as well as less fact-based speculation regarding how it might have been done.

The Great Pyramid is often seen as representing the zenith of ancient Egyptian culture, but it was built relatively close to the beginning of pharaonic history. The reasons for that rapid ascent are investigated in the chapters that follow. The Great Pyramid was not, however, isolated either geographically or historically. It was the central component of a huge funerary complex called Akhet Khufu, 'Khufu's Horizon' by the ancient Egyptians, and it was part of an ongoing tradition of royal tomb construction. It was the ultimate expression of an ideology whereby the pharaoh was the living earthly manifestation of a sky god, the falcon called Horus. He was thought to appear as the solar deity Re-Horakhty on the eastern horizon every morning, and to travel across the sky through the course of the day. The pharaohs who followed this ideology ruled during the glorious 4th dynasty and developed a culture that became a shining light in human history.

The ramifications of their achievements ran deep and wide through the centuries that followed. As the pharaonic era declined, the pyramids remained, like eternal shadows cast by that intense burst of creativity.

There was a darker side to the pyramid projects, however, that is not so apparent in the historical records. The pharaonic regime diverted all the state's resources towards a

monumental project intended to glorify one king. In order to support these huge projects, thousands of Egyptians were coerced into leaving their homes every year, and the majority of the work was undoubtedly gruelling.

During an intense phase of activity, which accelerated towards the end of the 3rd dynasty and which reached its peak during the 4th dynasty, the pharaonic culture developed unprecedented technical abilities and produced unsurpassable monuments. In this book, those monuments are reverse-engineered. Their architecture is described, and illustrated, using the latest evidence and the best available scholarship. This publication offers the most up-to-date description of the Great Pyramid and includes a discussion of current theories regarding its unusual internal layout. Finally, the history of all those who have explored the monument over the centuries is chronicled, from the accounts of the first explorers to the high-tech research projects carried out from the 1960s onwards.

The Great Pyramid remains as the largest, oldest and only surviving Wonder of the Ancient World. It undoubtedly ranks among the greatest cultural legacies of human history. A list of those who have visited it over recent centuries includes Napoléon Bonaparte, Winston Churchill and Barack Obama. It is very likely that Ramesses the Great, Alexander the Great, Cleopatra and Julius Caesar also saw the monuments at Giza when they ruled and travelled through Egypt more than 2,000 years ago.

The Memphite Necropolis is now a UNESCO world heritage site, and the Great Pyramid is the foremost monument overseen by the Egyptian Ministry of State for Antiquities. In many respects, however, the Great Pyramid belongs to everyone who has visited it, studied it and dreamed about exploring it someday.

ABOVE The Great Pyramid. Wonder of the ancient world.
(Franck Monnier)

'Akhet Khufu': Khufu's Horizon.
The Great Pyramid's original name.

Chapter One

Before the Great Pyramid

The Great Pyramid was the end result of a millennium of cultural, political and technical development. The pharaonic system had its roots in Upper Egypt, but soon controlled the entire lower Nile valley, all the way to the Mediterranean Sea. An architectural tradition evolved on these social foundations. It resulted in a sequence of exceptional monuments, and eventually led to the creation of the giant pyramids.

OPPOSITE The Step Pyramid and the *heb sed* court of Djoser at Saqqara. *(Franck Monnier)*

Neolithic origins

In order to understand why the great pyramids developed in Old Kingdom Egypt, it is necessary to appreciate the broader context that made the construction of these giant monuments possible. The fundamental factors were: Egypt's natural environment, the culture that developed there, and the economic and political systems that grew out of that culture. Only once these issues are understood can the specific historical events that occurred there, and the remarkable monumental architecture that developed, make good sense.

Neolithic Egypt's natural environment is dominated by the world's longest river. The Nile is supplied by two main tributaries; the Blue Nile, which draws seasonal rain falling in the mountains of Ethiopia, and the White Nile, which flows from Lake Victoria far to the south and then through the great wetlands of the Sudan. Once the tributaries join, the river flows north across the eastern edge of the Sahara Desert, through the territory that is today referred to as Egypt. Rain falls seasonally in the south, peaking in the summer months, and while there is little rain in Egypt itself, the flood waters that come down the valley once covered the flat lands around the river during the inundation season, leaving a thick layer of fertile silt behind. Steep desert cliffs overlook the Nile floodplain from the west and east. Further downstream, the wide Delta region also turned to marshlands during the inundation, and it took several months for the waters to subside and flow away north to the shores of the Mediterranean Sea.

During the Neolithic Subpluvial period, however, the climate became wetter and the East Sahara was turned into a savannah grassland. The hunter-gatherers of the Nile valley slowly developed into semi-nomadic pastoralists. They began tending herds of domesticated cattle, as well as goats and sheep, and travelling long distances over the grasslands on a seasonal basis. The rock art scenes they left behind are still visible at many outcrops in the Sahara today. They primarily depict cattle, but also scenes of abundant wildlife such as giraffes, flamingos, elephants and other now exotic species. Thanks to the increased rainfall, populations of animals and humans grew rapidly for around 2,000 years. Then the climate began to dry out again. The downturn in rainfall seems to have caused a gradual movement of people and their

livestock back to the Nile valley, which was more resistant to the effects of drought thanks to the river.

The constant supply of fresh Nile water and the annual influx of natural fertiliser meant that people in Egypt were ideally placed to benefit from the agricultural revolution that took place during the Neolithic Period, across the Fertile Crescent. New food production practices based on grain cultivation spread from upper Mesopotamia, through the Levant, and eventually into Egypt, from around 6500 to 6000 BC. The earliest evidence of agriculture comes from sites in the Delta and around the Faiyum, and over time the new practices spread south and were mixed with those already used by the pastoralists moving into Upper Egypt. The silt deposited by the Nile turned the soil black, and this is believed to be the reason that the Egyptians referred to their fertile land as *kemet*, the black land. Livestock husbandry began to be supplemented with sedentary grain agriculture, and bread became the dietary staple of the Egyptian people for the first time.

The Neolithic Subpluvial ended with the '5.9 kiloyear' drought event, named after the number of years before the present day when it happened. A new era of more arid conditions prevailed in the Sahara. Rains continued to fall in the distant south, which sustained the annual inundations, and over the northern parts of Egypt during the winter. Increasing numbers of nomads arrived in the Nile valley as the Sahara dried out, and the rising populations led to the development of the first substantial settlements.

BELOW The Nile carries an enormous volume of fresh water and silt through Egypt, which would otherwise be a desert landscape due to low levels of rainfall. This image shows the National Ferry at Luxor, which shuttles locals and tourists across the wide river channel. *(Franck Monnier)*

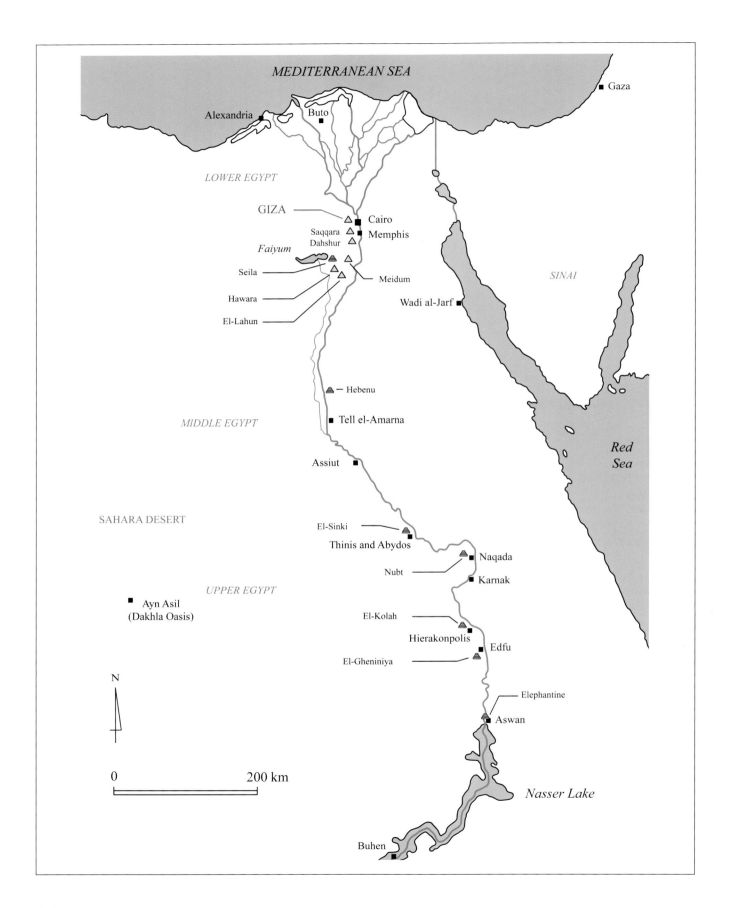

MEDITERRANEAN SEA

Gaza

Alexandria

Buto

LOWER EGYPT

GIZA

Cairo

Saqqara
Dahshur

Memphis

Faiyum

SINAI

Seila

Meidum

Hawara

El-Lahun

Wadi al-Jarf

Hebenu

MIDDLE EGYPT

Tell el-Amarna

Red
Sea

Assiut

SAHARA DESERT

El-Sinki

Thinis and Abydos

Naqada

Nubt

UPPER EGYPT

Karnak

Ayn Asil
(Dakhla Oasis)

El-Kolah

Hierakonpolis

Edfu

El-Gheniniya

N

Elephantine

Aswan

0   200 km

Nasser Lake

Buhen

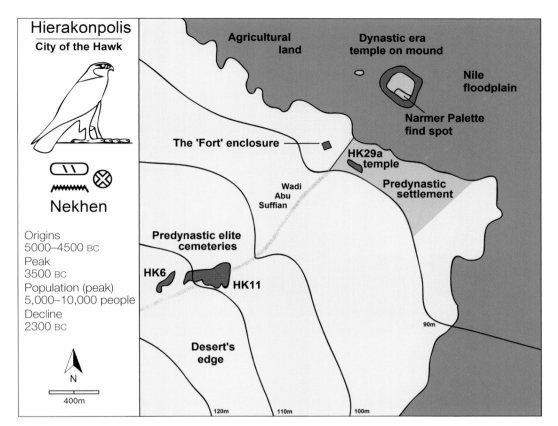

Hierakonpolis
City of the Hawk

Nekhen

Origins
5000–4500 BC
Peak
3500 BC
Population (peak)
5,000–10,000 people
Decline
2300 BC

N
400m

Agricultural land

Dynastic era temple on mound

Nile floodplain

Narmer Palette find spot

The 'Fort' enclosure

HK29a temple

Predynastic settlement

Wadi Abu Suffian

Predynastic elite cemeteries

HK6

HK11

Desert's edge

90m

120m   110m   100m

OPPOSITE Overview map showing the locations of sites mentioned in the text. *(Franck Monnier)*

LEFT Map of the early monumental cemetery on the desert edge near Hierakonpolis. *(David Ian Lightbody)*

Predynastic culture

The traditional vegetable and animal food products, from domesticated animals, hunting, fishing and gathering practices, were increasingly supplemented with cultivated grain products, including breads. Beer is also made from grain, and large breweries have been uncovered in predynastic settlements. These new products underpinned the growth of urban areas and the development of an economy in the Nile valley.

In turn, increasing population pressure appears to have led to a degree of conflict between neighbouring communities. The earliest mudbrick fortification walls surrounding settlements probably date to the end of the Naqada I period, around 3500 BC, and archaeological remains of walls indicate that they became more common towards the end of the predynastic era, around 3000 BC.

During the Predynastic Period, a number of significant cultural changes took place in the valley that set the scene for the start of the pharaonic era. The foundations of the pharaonic culture that became so prominent over many centuries were laid down, including the belief system that underpinned it.

Histories of the Great Pyramid age have traditionally traced the origins of pharaonic tomb architecture back to the tombs of the rulers of the 1st dynasty at Abydos, but in the last quarter of a century a settlement has slowly been uncovered in Upper Egypt that has been called the birthplace of 'the first Egyptians'. The predynastic town of Hierakonpolis had been identified at least a century ago, but intensive excavations led by Michael Hoffmann and Barbara Adams began only in the 1970s, and work continues today under the direction of Renée Friedman. Many of the cultural developments made at Hierakonpolis seem to be precursors of the elements and concepts that made pharaonic Egypt such a distinctive culture for the next 3,000 years. To the ancient Egyptians, the settlement was known as Nekhen. The town existed from as early as 4500 to 4400 BC. At its height, around 3400 BC, Nekhen had at least 5,000 and possibly as many as 10,000 inhabitants, and most likely controlled the southern part of Upper Egypt as far as Nubia. At its peak, the town stretched for 2.5 km

ABOVE
Reconstruction
of tomb T23 in
Hierakonpolis
cemetery HK6,
possibly belonging to a
leader of Hierakonpolis
who identified with
the falcon god Horus.
(David Ian Lightbody)

along the edge of the desert, back almost 3 km into the wadi, and an unknown distance into the cultivated land. Clearly, it was one of the largest urban units on the Nile in its day.

A sophisticated tomb group lies in an area referred to as cemetery HK6, built 2 km into the desert west of Hierakonpolis. It constitutes, like Naqada (Nubt), one of the earliest known elite necropolises in Egyptian history. Like the pyramid-age tombs of the Memphite Necropolis, and most of the tombs of this period, the cemetery was built away from the fertile agricultural land, out into the hot, dry, western desert. This area of the desert towards the setting sun was part of 'the red land', the *desheret,* and became associated with the afterlife. Although this land-use pattern was not unique to Hierakonpolis, it may be one of the fundamental traditions handed down to the pharaonic culture.

Several tombs here were built around a rectilinear chamber cut into the bedrock. Some of the graves were lined with matting, and some were also lined with mudbrick walls. The deceased were laid to rest along with fine pots and figurines and the graves were covered over with low mounds of earth. The mounds were then surmounted with a wooden and reed superstructure, like a small rectilinear house. These were possibly decorated with red paint on the exteriors, and perhaps with more matting. Each structure was surrounded by a

wooden post-and-reed panel enclosure wall that may have designated a sacred area.

Within some of these enclosure walls are what appear to be 'subsidiary graves', indicating that the elite rulers may have taken some of their loyal followers with them to the afterlife. There is similar evidence from the 1st dynasty royal tombs at Abydos that has led some scholars to conclude that large-scale human sacrifice was carried out on the death of the ruler. It is unclear if this would have been a voluntary or involuntary practice, and some scholars have questioned this interpretation of the evidence. By the Old Kingdom, the tradition, if it existed, had been abandoned.

An elite predynastic grave at Hierakonpolis, referred to as T23, was found to be 5.5 m by 3.1 m. Four large postholes to each side of the grave indicate that substantial effort was invested in supporting a large superstructure, and additional postholes on the east side of the grave show that a separate offering chapel was originally associated with the burial. The entire T23 tomb complex was once surrounded by a post fence that marked off an area of 16 m by 9 m. This type of tomb constitutes a major step toward the monumental tombs later built in Abydos, and eventually towards those built in the Memphite Necropolis near Giza.

Elements of the design of these tombs and the artefacts they contained appear to be simple precursors of elements familiar from the majestic pharaonic culture that developed later. For example, the deceased were provided with facemasks for the afterlife, although made of clay rather than the gold and precious stones of later eras. Grid-shaped arrangements of postholes also indicate the locations of larger chapels constructed with acacia wood pillars. These structures were precursors of the hypostyle halls of the pharaonic era, and of the mortuary temples where pharaonic cult rituals were performed.

The tombs also contained many knapped flint figurines of animals, possibly representing the first zoomorphic gods and goddesses. Many exotic animals were also found buried alongside the deceased humans in the cemetery.

From the earliest times, the ancient Egyptians were astute observers of animal behaviour in their natural environment, and they often referenced what they observed when trying to express concepts in other domains, such as in religion or politics. The archaeologists working at Hierakonpolis have found evidence that the inhabitants kept their own zoo containing monkeys, wildcats, hippos and crocodiles. Of the 780 hieroglyphs later developed, 176 are images of animals or parts of animals. Their language was also suffused with zoological metaphors. Giraffe glyphs, for example, were used as determinatives for the word foresight, and the first pharaoh of all Egypt adopted the deep-swimming Nile catfish as his emblem.

It was the symbol of the falcon, however, an apex predator in the zoological hierarchy, that came to be used more generically to represent the ruler of Hierakonpolis, and eventually the ruler of the first unified Egyptian political system. This symbol was retained for almost the entire pharaonic period. The falcon was probably considered sacred all over ancient Egypt in early times, but it seems to have become emblematic of the rulers from the town of Nekhen in Upper Egypt. Hierakonpolis was a name given to the town in Greek times that means the city of the hawk. As the power of Hierakonpolis grew around 3500 BC, the falcon became associated with centralised rule from that town, and with the official ceremonial buildings constructed by the Hierakonpolitan dynasty.

Small carved stone figurines of falcons have

ABOVE Watercolour sketch of a peregrine falcon, painted by Egyptologist Howard Carter. Horus is typically depicted as a falcon of this species. (© Griffith Institute)

LEFT *Serekh* of pharaoh Djet of the 1st dynasty. This is on a stele (vertical slab) that once stood outside his tomb in Abydos. Horus, the patron god of the pharaohs, stands guard above. (Louvre Museum, photo: Franck Monnier)

been found in the elite predynastic tombs there, including what may be the earliest statue of the god Horus, and many fragmentary wings from these modelled falcons show that they were relatively common. All the evidence suggests that the symbolism of the falcon seen during the Old Kingdom at Giza originated at Hierakonpolis.

The first proven association between Horus and the proto-pharaohs dates to dynasty '0', the Protodynastic Period just before the start of the dynastic era, when many of the pharaonic traditions were already being set in place. An emblem called the *serekh*, meaning 'to display', first appeared at that time. It is a rectangular, stylised representation of a niched-façade enclosure wall or building that was closely associated with the god Horus. The falcon can often be found perched on top of the emblem. Most scholars believe that the *serekh* represented the pharaoh's palace, but some believe it represented the pharaoh's tomb, a funerary enclosure or a false door. Inside, the *serekh* is generally divided into an upper part, which can be occupied by the pharaoh's own name, and a lower part that is framed by vertical lines representing the distinctive palace façade niches. These projections decorated the exteriors of pharaonic ceremonial buildings. In the classical royal titulary, the *serekh* name is the first of the five titles, representing the so-called Horus name (or *Ka*-name) of the pharaoh.

The falcon rested vigilantly over the residence of the reigning monarch. It is a very direct symbol;

the palace from where the pharaoh commanded was a like microcosm of the whole state territory over which he presided. The palace was also under the god's protection. The pharaoh's name in the *serekh*-palace is, however, written below the falcon, with evident implications about the nature of early divine kingship.

Political concepts of the early state

The ancient Egyptians believed that a pharaoh called Menes, possibly also known as Narmer, was the first to unify and rule over all Egypt. His reign is usually taken to mark the beginning of the dynastic era and the Early Dynastic Period. Egyptologists have studied this phase of Egyptian history for many decades, and although there is evidence that the first pharaohs were extensively involved in military actions, current theories see gradual cultural exchange between the regions of Egypt and economic colonisation to have been forces as significant as physical combat.

Although the details of the events that unfolded in both Upper and Lower Egypt are still being debated, it is clear that by the start of the dynastic era, there was standardisation in the production of many objects, and economic transformations were taking place throughout Egypt. This common culture retained the emblems of Horus and the *serekh*.

Evidence uncovered by the Polish Archaeological Expedition from Tell el-Farkha in the eastern Nile Delta of Lower Egypt shows that a valuable trade in luxuries was in place with the Levant (the eastern Mediterranean coast) at the time, and that by 3200–3000 BC, breweries and mastaba tombs similar to those found in Upper Egyptian sites were being built in the Delta. Wine jar inscriptions of Irj-Hor show that the symbolism of Horus was also present there. *Serekhs* of Narmer and Ka have likewise been found in the Levant, indicating an expanded exchange network that supplied raw materials and exotic goods to the rulers based in Upper Egypt.

Narmer is most famously known through his representations on the Narmer Palette, a large ceremonial plaque carved from stone and decorated on both sides. It was excavated from the dynastic era temple on a mound near the edge of the cultivated land at Hierakonpolis, and dates to approximately 3100 BC. One of the most important iconographic aspects of this palette is that he wears two different distinctive crowns, one on either side of the palette. These crowns are almost identical to the two crowns known in later Egyptian history to represent the white crown of Upper Egypt (the *hedjet*) and the red crown of Lower Egypt (the *desheret*), and so for the first time one of the fundamental concepts of the pharaonic culture was emerging, one that represented the pharaoh's most important function within the early Egyptian state: keeping it united.

The Narmer Palette seems to celebrate the military victory of Upper Egypt over Lower Egypt, and while the real history may not have reflected such a simplistic event, the later Egyptians did perceive this unification as real history.

Many of the principal symbols of the newly founded Egyptian state reflected this unification, and the two crowns were soon merged together to form the double crown of Upper and Lower Egypt, the *sekhmenti* or 'two powerful ones'. A pharaoh called Djet of the 1st dynasty is the earliest known to be shown wearing this classic hybrid emblem.

Another of the fundamental emblems of the emerging state was the *sema-tawi* symbol, first seen inscribed on three jars recovered from Hierakonpolis. Its name literally means 'unite the two lands'.

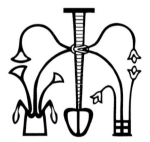

The *sema-tawi* motif was derived from three separate symbols. On either side are the emblematic plants of Upper and Lower Egypt, the lily and the papyrus reed. They are shown tied together around a central symbol that is thought to represent a heart and lungs with its windpipe attached. This central element forms the axis of the motif, and may represent both the pharaoh, as the heart who unites all Egypt, and

the Nile river, which is the channel that brings life to all Egypt in the form of fresh water. In the early examples, the motif is shown grasped by Horus's counterpart, the vulture goddess Nekhbet, who stands upon another emblem that became central to the Egyptian iconographic culture, the *shen* ring. There have been various theories as to what the glyphs inside the *shen* ring represent, but the most convincing suggest that they spell out the word 'rebels', and that the arrangement shows that the rebels have been encircled, contained and crushed. Already it seems that keeping the immense territory that was Egypt together under one ruler may not have been an easy task.

Other pairs of symbols represented this duality. The bee symbol of Upper Egypt and the sedge symbol of Lower Egypt were important motifs representing the pharaoh, while the vulture Nekhbet and the snake Wadjet were the two regional goddesses who protected the pharaoh as ruler of Upper and Lower Egypt. The *sema-tawi* symbol was later applied in important contexts at Giza. It appears on

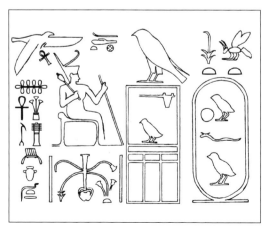

LEFT Symbolic arrangement interpreted as commemorating the crushing of rebels to maintain the unification of Egypt. The protective vulture goddess Nekhbet grasps the *sema-tawi* motif and faces the falcon Horus, who is wearing the white crown of Upper Egypt. *(David Ian Lightbody)*

LEFT Symbolic arrangement carved on the rock face at the quarry of Hatnub. Khufu sits on his throne over the *sema-tawi* motif. Horus flies above in eternal protection. *(David Ian Lightbody)*

the sides of stone thrones of the statues of pharaohs Khafre and Menkaure and would presumably have appeared on the sides of Khufu's thrones as well, although no major statues of Khufu have survived to prove this.

Another symbol to emerge from the Early Dynastic Period was the *heb sed* ritual. It remains unclear precisely what this was supposed to represent, other than the pharaoh's periodic physical renewal and fitness to rule Egypt, but elements of the ritual seem to express the specific concept that the pharaoh was the one keeping Egypt united. His encirclement of the territory as he ran around the cairns representing the extents of Egypt may have expressed his ability to keep the country bound together and unified under one state system. Horus the falcon often flies above, holding the *shen* ring, and in fact it seems likely that the Horus king's primary role in the Egyptian culture at the start of the pharaonic era was to keep Egypt united. Reliefs representing the *heb sed* ritual were most likely displayed prominently in most, if not all, of the pyramids of the Old Kingdom. Depictions clearly showing

the ritual have been found on artefacts and monuments attributable to Early Dynastic and Old Kingdom pharaohs, including Den, Djoser, Snefru and Niuserre.

A further important object, the Narmer Macehead, was recovered alongside the Narmer Palette in the dynastic era temple at Hierakonpolis. It depicts the pharaoh performing the *heb sed* ritual, and the arrangement is clearly a precursor of the scenes found in Old Kingdom pyramids. This artefact was probably made in late dynasty '0' or the early 1st dynasty, but what it shows is that key motifs of the early state, the *serekh*, Horus and the *heb sed* ritual, were in place at the start of the dynastic era and were certainly associated with Hierakonpolis.

Towards the end of dynasty '0', power in Upper Egypt seems to have consolidated around a town called Thinis, around 250 km downstream from Hierakonpolis. A cemetery at nearby Abydos, 1.5 km into the margins of the western desert in that area, had been in use since as far back as 4000 BC, and elite tombs were constructed there from around 3300 BC. One substantial multi-chambered mudbrick tomb, referred to as U-j, contained evidence of the earliest known phonetic writing. From the start of the dynastic era, the pharaohs of all Egypt who used the symbols of Horus and the *serekh,* were buried there. Manetho, the Greek historian, referred to Thinis as the first capital of all Egypt, before Memphis, and the elite cemetery at Abydos was probably the first pharaonic necropolis.

Closer to the edge of the agricultural land at Abydos are the remains of giant ritual enclosures, made of mudbrick and decorated with the palace façade motif. They were built, destroyed and reused, probably as part of ceremonies held at the time of each pharaoh's funeral. The exact function of these enclosures remains enigmatic. Australian Egyptologist David O'Connor studied the largest and only surviving one that belonged to the last pharaoh of the 2nd dynasty, Khasekhemwy, whose name means 'Horus, whose two powers appear'. The structure is now known as the Shunet el-Zebib, and after studying it, O'Connor concluded that encircling rituals, perhaps similar to those that might be expected during the *heb sed* ceremony, were held there. He reached this conclusion in part due to the existence of a double wall around the enclosure, which formed what might have been a ritual passageway surrounding the entire monument.

Administration and economy

During the 1st dynasty, when all Egypt was first united, the town of Memphis was established as the administrative capital of the new Egyptian state. It was situated far downstream from Hierakonpolis and Abydos, between the two major geographical regions of Egypt: the long, winding, fertile valley of Upper Egypt running to the south, flanked on both sides by steep desert mountains, and the wide, flat, fertile lands of the Egyptian Delta of Lower Egypt to the north, which was also flooded seasonally, forming marshlands as far as the eye could see. Settlements, including Memphis, were built on raised mounds that remained above the annual flood waters.

The pharaoh carried out regular tours of these immense territories, to gather information and also share it between his various representatives who ruled each *nome* region. These tours were called the 'Following of Horus' and incorporated one of the most fundamental tasks of the pharaoh's accounting trip, the biannual cattle count.

Careful management of cattle herds, grain production, allocation of land and taxation of surplus produce meant that the officials in the administration became important members of the emerging state, and by the early dynasties they were able to commission their own impressive mastaba tombs, so-called because they resemble the low wooden mastaba benches familiar from Egyptian homes. These tombs were built in an impressive row overlooking the new capital Memphis from the cliffs along the edge of the western desert. They were among the first major tombs to be built in the Memphite Necropolis. The mastabas were decorated with the same palace façade motif that the pharaohs themselves were using at Abydos and Hierakonpolis, in distant Upper Egypt.

The power of the members of the administration grew as they expanded the industrial-scale grain agriculture and

RIGHT Reconstruction of a classic palace façade as it would have appeared when newly painted.
(Franck Monnier)

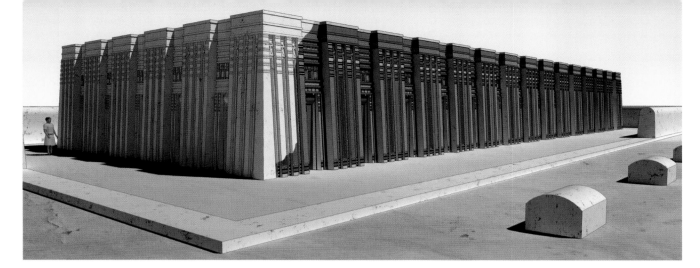

the complexity of the Egyptian state. This organisation provided more and more surplus grain for making bread and beer, and undoubtedly increased the power of these officials. It may have been for this reason that the pharaohs began to move elements of their own funerary monuments to the Memphite Necropolis.

Elevating the pharaoh's status through monumental architecture

Rituals that described the pharaoh as the primary force that kept Egypt unified were emphasised through iconography, the performance of rituals, and increasingly through the creation of monumental architecture that embodied this ideology.

At the end of the 2nd dynasty, it seems that the pharaohs began to build ritual enclosures using layouts similar to those already built at Abydos, out in the desert at Saqqara. The great enclosure known as the Gisr el-Mudir is the oldest known Egyptian structure built of stone. Recent excavation by Ian Mathieson's team from the National Museum of Scotland demonstrated that it was most likely built during the 2nd dynasty.

At the start of the 3rd dynasty, the pharaoh Djoser began building his extraordinary tomb, in an enclosure of unprecedented size, at Saqqara. Over time, and over several phases of construction, this evolved into the world's first pyramid. It was built in sight of the capital Memphis, and by the time it was finished it overshadowed the Early Dynastic tombs of his predecessors and the mastabas of the most powerful members of the administration.

At Saqqara, it seems that Djoser built a monument to highlight that his own role transcended the mundane world of the officials. It showed that he was a sacred leader who had inherited a divine right to rule, given by the ancient god Horus. Only the pharaoh could hold the two lands together, and only the pharaoh could perform the special rituals, immortalised within this monument, that ensured that this remained the case. The iconography used for the pharaoh was special and used discretely, extending only to his closest family members. Only the pharaoh was shown under Horus, providing eternal protection. The flying solar disc also appeared at that time. From then on, almost all the surplus energy produced by the state was redirected towards one end: feeding the workers who were to glorify and elevate the pharaoh through the erection of cult monuments of unprecedented dimensions.

Chronology of Khufu's reign

The Greco-Egyptian historian Manetho lived in the 3rd century BC and was the first to group and subdivide Egyptian history into the 30 dynasties that are still used today. Even if the actual historical events may not fit neatly into this chronological system, it remains a practical way for Egyptologists and historians to locate events and reigns on the historical timeline. Scholars of the 19th century then introduced a grouping of these dynasties into major periods which are, in chronological order: the Predynastic Period, the Early Dynastic Period, the Old Kingdom, the First Intermediate Period, the Middle Kingdom, the Second Intermediate Period, the New Kingdom, the Third

ABOVE

Reconstruction of an Early Dynastic mastaba tomb belonging to an official or member of the pharaoh's family.
(Franck Monnier)

Chronology of Egypt from Prehistory to the Protodynastic Period

Architecture

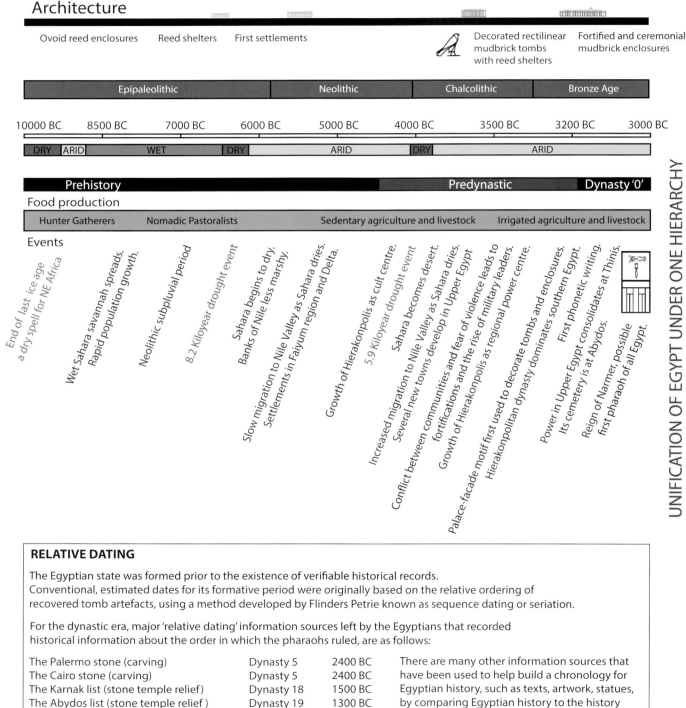

Ovoid reed enclosures   Reed shelters   First settlements   Decorated rectilinear mudbrick tombs with reed shelters   Fortified and ceremonial mudbrick enclosures

Epipaleolithic		Neolithic	Chalcolithic	Bronze Age

10000 BC	8500 BC	7000 BC	6000 BC	5000 BC	4000 BC	3500 BC	3200 BC	3000 BC

| DRY | ARID | WET | DRY | ARID | DRY | ARID |

Prehistory   Predynastic   Dynasty '0'

Food production

| Hunter Gatherers | Nomadic Pastoralists | Sedentary agriculture and livestock | Irrigated agriculture and livestock |

Events

End of last ice age a dry spell for NE Africa

Wet Sahara savannah spreads. Rapid population growth.

Neolithic subpluvial period

8.2 Kiloyear drought event

Sahara begins to dry. Banks of Nile less marshy.

Slow migration to Nile Valley as Sahara dries. Settlements in Faiyum region and Delta.

Growth of Hierakonpolis as cult centre.

5.9 Kiloyear drought event

Sahara becomes desert.

Increased migration to Nile Valley as Sahara dries. Several new towns develop in Upper Egypt

Conflict between communities and fear of violence leads to fortifications and the rise of military leaders.

Growth of Hierakonpolis as regional power centre.

Palace-facade motif first used to decorate tombs and enclosures. Hierakonpolitan dynasty dominates southern Egypt.

Power in Upper Egypt consolidates at Thinis. First phonetic writing. Its cemetery is at Abydos.

Reign of Narmer, possible first pharaoh of all Egypt.

UNIFICATION OF EGYPT UNDER ONE HIERARCHY

RELATIVE DATING

The Egyptian state was formed prior to the existence of verifiable historical records.
Conventional, estimated dates for its formative period were originally based on the relative ordering of recovered tomb artefacts, using a method developed by Flinders Petrie known as sequence dating or seriation.

For the dynastic era, major 'relative dating' information sources left by the Egyptians that recorded historical information about the order in which the pharaohs ruled, are as follows:

The Palermo stone (carving)	Dynasty 5	2400 BC	There are many other information sources that have been used to help build a chronology for Egyptian history, such as texts, artwork, statues, by comparing Egyptian history to the history of neighbouring states, and by dating recorded astronomical events.
The Cairo stone (carving)	Dynasty 5	2400 BC	
The Karnak list (stone temple relief)	Dynasty 18	1500 BC	
The Abydos list (stone temple relief)	Dynasty 19	1300 BC	
The Saqqara list (stone tomb relief)	Dynasty 19	1300 BC	
The Turin canon (on papyrus)	Dynasty 19	1300 BC	
Manetho's list (papyrus/stone)	Greek period	200 BC	

Chronology of Egypt from the Early Dynastic Period to the Old Kingdom

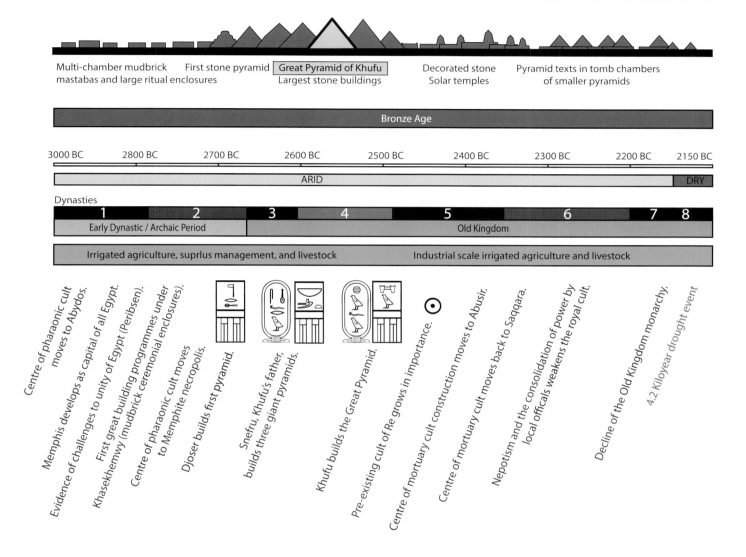

Multi-chamber mudbrick mastabas and large ritual enclosures

First stone pyramid

Great Pyramid of Khufu — Largest stone buildings

Decorated stone Solar temples

Pyramid texts in tomb chambers of smaller pyramids

Bronze Age

| 3000 BC | 2800 BC | 2700 BC | 2600 BC | 2500 BC | 2400 BC | 2300 BC | 2200 BC | 2150 BC |

ARID — DRY

Dynasties

1 | 2 | 3 | 4 | 5 | 6 | 7 | 8

Early Dynastic / Archaic Period — Old Kingdom

Irrigated agriculture, suprlus management, and livestock — Industrial scale irrigated agriculture and livestock

Centre of pharaonic cult moves to Abydos.

Memphis develops as capital of all Egypt.

Evidence of challenges to unity of Egypt (Peribsen).

First great building programmes under Khasekhemwy (mudbrick ceremonial enclosures).

Centre of pharaonic cult moves to Memphite necropolis.

Djoser builds first pyramid.

Snefru, Khufu's father, builds three giant pyramids.

Khufu builds the Great Pyramid.

Pre-existing cult of Re grows in importance.

Centre of mortuary cult construction moves to Abusir.

Centre of mortuary cult moves back to Saqqara.

Nepotism and the consolidation of power by local officals weakens the royal cult.

Decline of the Old Kingdom monarchy.

4.2 Kiloyear drought event

ABSOLUTE DATING tells how many solar-earth years ago something happened. This can be expressed using the BC/BCE system, or as a BP (Before Present) number. BP numbers are used here for the Kiloyear drought events shown in red, as this is the system typically used by scientists who use ice cores and sedimentary layer cores to date distant events. They may compare how much volcanic ash or vegetal matter was laid down each year, to measure climate changes, or examine disrupted rock structure to date catastrophic events.

A new, comprehensive, study of carbon 14 dates from ancient Egyptian artefacts was published in 2013. The new samples were all taken from biological materials in museum collections outside Egypt, including plant remains, hair, and bone. Levels of C14 in the artefacts were compared to known continuous sequences of C14 values derived from overlapping tree ring sequences taken from many wood samples from many regions. This system works because carbon levels in the atmosphere change on a global basis, and trees all grow one ring a year. All trees show similar tree-ring sequences over a given time period due to global climate variations. The C14 levels in rings from a particular year in those known sequences can then be measured and compared to those in artefacts.

Intermediate Period and finally the Late Period, which included several successive invasions of the country.

The 30-dynasty system ended around the time Manetho lived, which was just after the arrival of Alexander the Great in Egypt. Alexander took power over the country, signalling the start of the Hellenistic or Ptolemaic Period, which is why Manetho apparently wrote in Greek and is sometimes referred to as a Greek historian. This period is often extended and referred to as the Greco-Roman Period.

The reign of Khufu was relatively early in dynastic history, during the 4th dynasty of the Old Kingdom (approximately 2600–2500 BC). This absolute dating has been narrowed down with increasing degrees of accuracy over the years. Carbon 14 dating has been carried out on numerous samples taken from the Giza site. Meanwhile, an ancient text that refers to the latest known date during his reign indicates that he was on the throne for 27 years at most.

Khufu was the son of the pharaoh Snefru, who is remembered in Egyptian tradition as a good pharaoh, but the situation with Khufu himself is more ambiguous. A group of stories recorded on a papyrus now held in the Berlin Museum, referred to as the Westcar papyrus, describes Snefru as someone who enjoyed the pleasures of life but was close to his subjects. Khufu, on the other hand, is described as an unscrupulous and misguided ruler, seeking only to be entertained. He demands to know 'the number of chambers in the sanctuary of Thoth' for the benefit of his own funerary complex. This tale was written long after these pharaohs lived, at the earliest in the Middle Kingdom, but it is the only Egyptian document that relates to specific events that included Khufu, and so it may retain some information that was based on historic or remembered events.

Now Prince Hardedef stood up to speak and said: "So far you have heard examples of the skills of those who have passed away… But there is a subject of your majesty in your own time, unknown to you, who is a great magician." Said his majesty: "What is this about, Hardedef, my son?" Said Prince Hardedef: "There is a man named Djedi who lives in Djed-Snefru. He is a man of a hundred and ten years who eats five hundred loaves of bread, half an ox for meat, and drinks one hundred jugs of beer to this very day. He can join a severed head. He can make a lion walk behind him, its leash on the ground. And he knows the number of the secret chambers of the sanctuary of Thoth."

"Now his majesty Pharaoh Khufu had been spending time searching for the secret chambers of the sanctuary of Thoth in order to copy them for his 'Horizon'." Said his majesty: "You yourself, Hardedef, my son, shall bring him to me!" ... A goose was brought to him and its head was cut off. The goose was placed on the west side of the great hall, its head on the east side of the great hall. Djedi said his say of magic: the goose stood up and waddled, its head also. When one had reached the other, the goose stood cackling. Then he had a 'long-legged' bird brought to him, and the same was done to it. His majesty had an ox brought to him, and its head was cut off. Djedi said his say of magic, and the ox stood up. Then his majesty Pharaoh Khufu said: "It was also said that you know the number of the secret chambers of the sanctuary of Thoth." Said Djedi: "Please, I do not know their number, oh king, be alive, strong and healthy, my lord, but I know the place where it is." Said his majesty: "Where is that?" Said Djedi: "There is a chest of flint in the building called 'Inventory' in Iunu [Heliopolis]. It is in that chest." Said his majesty: "Go, bring it to me." Said Djedi: "King, my lord, it is not I who shall bring it to you." Said his majesty: "Who then will bring it to me?" Said Djedi: "It is the eldest of the three children who are in the womb of Ruddedet who will bring it to you." Said his majesty: "I want it; but say: who is this Ruddedet?" Said Djedi: "She is the wife of a priest of Re, lord of Sakhbu, who is pregnant with three children of Re, lord of Sakhbu. He has said concerning them that they will assume this beneficent office in this whole land, and the eldest of

them will be high priest in Iunu." (based on a translation from Miriam Lichteim's book, Ancient Egyptian Literature)

It has often been proposed that the reference to the 'secret chambers of the sanctuary of Thoth' reflected the pharaoh's obsession with endowing his own pyramid with similar rooms of special design, but other than the name there is nothing in the text to indicate the nature of these 'chambers', and nothing to say that they reference the plan of a pyramid. According to recent interpretations, this tale presents the pharaoh as an indecisive person, distracted by futile tricks more than by the search for the number of Thoth's chambers. Moreover, as the answer to his quest is denied to him, he remains in the dark. Djedi the magician predicts that his lineage will end with the advent of a ruler, the son of Re, and it is one of the sons of Ruddedet who will be responsible for revealing the knowledge he seeks. As the text has a mythological nature, specific architectural links with the design of Khufu's pyramid are unlikely.

The famous Greek historian Herodotus recorded that the Egyptians remembered Khufu as a tyrant who enslaved his people, and it is possible that an unflattering oral tradition gradually turned into a persistent hatred. In general, although his monument has ensured that he is not forgotten, there are too few historical or contemporary documents available to reconstruct even a basic picture of his reign or his personality with any degree of confidence. His legacy is certainly dominated by his funerary monument and his reign must have been dominated by the search for the mass of resources required to complete it. A few inscriptions bearing the name of Khufu have been found outside of Giza, for the most part near stone quarries and copper mines (at Hatnub, Gebel el-Asr, Wadi el-Maghara and Aswan), but the most numerous examples are found in his funerary complex.

The full extended set of the pharaoh's personal and ceremonial names is known as the royal titulary of the pharaoh. It comprised several parts that had different meanings: the Horus name was the oldest and was usually included in the *serekh* surmounted by the falcon deity; the golden Horus name was not contained

in a cartouche or *serekh*; the throne name or prenomen was encircled by a cartouche and preceded by the *nsw-bity* signs (the sedge and the bee representing Upper and Lower Egypt); and finally the Nebty name comprised the two goddesses of Upper and Lower Egypt, Nekhbet the vulture and Wadjet the snake. For Khufu, these names were, in the following order: Medjedu 'He who crushed enemies (for Horus)', Nebouy 'twice golden', Khufu (or Khnum-Khufu) 'He protects me' or 'Khnum protects me', and Medjeder 'He who crushes the enemies of the two ladies'. The most commonly found of these names is the one by which he is known today; Khufu. This name is also included in the name of his funerary complex, Akhet Khufu, which translates as 'The Horizon of Khufu'. In older Egyptology publications he is sometimes referred to as Cheops, a later corruption used by the Greeks for the pharaoh.

Because there are no ancient carved inscriptions or reliefs within the Great Pyramid, many amateur scholars questioned if it was actually built during the Old Kingdom at all. However, red-painted cartouches and informally painted names of teams of workers were left behind by the builders inside the pyramid. These were discovered in the early 19th century by the English explorers Howard Vyse and John Shae Perring in the so-called 'relieving chambers' above the King's Chamber. The authenticity of these too has been questioned, but some of them continue into joints between the monoliths, which would have made it extremely difficult to add them later on. In addition, the format of the team names matches perfectly with those written on the papyrus containing the Journal of Merer that was first uncovered in 2013. Finally, similar red-painted

ABOVE, RIGHT AND BELOW Fragments of reliefs dating to Khufu's reign that were reused in pyramid complexes at Lisht. *(Metropolitan Museum of Arts)*

inscriptions were found behind the so-called door in the Queen's Chamber's southern shaft, which was closed off completely until recently. When the evidence is taken together, there is little doubt that the inscriptions spelling out Khufu's name are authentic and were left behind by Khufu's builders.

A further indication has been found outside the pyramid testifying that Khufu was the builder of the monument: a cartouche found in the 1940s by the French Egyptologist Georges Goyon was also rendered in red ink. It was found at the level of the fourth layer of stone blocks on the west side, on the 71st stone from the north corner. Additionally, Egyptian archaeologist Selim Hassan cleared the foundations of the mortuary temple and the causeway linking it to the valley temple and recovered fragments of the reliefs that decorated the corridor and the temples. Fragments included a portion of Khufu's cartouche, an image of the pharaoh himself and a depiction of the *heb sed*, the ritual ceremony that symbolically demonstrated the pharaoh's ability to rule all Egypt, on earth and in the afterlife.

Other inscribed blocks from Khufu's complex were reused by the pharaohs of the 12th dynasty (Amenemhat I and Senwosret I) to adorn their own funerary temples. Some of those pieces also mention Khufu. Furthermore,

a mace head was discovered near Khufu's causeway, engraved with his Horus name. Finally, many of the tombs of the officials that were constructed close to the Great Pyramid are adorned with the name of Khufu on their walls, further attesting to the historical authenticity of the painted names found in the 'relieving chambers' of the Great Pyramid itself.

The development of the first pyramids

The first building that attained a pyramidal form of sorts was the Step Pyramid of pharaoh Djoser. It was built on the highest rise at the edge of the desert plateau at Saqqara, overlooking the capital Memphis from the west. The huge funerary complex immortalised

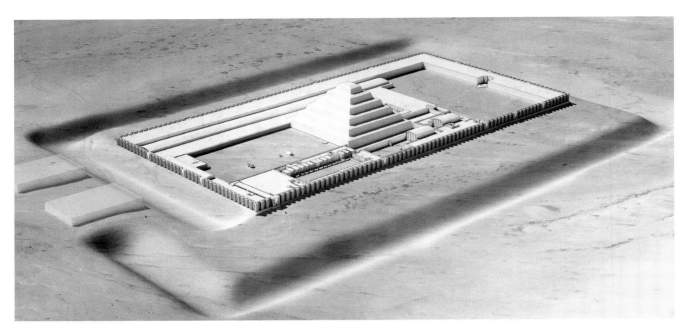

the memory of the first pharaoh of the 3rd
dynasty and is reputed to be the first Egyptian
monument built entirely of stone. A massive
enclosure wall surrounded the tomb and its
religious buildings. This monumental wall was
decorated with the traditional palace façade
niches all around its exterior faces. It was
1,645 m or nearly 3,141 cubits long and
covered an area of 15 hectares. The formidable
complex of buildings within it was a city for the
afterlife, a necropolis intended to ensure the
worship of the deceased pharaoh in perpetuity.
The rituals and ceremonies maintained there
ensured that he lived on in the afterlife.

The multi-talented architect Imhotep ensured
that the pharaoh's burial place dominated the
complex and overshadowed the tombs of his
predecessors and the mastabas of important
officials nearby, both in order of magnitude and
by inventing a unique new distinctive form for
the structure. Here, under the direction of the
brilliant architect, the first pyramid was born: a
colossal tomb the like of which had never been
seen before.

The pyramid is located near the centre
of the huge enclosure and initially took the
classical form of a mastaba. It was built on a
square base 63 m on each side and raised
to a height of 8.4 m using only rough blocks
of limestone. The innovative use of stone did
not immediately impact the appearance of the
structure, as it initially resembled the mastabas

and enclosures that had, until then, mostly been
built using mudbrick. At that stage the workers
began to excavate chambers and galleries
deep underground, and to dig a huge shaft into
which red granite monoliths were lowered so
that a burial chamber for the pharaoh could be
assembled at its bottom.

Outside the original mastaba, running along its
eastern side, were the now-covered entrances
to a series of 11 shafts that were sunk more
than 30 m down into the bedrock. At the bottom,
each connects with a horizontal chamber. The
initial phase of the superstructure had been
completed when the first of these subterranean
excavations were sunk, and some of the
chambers below were filled with vast quantities
of fine cut-stone vessels commemorating the
pharaoh and his predecessors. No less than
40,000 vessels made from a variety of stone
types were placed in these corridors. The
perimeter of the mastaba's base was then
enlarged by encircling it with an envelope 4 m
thick at the base using blocks of limestone
masonry laid in horizontal layers. In this way,
the area covered by the building was increased
to 71 m by 71 m. Afterwards, it was decided
to extend the structure further to the east by
adding another masonry wall 8.50 m thick
against the eastern face of the mastaba. Another
enlargement was then built using a new and
revolutionary technique for placing the masonry,
by adding thick external walls built upwards, but

LEFT The Step Pyramid in 2012, which was undergoing reconstruction work. (Franck Monnier)

with courses inclined towards the centre of the monument, with each wall leaning on the next and those in turn leaning on the existing structure at the centre of the layer.

Adding inclined walls and then additional layers in this way may have resulted in the creation of the first stepped pyramid, at that stage, although there is no way to verify that it was in fact completed. A final redesign that further enlarged the dimensions of the monument did result in the form that is still familiar today. The final stage consisted of increasing the area covered by the base of the monument, most notably towards the north and west, using limestone blocks around half a metre on each side, using inclined walls leaning against each other around the central core. Additional layers were added and enlarged using

BELOW Cutaway view of the Step Pyramid showing its subterranean tunnels and burial shaft, looking north-east. (Franck Monnier)

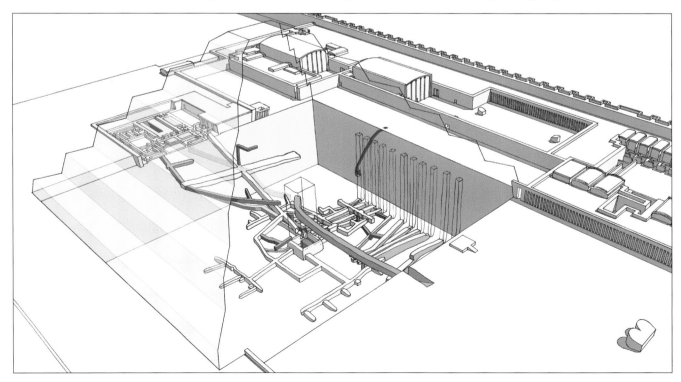

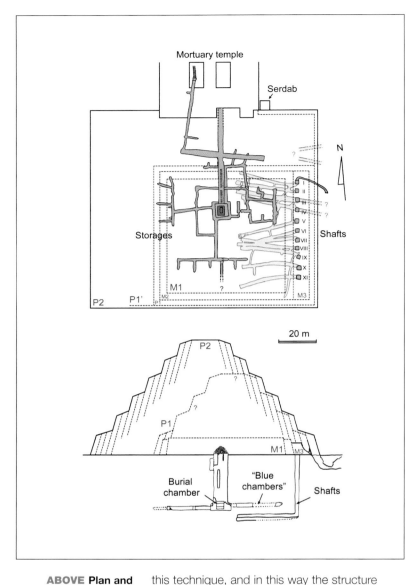

ABOVE Plan and section of Djoser's Step Pyramid showing the main subterranean chambers.
(Franck Monnier)

of six steps with a distinctive silhouette that is immediately recognisable today. The finished building was covered with a fine limestone cladding, although only a few scattered blocks of this now remain in situ. The monument finally covered a rectangular area 109 m from north to south by 121 m from east to west and rose to more than 60 m in height. In the context of the inherently conservative traditional forms used for dynastic funerary architecture, the pyramidal form used for Djoser's tomb must have represented a striking and unexpected development. The overall increase in size also meant that the superstructures created earlier in the project were no longer visible or accessible.

The hypogeum or underground funerary chambers of Djoser's complex comprise two distinct areas. An area dedicated to the pharaoh extends under the centre of the pyramid, and another area dedicated to the pharaoh's children and close family members lies to the east and just below this part of the pyramid. Eleven galleries are located on the eastern side, at a level below that of the funerary apartments of the ruler which lie around 33 m below ground level. While the walls of the storage magazines were left roughly finished, the walls of the rooms on the east side of the burial chambers were partially dressed with carefully fitted limestone blocks and decorated with inlaid tiles of green and blue faience, a type of artificial ceramic coloured with copper ores. German Egyptologist Karl Richard Lepsius removed one inscribed door frame encrusted with the faience tiles from these rooms in order to display it in the Berlin Museum. In total, there are four decorated rooms. All of them were adorned with wall decoration imitating the reed wickerwork that would have ornamented the pharaoh's palaces, but here made up from numerous faience tiles. They are ingeniously embedded into the walls and are fixed there using a mortar that holds cords that were threaded through perforations in tenons protruding from the reverse of the tiles.

An analysis of the decorated reliefs in the two easternmost rooms showed that each of them was prefabricated outside the pyramid before being brought underground in one piece. These tiled reliefs comprise panels containing hundreds of rows and columns of the faience pieces,

this technique, and in this way the structure was raised into a stepped pyramid with six major layers of regularly decreasing sizes. The superstructures of the unfinished pyramids of Sekhemkhet at Saqqara and the surviving layers at Zawiyet el-Aryan, which were built using the same method, show that the pyramidal form was not created by expanding out from a tall core at the centre, but by laying a sequence of horizontal layers from the bottom to the top.

The protrusion of each step towards the sides was created with two different leaning wall-layers of masonry, with an outer wall leaning against an inner and both inclined towards the centre of the structure. These inclined outer slices are still discernible in the masonry today. Altogether, the structure formed a staircase with some of them surmounted by further tiles arranged in arched forms that are depicted as supported by rows of *djed* pillars. The most significant part of the decorated corridors is, however, a chamber containing three relief scenes sunk into false doorways within the walls. The reliefs imitate statues or stelae of the pharaoh and show him in the act of performing the *heb sed* rituals. These are sunk into the doorways or alcoves, which are surrounded by finely decorated frames. The vertical sides of the frames are adorned with columns of the pharaoh's name in *serekhs*, perhaps alluding to the palace façade walls encircling the pharaoh's monument and the ceremonial courtyard above.

Three of these alcoves or false doors are aligned along a short corridor or chamber running north–south under the main pyramid. To the south of the main complex, near the southern wall of the main enclosure, is another deep shaft that leads down to a secondary burial chamber known as the 'south tomb', again around 33 m below ground level, the purpose of which remains unclear. A short corridor near this southern tomb contains another three of these false sunken doorways containing reliefs showing the pharaoh performing the *heb sed* ritual. All six of these scenes are carved in low raised relief and show the pharaoh performing various ceremonies, or parts of a single ceremony. Analysis of a survey of the monument by American Egyptologist and art historian Florence Friedman has demonstrated that these two short corridors are actually aligned with each other, despite the fact they are almost 200 m apart, and it is likely that all six scenes relate to one ritual that included several components.

Furthermore, in the last decade, a Latvian scientific expedition led by French architect Bruno Deslandes has detected evidence indicating the existence of previously unknown long corridors under the pyramid, including one that seems to link the subterranean complex in the north to the smaller subterranean complex under the south tomb.

This *sed* festival ritual, or *heb sed*, seems to have been the most ancient and fundamental of all the pharaonic rituals. In this ceremony, the pharaoh ran around northern and southern bollards representing the northern and southern extents of Egypt. In this way,

ABOVE The entrance colonnade to Djoser's Step Pyramid complex. The roof was supported by ribbed stone columns representing bundles of reeds. *(Franck Monnier)*

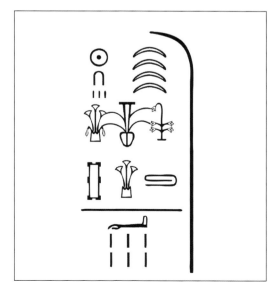

LEFT The Palermo stone records a unification ritual performed on the 13th day of the fourth month, during the reign of the 1st dynasty pharaoh, Djer. *(David Ian Lightbody)*

RIGHT The statue of Djoser as it would have appeared through the holes cut in the north side of his *serdab* shrine, on the north side of the pyramid.
(Franck Monnier)

door, in order to encircle the walls outside. This would mirror the rituals recorded on the Palermo Stone and elsewhere in which the pharaoh performed ritual runs around the walls of the palaces and towns of his territory, such as Memphis, the city called 'White Walls'.

Stars on the ceilings of the burial chambers of the Step Pyramid complex suggest that the underground chambers were also associated with the heavens above, and in this context it is notable that Geb, the Egyptian god of the earth, and Nut, the Egyptian goddess of the sky and heavens above, were considered to be brother and sister. These scenes thus represent the rites that Djoser had to carry out for eternity, in the world of the afterlife, above in the sky (*pet/ Nut*) and below in the ground (Nun/Geb). The cardinal alignment of the whole complex, whose north–south axis deviates only a few degrees from true north, also indicates a desire to align and associate the complex, and by extension the pharaoh who was to be buried there, with the heavens above.

The only useable entrance to the funerary enclosure is a door located near the south-east corner of the complex. It opens into a corridor that cuts right through the massive exterior wall and then steers through a magnificent colonnade that leads west and opens directly into the huge southern courtyard, which contains the 'B'-shaped bollards.

Another long open-air space running north–south is located within the complex, to the east of the southern courtyard. It contains a series of adjoining monumental chapels that were built out of solid stone and were therefore inaccessible. Each of them incorporates a small courtyard and a stone staircase leading to a statue niche, although the statues, which may have represented the gods and goddesses of each region (nome) of Egypt, are now lost. In front of this row of chapels at the southern end of this *heb sed* court is a stone platform with a double staircase leading up to it on which a throne or a pair of thrones would have been placed. Representations of this royal kiosk show it used in the *heb sed* ceremony and it was represented many times on jar labels of the period and in later reliefs that show the pharaoh sitting back to back with himself, wearing the crowns of Upper and Lower Egypt, one

he would symbolically unite Upper and Lower Egypt, demonstrate his fitness to achieve this feat and take possession of the territory he had encircled. Two huge double half-moon or 'B'-shaped bollards were placed at the northern and southern ends of the open courtyard above. They resemble the icons positioned behind the feet of the pharaoh shown in the reliefs, so that it seems the whole complex, above and below, was intended to represent or be used for this one ritual, either in reality or symbolically in the afterlife.

Friedman notes that the corridors are also aligned with a false door designed into the southern face of the main enclosure wall, and she suspects the pharaoh was also understood to leave the complex symbolically through this

BELOW
Reconstructed shrine with an arched roof in the pyramid complex of Djoser at Saqqara.
(Franck Monnier)

on each throne. The theme of the unification of Upper and Lower Egypt is evident in this courtyard, as it is throughout the complex.

To the north of this courtyard are two large rectangular stone buildings with vaulted roofs that dominate the north-eastern corner of the complex. The southern one is positioned in front of the northern building, but they are offset and both open onto their own small courtyards. They are sometimes referred to as the houses of the north and south, although there is no real evidence to suggest such a designation. The latest research conclusions reached by the Latvian mission are they may in fact have been funerary chapels for two of Djoser's daughters.

The main mortuary temple for the Step Pyramid was attached to its north face, unlike the arrangement from the 4th dynasty onwards when mortuary temples were placed against the eastern faces of the pyramids. A small, closed building containing a life-sized statue of the pharaoh was attached to this temple, on the eastern side of the entrance passage leading into the pyramid. It is referred to as a *serdab*; a small funerary chapel where libations and ritual foods could be offered to a statue of the deceased. A pair of circular holes drilled in the northern wall of the chapel at the level of the statue's eyes allowed the deceased to enjoy the offerings that were brought to him on a daily basis.

The entire *serdab* chamber is inclined back towards the south, possibly to allow the pharaoh to view the circumpolar stars at night through the holes. The priests of the pharaoh's cult would have presented themselves in front of this representation of the deified ruler, left their offerings outside, and dedicated their prayers to the eternal memory of the pharaoh. They would then have departed through the maze of corridors that ran through the mortuary temple, censing and cleaning the space to maintain its ritual purity as they went, until they reached two central courtyards flanked by engaged, fluted columns.

Djoser demonstrated architectural ambitions well beyond those of his predecessors. By utilising the skills of Imhotep, high priest of Heliopolis, and by mobilising a workforce capable of creating a structure of this magnitude built entirely of cut stone, he ensured that his memory transcended the mundane. On the day of his burial, the visual and symbolic impact of this architectural jewel must have been striking. The palace façade walls would have dazzled with white polished limestone and created a bright cut across the red desert landscape, overlooking the green fields of the Nile valley and the walls of Memphis below. The cult buildings were lavishly painted and the lively colours would have brought the stone elements to life. Fluted and ribbed columns, like bundles of reeds with palmiform capitals at the top, supported walls decorated like

LEFT Fragmented statue of Snefru wearing the white crown. *(Cairo Museum, photo: Franck Monnier)*

coloured matting, giving the illusion of life to the pharaoh's petrified domain.

Djoser's immediate successors attempted similar pyramid building projects during their reigns, but no other pharaoh of the 3rd dynasty managed to match or even come close to completing a monument that rivalled his architectural feats. All of them died prematurely, leaving largely unfinished buildings behind. It was not until the advent of the 4th dynasty and the coronation of Snefru that pyramid construction projects rivalling Djoser's achievements were finally commenced.

Snefru's great pyramids

The Meidum Pyramid

For reasons that remain under discussion, Snefru completed three great pyramids: one at Meidum, more than 60 km south of Giza, and two at Dahshur, approximately 20 km south of Giza. Like their predecessor at Saqqara, all three were built on the west bank of the Nile and on the edge of the Sahara Desert. Snefru was undoubtedly the most ambitious builder of the ancient world since his three large pyramids employed a volume of quarried stones amounting to nearly 3.9 million cubic metres. The first pyramid, now known as the False or Collapsed Pyramid, was built at Meidum near the entrance to the Faiyum, approximately 45 km south of the ancient capital Memphis. The other two, the Bent Pyramid of Dahshur-South and the Red Pyramid of Dahshur-North, were built closer to Memphis, although still 8 km south of the capital and Djoser's Pyramid at Saqqara. The Meidum complex was very different to those of the previous dynasty, as the pyramid became an even more prominent part of the complex, while the enclosure walls and subsidiary buildings were reduced in scale. Today the pyramid is partially destroyed and part of its internal core is clearly visible. The cult buildings, varied and numerous in Djoser's complex, appeared at Meidum in a simplified form and reduced in number, down to a single chapel adjoining the centre of the eastern face of the pyramid. Although small, the structure represents the first of the prototypical mortuary temples that became more prominent throughout the 4th dynasty.

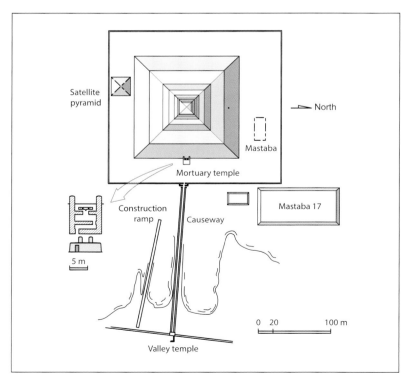

Satellite pyramid

North

Mastaba

Mortuary temple

Construction ramp

Causeway

Mastaba 17

5 m

0 20   100 m

Valley temple

The chapel stands at the centre of the pyramid's east side. After entering the building, it is necessary to negotiate four right-angled turns as the short passage doubles back on itself, before a door opens out onto a small open-air courtyard containing an offering table sitting between two tall monolithic stelae with rounded tops. A few small Old Kingdom figurines representing Horus were recovered from this area by English Egyptologist Flinders Petrie as the chapel was being excavated from the rubble around the collapsed monument.

The stelae were left blank with finely finished surfaces. They may have been designed to display iconography commemorating and celebrating the ruler, but this was never started. The structure was completed, but not decorated in any way. Despite the unadorned walls and blank stelae, the temple was similar to the mortuary temple later constructed for the Bent Pyramid at Dahshur-South, which contained finely carved stelae described below. The chapel and the main pyramid stood within a wide stone enclosure wall almost 2 m in height, which created a sacred space around the pyramid. The enclosure was 236 m or 450 cubits long from north to south, and 217 m or 415 cubits from east to west. A small satellite pyramid was also built near the south side of the pyramid, and a small mastaba was constructed in the northern side of the enclosure. Crossing the pavement outside the mortuary temple led to the only entrance into the sacred area, near the centre of the east side and slightly to the south of the temple. The entrance opened onto the top of a 210 m long causeway that was very different to the enclosed corridors and massive embankments of later eras, including at Khufu's Great Pyramid. A simple path linked the pyramid and the valley temple below, consisting of an open-air pavement flanked by two low walls.

The Meidum Pyramid's valley temple has been located, but Nile flood silt and agricultural land has covered it and has prevented large-scale excavations taking place. The layout of the complex of monumental buildings at Meidum, just like at the Bent Pyramid that

RIGHT Section showing the Meidum Pyramid's three main phases of construction. *(Franck Monnier)*

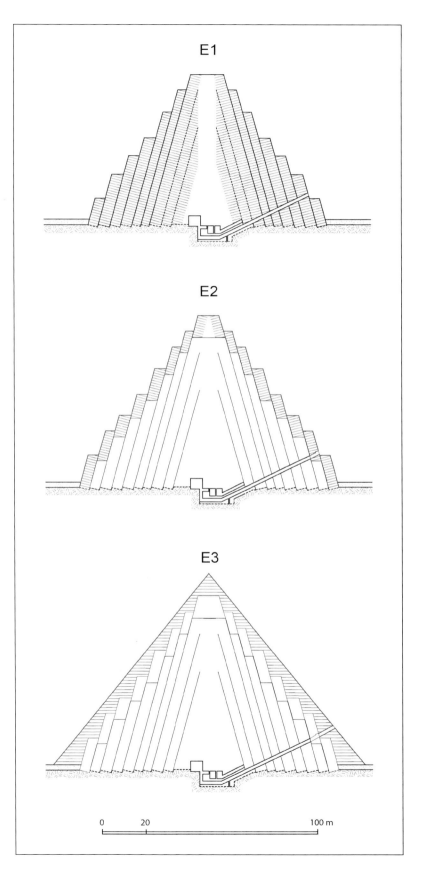

E1

E2

E3

0   20   100 m

ABOVE The Meidum
Pyramid's mortuary
temple.
(Franck Monnier)

was built around the same time, is among the
earliest examples of the classic royal funeral
groups of the Old Kingdom. These groups
comprised a pyramid, a small satellite pyramid,
a mortuary temple on the high ground near the
pyramid's east face and a valley temple down
on the Nile floodplain, which would have been
accessible by boat. The two temples were
connected by a long pavement or causeway.

The Meidum Pyramid in its ruined state
might provide Egyptologists with an insight

RIGHT Descending
passage leading into
the Meidum Pyramid.
(Franck Monnier)

into the internal structure of a great pyramid.
Ludwig Borchardt was the first to understand
the different stages of construction that had
produced the monument. In total there were
three separate phases that he named E1,
E2 and E3. The first stage, E1, followed the
construction principles used for the step
pyramids of the 3rd dynasty. E1 was made
up of concentric stepped walls of masonry
leaning onto a central core. A seven-step
pyramid was raised using this method of
construction to a height of nearly 65 m, and
then the outer faces were carefully finished. It
was then decided to increase the dimensions
of the whole building by adding an additional
outer layer of masonry to produce phase E2.
Each step was enlarged in such a way that the
existing regular succession of steps was not
upset, and the result was that the seven-step
pyramid was increased to eight even steps. This
phase of construction was also completed, as
is demonstrated by the finished walls exposed
today. Finally, Snefru's architects radically
modified the external form of the building, by
adding a masonry envelope in horizontal layers
until the building acquired a new form, that of a
true pyramid with a triangular profile.

The external slope of the faces was determined
to some extent by the shape of the existing
underlying structure, but they had a final inclination
that was a consistent 51° 50' throughout, the
same slope that was subsequently used to
construct the faces of Khufu's Pyramid at Giza.
Flinders Petrie noted this similarity in his survey
report, and he discussed the symbolic proportions
that this represented, which are analysed later
in this publication. Although identical in profile to
the Great Pyramid, the Meidum Pyramid was
nevertheless smaller in scale. In its final finished
state, phase E3 stood on a square base of
144.32 m average on each side and reached a
height of 91.90 m at its peak. In Egyptian cubits
this equates to 1,100 cubits around by 175 cubits
in height; still monumental by any measure.

The main entrance to the internal passages
and chambers of the Meidum Pyramid is
located on the north face, at a height of 18.50 m
(35 cubits), and slightly offset to the east with
respect to the building's north–south axis. It
opens into a long descending corridor that
begins with a section that is an extension of the

corridor further down, completed during phases E2 and E3. The first section ends 13.35 m from the entrance before continuing within the older structure. At the interface between the two sections, the slope of the corridor changes slightly from 30° 23' to 27° 36'. It then continues down into the core structure and into the bedrock below ground level for a distance of approximately 44 m, before levelling off to reach an antechamber.

Although the material used for the masonry is a fine-grained limestone, the general condition of the walls surrounding the descending corridor beyond the first section is extremely poor. The nature of the rock has resulted in exfoliation to such an extent that the passage now has the appearance of a long cavern. According to analyses carried out by German geologists Dietrich and Rosemarie Klemm, the first two stages of construction used materials from a local limestone quarry, whereas the final stage combined these with a fine limestone from the Maasara quarries in the hills on the opposite bank of the Nile, which was used for the exterior casings of all later pyramids. The local

LEFT The corbelled burial chamber of the pyramid looking north. *(Franck Monnier)*

source was most likely exhausted during the E3 construction phase, and good building materials were sought elsewhere to complete the building. Two antechambers, also in poor condition, follow one another within the horizontal corridor which is nearly 10 m long. The corridor is 1.80 m high and opens into the first chamber, offset slightly to the east side of the corridor. This chamber is 2.60 m long and 2.20 m wide. The second chamber has almost identical dimensions and is offset to the west side of the corridor.

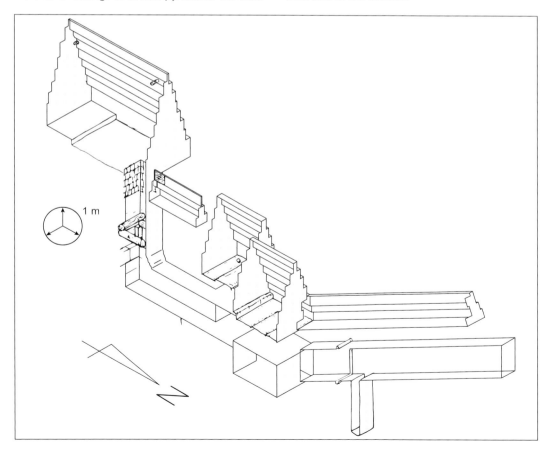

1 m

LEFT Perspective view of the inner arrangement of the Meidum Pyramid. *(Franck Monnier)*

ABOVE Snefru's Bent Pyramid at Dahshur.
(Franck Monnier)

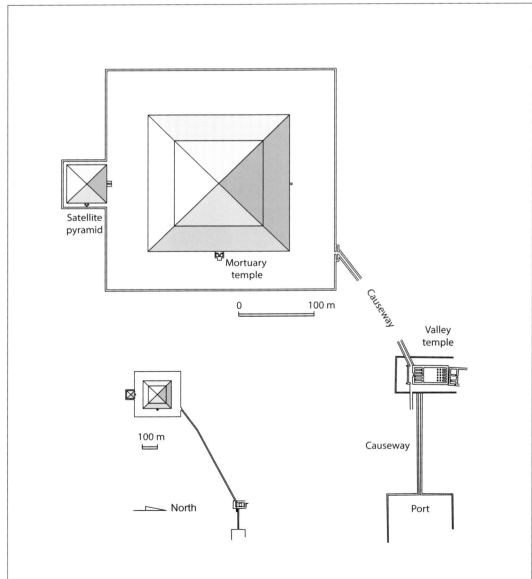

Satellite pyramid

Mortuary temple

Causeway

Valley temple

Causeway

Port

0   100 m

100 m

North

RIGHT Plan of the Bent Pyramid complex.
(Franck Monnier)

Two separate corbelled vault spaces (with ceilings like an upturned set of steps narrowing towards a point) were recently discovered directly above these two chambers by a French team led by Gilles Dormion and Jean-Yves Verd'hurt. Below, the corridor continues to the southern end where it joins an irregularly shaped vertical shaft that provides access up to the most important chamber in the pyramid, the burial chamber. Compared to the funerary chambers of Snefru's other two pyramids at Dahshur, this room has very modest dimensions. Its floor is 5.90 m in length by 2.65 m in width, approximately 11 by 5 cubits. A vault rises up to 5.05 m, around 10 cubits. Flinders Petrie discovered broken pieces of a plain wooden sarcophagus at the bottom of the vertical shaft leading up into the tomb chamber and judged that they were of a type known in the Old Kingdom, but fragments were not sufficiently preserved to allow C14 verification of this claim.

The Bent Pyramid

The Bent Pyramid at Dahshur-South, which was probably the second great pyramid begun during Snefru's reign, was located in the centre of an open area surrounded by a square enclosure wall, 299 m along each side and 2 m thick. A single entrance opened on the north side of the enclosure and connected the sacred temenos area around the pyramid with its causeway. A pair of wooden doors flanked the entrance into the open area. Several discrete structures were located inside the enclosure, including a small mudbrick chapel with a limestone offering table. This was located on the ground directly below the entrance to the pyramid, which was up on its north face. A slightly larger mortuary temple sat at the foot of its eastern face. The mortuary temple's own high wall surrounded two tall monolithic limestone stelae and an offering table. The stelae had rounded tops like those at Meidum, but were more than twice as tall, reaching almost 10 m. These were elaborately carved with iconography representing the pharaoh's titulary contained within huge *serekhs* surmounted by Horus. The arrangements recall the groups of symbols used by the pharaohs of previous dynasties, but here they included

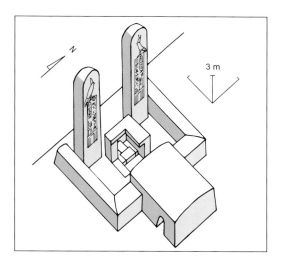

LEFT Reconstruction showing the Bent Pyramid's mortuary temple or chapel with its pair of monumental stelae in situ.
(Franck Monnier)

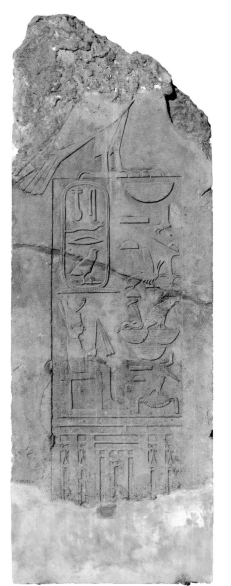

LEFT The recovered stele that was erected on the west side of the mortuary chapel.
(Cairo Museum, photo: Franck Monnier)

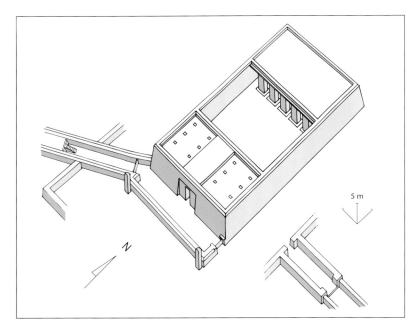

5 m

N

ABOVE
Reconstruction of the
Bent Pyramid's valley
temple.
(Franck Monnier)

BELOW The Bent
Pyramid's internal
chambers and
passages shown in
cutaway view.
(Franck Monnier)

pharaoh as they travelled from the valley temple below, up to the pyramid and back again. The valley temple was 26.20 m wide and 47.16 m long, or 50 by 90 cubits. This size was unprecedented for a funerary temple, as was the decorative programme of reliefs on its walls. A date marked beneath one of the stone building blocks indicates that it was inaugurated during the 15th census of the reign of Snefru. The construction of this temple was, therefore, contemporary with the final stages of construction of the Bent Pyramid, as well as the foundation of the Red Pyramid at Dahshur-North, and the final stages of construction of the Meidum Pyramid. The temple was divided into three distinct parts: storage magazines, a courtyard bordered on its north side by a double row of decorated pillars and finally a row of six chapels, each of which contained a large statue of Snefru.

The walls were decorated in low reliefs showing various scenes, including the foundation ceremony and the *heb sed* festival ritual. Scenes depicting the pharaoh visiting various sanctuaries and representations of royal estates made up an iconographic programme of unprecedented richness. A second pavement, brick this time and 148 m long, connected this religious complex to a rectangular pond, 145 m by 95 m, which was filled with water when the Nile was in flood

a representation of a cartouche containing the pharaoh's prenomen, Snefru, 'He who makes things perfect'.

The proportions of the temples were, on the whole, modest, and in no way anticipated the monumental dimensions that Snefru's successors gave to their own buildings. This temple was reused and enlarged many times during the Middle Kingdom.

The open causeway was flanked by two parallel walls for the full 704 m, providing protection for the priests of the cult of the

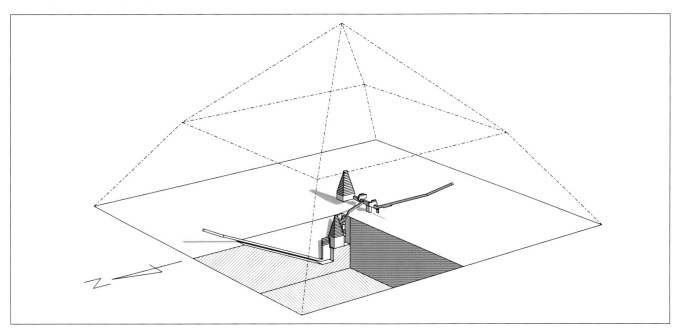

N

and the canals were full. It is the oldest known harbour attached to a royal funerary complex. These places of worship were reoccupied and reused during the Middle and New Kingdoms, until the 18th dynasty when they were dismantled and plundered for building materials.

The Bent Pyramid rises to 104.71 m and stands on a square base 189.43 m on average on each side. Its faces are oriented to the cardinal directions with only a slight error of a quarter of a degree on average. It could be classified as a true pyramid if its faces did not suddenly 'bend' at a height of 47.04 m above the ground, from a steep incline of 55° to a reduced slope of 44°. This pyramid is also unique in that it has two separate internal systems of chambers and passages: one whose entrance is located on the north face at 11.33 m above ground level, and the other which is the only example from the Old Kingdom of an entry located on the west face, at 32.76 m above ground level. Both internal passage systems have large chambers covered with corbelled vaults. They were interconnected by a tunnel dug through the masonry by the builders themselves at a late stage of construction, but before the western entrance was permanently closed. The northern entrance passage consists of a first section 12.60 m long inclined at 28° 38' that then connects to the rest of the corridor, which plunges 66 m into the pyramid down a 26° slope.

There are significant cracks in the walls at the interface joints between the two tunnel sections. At the bottom is a narrow vestibule chamber covered by a tall corbelled vault. On the opposite wall on the southern side of this chamber, at a height of 6.75 m above ground level, is a large opening that provides access into the lower of the two larger chambers. The chamber, which measures 4.96 m from east to west and 6.30 m from north to south, is covered with a magnificent corbelled vault that reduces in width gradually up to a full height of 17.30 m. Significant traces of mortar on the walls of the room show that the volume was once filled with masonry leaving only the space under the vault open. At floor level in the south wall of this chamber is a doorway that opens into a short passage leading to a vertical shaft known as the 'chimney'. The shaft

rises more than 15 m before ending in a dead end where the passage is obstructed by two blocks leaning against each other. Two other slabs standing on edge in alcoves at the side of the chimney seem to be in waiting positions and were intended to be closed down like hatches to permanently block the shaft, once its purpose was achieved.

Certain aspects of the internal layout recall the design of the Meidum Pyramid, in particular the passage associated with the relieving chamber vault, and the chimney that was probably intended to lead up to a funerary chamber. Overall, it seems from the closed-off shaft and the two unused closing blocks that the architects modified their plans early in the project, and the chimney never connected to a burial chamber that had originally been planned but never built. This hypothesis is supported by the existence of a long tunnel dug through the top of the south wall of the corbelled chamber, 12.60 m above the floor, which bypasses the top of the closed-off chimney and connects this lower chamber system with the upper system.

The passage leading into the pyramid from the western entrance was designed with a double slope. The first section is inclined at a relatively steep 30° 9' for 21.81 m before it connects to a longer section inclined at 24° 17' for 45.85 m. The descent ends in a horizontal corridor that is still a few metres above the ground level outside. The horizontal corridor contains two consecutive lateral sliding block chamber systems of similar design that were intended to store and then install stone slabs

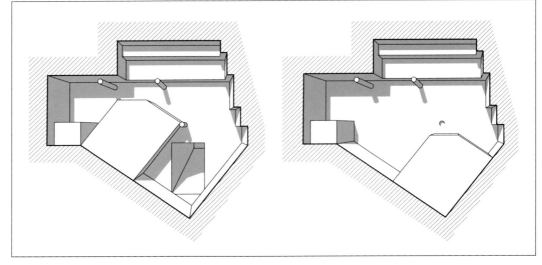

to close off the corridor, but only the western one was ever activated. This was then cut through in the distant past by looters. Plastering around the joints on both sides of this sliding block shows that this passage system, entered from the west, was closed off with this stone before the western entrance was shut, and that the northern chamber system was also still accessible at that time. The tunnel connecting the two systems was, therefore, not the work of looters, but of the builders themselves, so that they could continue to access the upper system from the lower system, and eventually exit via the northern entrance.

Each of the closing mechanisms consists of a transverse housing space containing a limestone slab of more than five tons. Each slab was held up a slope inclined at 35° from the horizontal by a large wooden beam. These were to be removed when the pyramid was being closed, thus allowing the blocks to slide into place using the force of gravity alone. At the far end of this corridor, past the closing mechanisms, is the large corbelled funerary chamber, at a higher level than the equivalent chamber in the northern passage system. The ground plan of this room is rectangular, and the top of the corbel runs north to south. It measures 7.97 m in this orientation and is 5.26 m wide east–west. The room is covered by a corbelled vault on all four sides, starting at 3.20 m above the floor level and rising to a maximum height of almost 16.50 m.

The surfaces of this corbelling are so eroded that it is extremely difficult to discern the steps of the vault. There are many gaps in the walls and finishing work has not been done. A solid stone mass once filled a large proportion of the lower part of this burial chamber to a height of 6.54 m, but much of it was broken up and removed in modern times. A substantial framework made from cedar trees from Lebanon was installed during construction and was discovered in situ within this fill. It still occupies part of the space in the floor volume between the back walls of this room.

A study undertaken by Franck Monnier and Alexander Puchkov showed that this room underwent several changes of form during construction, including a raising of the floor on two separate occasions. The corbels of the upper part of the space were then recut to form wall surfaces that were almost flat.

The Red Pyramid

The 'Red' or Northern Pyramid is located less than 2 km north of the Bent Pyramid. It owes its nickname to the brown or reddish colour of the local limestone used for its construction. It is the third-largest pyramid of all and competes with the Bent Pyramid's satellite pyramid and the

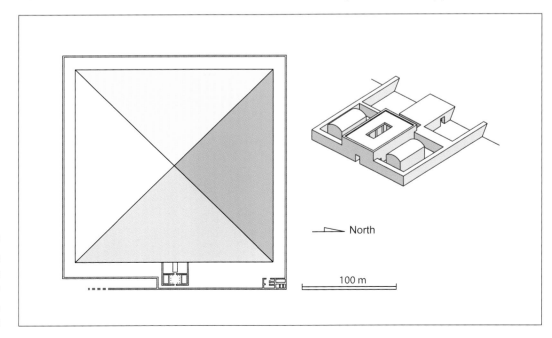

North

100 m

Meidum Pyramid for the status of the first true pyramid, with the classic isosceles triangular section. It is certainly the oldest example to have survived to the present day in this special form.

The complex seems to have been very simple. A funerary temple was attached to the eastern face of the pyramid and an enclosure closely encircled them both. No satellite pyramids were built nearby, and it seems that no causeway was built to connect the mortuary temple to a valley temple below, or to a port of arrival down on the Nile floodplain. The mortuary temple had modest dimensions, but its ground plan marked a clear evolutionary step compared to those of the pyramids of Meidum and Dahshur-South. The entrance vestibule opened into a small peristyle courtyard flanked by alcoves. The court contained an offering table in front of a covered chapel. Outside the enclosure to the south-east, a necropolis was developed for the monumental tombs of Snefru's court officials.

The base of the Red Pyramid is set out on a square 219 m on each side (almost 420 cubits). Its faces are oriented to the four cardinal directions with great accuracy. The eastern face deviates from the true north–south axis by only 8.7' (around one-seventh of a single degree). The average inclination of the faces is approximately 44° 44', although there is some disagreement over the final intended angle, and so the original height of the pyramid can only be estimated at 109.54 m. Although the casing stones and backing stones made of fine Tura limestone were mostly exploited for reuse from Antiquity to the Arab period, some remain in situ, especially at the foot of the eastern face. The base layer shows a vertical levelling difference of less than 10 cm between the western and eastern sides.

Apart from losing the majority of its external casing stones, the building is in very good condition. The cuboid stones were placed in horizontal layers of varying heights, which generally decrease from the bottom to the top, from 0.9 m to 0.6 m (or just over 1 cubit). This construction method most closely resembles the construction method subsequently used for Khufu's pyramid, and it may be that the system was developed following the structural problems encountered during the construction of the Bent

LEFT The second of the Red Pyramid's enormous corbelled chambers.
(Franck Monnier)

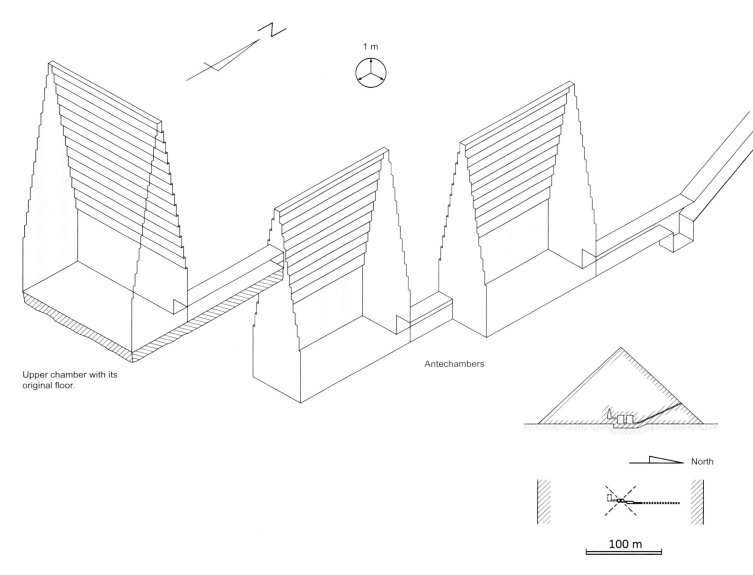

Upper chamber with its
original floor.

Antechambers

1 m

North

100 m

Pyramid. The reduced slope of the Red Pyramid
when compared to those near-contemporary
buildings also supports this hypothesis. The
new method clearly worked well, and its solidity
may have persuaded the next generation of
architects and builders to attempt the steeper
slope angle again, for Khufu's monument.

The main entrance to the internal passages
and compartments is on the north face, slightly
offset to the east with respect to the central
north–south axis of the pyramid, and at a height
of 30.92 m above ground level. The descending
passage is 1.04 m wide by 1.16 m high; the
same dimensions as the passages later used in
Khufu's pyramid. The passage penetrates down
into the core of the pyramid to a level almost
equivalent to the exterior ground level, at an

inclination of 27° 36'; close to the inclination
also used for Khufu's passages. After 55.55 m
it levels out into a horizontal stretch of corridor
1.35 m high by 7.43 m in length. The corridor
leads to the first of three massive spaces, a
finely finished anteroom 8.33 m long by 3.65 m
wide, covered with a corbelled vault, which
slopes in on the east and west sides only. The
total height of the room rises to 12.31 m.

A connecting corridor comparable to the
previous one opens in the south wall of this
space near the south-west corner of the room.
It leads into a second massive antechamber
located directly under the summit of the
pyramid. It is almost identical to the first, but
in the southern wall of this one, at a height of
7.80 m above the floor, is the opening to a third

LEFT The excavated floor of the final corbelled chamber exposing the core construction blocks below. *(Franck Monnier)*

passage that, once blocked off with a finishing stone, must have been almost impossible to detect by torchlight. A wooden staircase now leads up to this entrance. It opens into a corridor that continues for a distance of 7.38 m to the third massive corbelled chamber. This third and final chamber may have been the pyramid's principal tomb chamber. The chamber is similar to the other two described above but is oriented east–west and is a little larger. The passage leading to it was originally 1.05 m high (or 2 cubits), but an excavation of the floor at some unknown time in the past increased its vertical height to 1.88 m.

The burial chamber is 8.35 m long by 4.18 m wide and follows the form typical for the reign of Snefru, as its ceiling width gradually reduces via a succession of corbels up to a height of 14.67 m. The walls slope in on the north and south sides only. The floor of this chamber was dug out and dismantled to a depth of more than 4 m by looters who revealed that the foundations, like the external layers, were made up of large cuboid, and closely fitted, limestone blocks. There is little doubt that the excavated pit was created by looters, who were clearly enthusiastic about their quest for treasure, and it is likely that it was these same looters who lowered the floor of the entrance passage

between the tomb chamber and the southern antechamber, to facilitate the extraction of loose spoil materials from their excavations. They also dug a few feet below the level of the floor under the north wall of the room. The reasons why they attacked this particular spot remain unknown, but as no fragments of a sarcophagus have ever been found, it might be assumed that the absence of one led former explorers to look elsewhere for a burial location. Their project appears to have been futile, but the high quality of the masonry they exposed contrasts with the disorderly appearance of the core fabric materials used to build the Meidum and Bent Pyramids. Similarly, the corbelled vaults of the Red Pyramid are in such exceptional condition that it is difficult to believe that they are so ancient.

In 1950, the analysis of human remains found in the chambers led Ahmed Batrawi to propose that they dated back to the Old Kingdom, therefore implying that they may be the remains of Snefru. Similar studies of this type carried out in the 1940s and 1950s, however, have been invalidated by more modern analytical techniques. Other experts note that this monument was probably entered and reused many times, like most of the great burials of the Old Kingdom, by looters and inquisitive Egyptians of later dynasties.

Symbolic meanings

The reasons for adopting the pyramidal form and the meanings it represented for the ancient Egyptians have been the subject of many amateur and academic theories. The first stage of Djoser's Step Pyramid was a square, smooth-faced mastaba. It contrasted with the conventional rectangular tombs with their palace façades built from the Early Dynastic Period onwards. The Step Pyramid does bear some comparison to a nearby tomb (Mastaba 3038) that was built in the form of a stepped platform. Only after several enlargements, however, did Djoser's stepped monument obtain a form approaching that of a pyramid. Some have seen in these tombs and early pyramids a desire to represent the primordial mound that often appears in Egyptian religious tradition, emerging from the waters of Nun which covered the primordial world. According to later traditions, Horus the falcon first alighted on earth upon one of these emerging mounds.

The 5th dynasty unfinished pyramid of Neferefre at Abusir was referred to with the word for hill or mound, *iat*, as it never surpassed the partially built state of a square mastaba. The Step Pyramid, on the other hand, was later designated using the term *mer*, which was also used for the true pyramids. From the start of the 4th dynasty, the true pyramids were capped with pyramidions known by the feminine form of *benben*, *benbenet*, which certainly referred to the primordial mound. A sculpted model of the *benbenet,* which was considered a sacred stone, was installed in the temple of Heliopolis, the centre of solar worship, 20 km north-east of Giza. There are diverging views about what pyramids meant to the ancient Egyptians. Some consider that the pyramid was seen as a mound emerging from the primordial ocean. Other scholars also believe that it was associated with solar symbolism, where the faces of the pyramid manifested the rays of light that the pharaoh was to climb to reach the sky and reign alongside Re.

During the Old Kingdom, the steps of the first pyramids seem to have represented steps of a gigantic staircase erected by the gods for the deceased ruler, and this idea is often expressed in the Pyramid Texts. These texts were written on the walls of pharaonic tomb chambers from

BELOW The rays of the sun falling on the 'Red' land at Saqqara. *(Franck Monnier)*

ABOVE Menkaure's pyramid at Giza.
(Franck Monnier)

the end of the 5th dynasty: 'The earth is made into steps for him towards heaven, so that he may ascend on them to heaven!' (Pyramid Texts of Pharaoh Unas, utterance 267, §365).

This idea of elevation was also expressed within the funerary chambers that were first built underground during the 3rd dynasty, and then also located above ground level from the reign of Snefru at the start of the 4th dynasty. Some scholars have linked the emergence of the pyramidal form to the solar doctrine of the Egyptian religion, whose highest representative, the high priest of Heliopolis, Imhotep, possibly designed the first pyramid. It is possible that he was responsible for adopting the iconic shape.

According to this theory, at the dawn of the 3rd dynasty there was an evolution in the Egyptian belief system regarding the afterlife of the pharaoh, from a chthonic underworld concept to a Heliopolitan solar doctrine, where the deceased pharaoh also ascended to a celestial kingdom. The rise of the solar religion was probably related to the omnipotence increasingly sought and attained by the pharaoh as the 4th dynasty proceeded, which was materialised by the towering monumentality of the tombs compared to those of relatives and court officials. The iconography associated with the pharaoh's patron god Horus, the ancient sky god of his ancestors, was very discretely used, only for the pharaoh and his closest family members, and was not extended even to the highest officials.

By monopolising the available human and material resources for his own projects, the sovereign used the energy of the state to validate his supremacy over all his subjects. He expressed his claim to divine status by demonstrating his ability to execute monumental projects as much as through the finished monument itself. His pyramid, and the concepts associated with it, articulated the idea that he was the earthly manifestation of Re, the absolute ruler over the Egyptian universe.

The era of the giant pyramids ended with the reign of Menkaure. His successor Shepseskaf, the final pharaoh of the 4th dynasty, was content to relocate his burial site to Saqqara, where he constructed a mastaba. At 100 m in length it was still a massive building, but it was considerably smaller than his predecessor's pyramid. From the start of the 5th dynasty, pharaonic tombs took on more consistent and

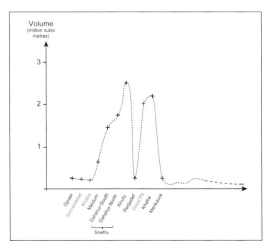

LEFT Diagram depicting the relative quantities of stone used for pyramid construction during the reigns of the Old Kingdom (in light grey are estimates for incomplete projects).
(Franck Monnier)

OPPOSITE The
layouts and concepts
used in funerary
complex design
through the centuries
leading up to the
4th dynasty.
(Franck Monnier)

somewhat standardised dimensions, certainly inferior to the giants of the early 4th dynasty by an order of magnitude. The reasons for halting the frantic race for gigantism are obscure, but it is likely that reduced efforts were invested in the pyramid projects and workers were simultaneously redeployed towards developing and decorating the temples. This created more elaborate and finely finished relief programmes that could communicate more sophisticated messages. The iconic signs that were the giant pyramids slowly gave way to more elaborate compositions that culminated in the compilation/creation of the Pyramid Texts at the end of the 5th dynasty. Another likely cause is the possible weakening and decentralisation of royal power as court officials became more influential again. This process could have been the end result of economic difficulties resulting from the titanic projects undertaken during the early 4th dynasty, which ultimately proved both resource-consuming and materially unproductive. Without external inputs, an economic imbalance was inevitable and the hierarchy began to collapse outwards to some extent.

Records contained on the Palermo Stone are enlightening in that they show intense activity by Snefru in foreign lands, to bring back slaves and valuable material produce of all kinds, but there is little evidence regarding the efforts of his successors in this respect. Such missions could have been economically significant. After many decades during which construction projects employed all the manpower available, it is not clear, for example, that the army retained the ability to conduct large-scale expeditions to foreign lands. These missions may have been essential to support the economic foundations that underpinned the giant pyramid projects, but the documentary evidence currently available does not reveal whether this ability was lost or not.

It seems very likely, however, that the economy was a factor in Menkaure's decision to reduce the proportions of his third pharaonic pyramid at Giza, and it is worth noting that Djedefre, whose reign was between Khufu's and Khafre's, established a similarly sized project several kilometres to the north of Giza. There was, therefore, a precedent for Menkaure's degree of restraint. Whether it was foresight on

Djedefre's part, or because economic warning signs were becoming apparent, Djedefre seems to have decided to put an end to the excessive undertakings of his ancestors, but he did not succeed in convincing his successor Khafre to show the same degree of restraint. Despite the return to gigantism under Khafre, it is clear that a policy that diverted all the resources of the state to erect a practically useless monument to legitimise the ruler's claim to the rank of solar god was doomed to failure, particularly in the face of any external challenges.

Over the course of the development of the classic pyramid complex, the main monument and its ancillary buildings underwent many changes before they reached a cohesive form that reflected the funerary beliefs that were also consolidating at the time. The early complexes such as Djoser's Step Pyramid and its enclosure were profoundly innovative from a technical point of view but retained most of the architectonic traditions of the Early Dynastic tombs and enclosures. Djoser and Sekhemkhet merged the tomb mounds with the funerary enclosures, and although these had previously been separate entities during the 2nd dynasty, they were both retained. The general ground plans of the enclosures were also oriented north–south according to the old custom. The underground chambers, on the other hand, were extended over a vast subterranean expanse, running through intertwined galleries, chambers and storage magazines, like those dug for Djoser's predecessors Ninetjer and Hotepsekhemwy.

Mortuary temples abutted against the north sides of the pyramids welcomed daily offerings left by the cult attendants. They were constructed for eternity, petrifying building types originally made of perishable materials. They were now required to maintain the deceased pharaoh's afterlife on a permanent basis.

Despite the incomplete nature of the funerary complexes erected during the reigns that followed up to the end of the 3rd dynasty, it seems that the building conventions were maintained with few exceptions. It was not until the reign of Snefru at the start of the 4th dynasty that a radical break was made with the past, as several elements that had been present since the Thinite period were finally abandoned. The enclosure with the stepped pyramid and underground

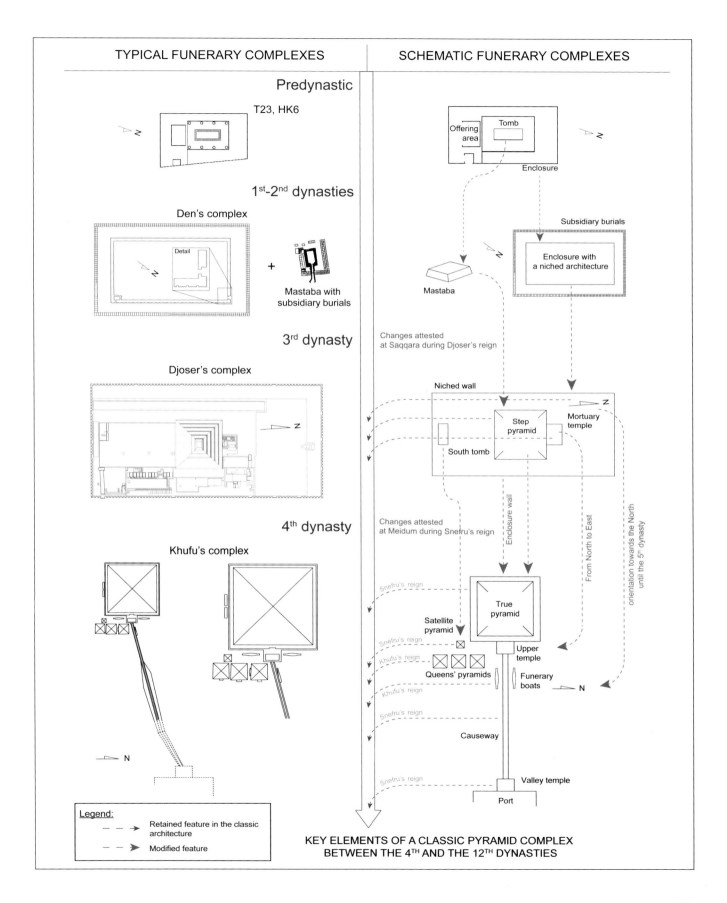

TYPICAL FUNERARY COMPLEXES

SCHEMATIC FUNERARY COMPLEXES

Predynastic

T23, HK6

N

Tomb

Offering area

Enclosure

N

1st-2nd dynasties

Den's complex

Detail

N

+

Mastaba with subsidiary burials

Subsidiary burials

Enclosure with a niched architecture

Mastaba

N

3rd dynasty

Djoser's complex

N

Changes attested at Saqqara during Djoser's reign

Niched wall

N

Step pyramid

Mortuary temple

South tomb

Enclosure wall

From North to East

orientation towards the North until the 5th dynasty

4th dynasty

Changes attested at Meidum during Snefru's reign

Khufu's complex

N

Snefru's reign

Snefru's reign

Khufu's reign

Khufu's reign

Snefru's reign

Snefru's reign

True pyramid

Satellite pyramid

Upper temple

Queens' pyramids

Funerary boats

N

Causeway

Valley temple

Port

Legend:
- - - → Retained feature in the classic architecture
- - - → Modified feature

KEY ELEMENTS OF A CLASSIC PYRAMID COMPLEX BETWEEN THE 4TH AND THE 12TH DYNASTIES

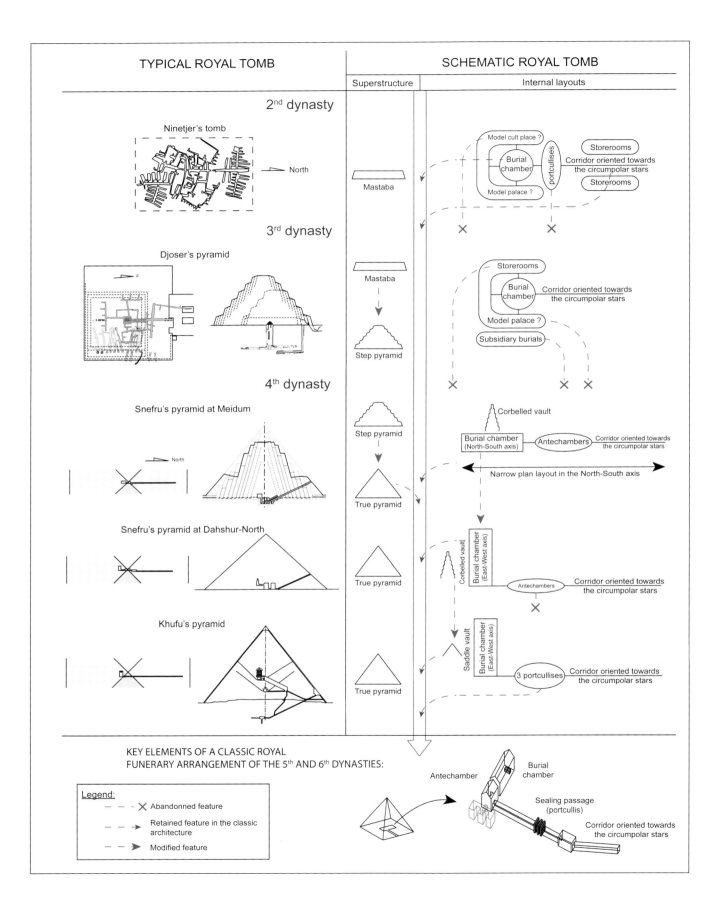

TYPICAL ROYAL TOMB

SCHEMATIC ROYAL TOMB

Superstructure

Internal layouts

2nd dynasty

Ninetjer's tomb

North

Mastaba

Model cult place ?

Burial chamber

portcullises

Storerooms

Corridor oriented towards the circumpolar stars

Storerooms

Model palace ?

3rd dynasty

Djoser's pyramid

z

Mastaba

Step pyramid

Storerooms

Burial chamber

Corridor oriented towards the circumpolar stars

Model palace ?

Subsidiary burials

4th dynasty

Snefru's pyramid at Meidum

North

Step pyramid

True pyramid

Corbelled vault

Burial chamber (North-South axis)

Antechambers

Corridor oriented towards the circumpolar stars

Narrow plan layout in the North-South axis

Snefru's pyramid at Dahshur-North

True pyramid

Corbelled vault

Burial chamber (East-West axis)

Antechambers

Corridor oriented towards the circumpolar stars

Khufu's pyramid

True pyramid

Saddle vault

Burial chamber (East-West axis)

3 portcullises

Corridor oriented towards the circumpolar stars

KEY ELEMENTS OF A CLASSIC ROYAL
FUNERARY ARRANGEMENT OF THE 5th AND 6th DYNASTIES:

Antechamber

Burial chamber

Sealing passage (portcullis)

Corridor oriented towards the circumpolar stars

Legend:

— – - ✕ Abandonned feature

– – ➤ Retained feature in the classic architecture

— – ➤ Modified feature

maze made way for the true pyramid with overwhelming dimensions compared to the ancillary buildings. The key elements of the classic royal funeral complexes of the Old Kingdom fell into place: the mortuary temple up near the pyramid, the causeway that connected to the port and the valley temple below, the satellite pyramid established to the south of the main monument, the massively reduced enclosure wall and the subsidiary pyramids nearby. The general orientation also changed. From then on, the centre line of the complex followed the course of the sun through the day, running from east to west. The causeway also ran up from the east, from the valley towards the mortuary temple that was then placed against the eastern side of the pyramid. The journey up the causeway led from the world of the living below, on the black land, to the realm of the dead above, on the red land at the desert's edge.

The more clearly defined arrangements of the 4th dynasty showed greater abstraction and expressed deeper symbolism. The mortuary temple became a chapel celebrating the pharaoh's cult where offerings could be made. The pyramid had four perfectly flat and finely polished faces and had the appearance of a stark shining chevron pointing to the sky.

The minimalist design and simple layout of the funerary chambers was retained. They were still accessed via an entrance on the north face that led down a sloped passage to the mortuary chambers, but the deep underground character of the chambers was abandoned in favour of placing them higher within the masonry, sometimes above ground level. From the time of the Red Pyramid of Dahshur-North the main burial chambers were oriented from east to

west. During the reign of Khufu, it seems as if some effort was made to begin construction of a burial chamber entirely underground again, as a large cavern was excavated at a depth of approximately 30 m. This first project, however, was abandoned, and the architects finally decided to position the funerary chambers higher up than had ever been attempted before. The structural problems associated with this new engineering challenge, however, did not increase the pharaoh's chances of reaching his eternal rest, and subsequent generations resolved never to build funerary chambers above ground level again. The antechamber with granite portcullises was a successful new innovation, and similar systems were reproduced many times thereafter. The typical internal arrangement became a burial chamber oriented according to the daily path of the sun and covered with an apexed vaulted roof. The sarcophagus was still placed in the western part, towards the realm of the afterlife.

One of the most important ritual elements was the long descending passage opening in the north face that allowed the pharaoh's soul to join the circumpolar stars of the northern sky:

'May he ascend to heaven among the stars, the Imperishables' (Pyramid Texts of pharaoh Pepi II, utterance 474, § 940a).

Outside, large pits were excavated to receive the great royal boats, and the pharaoh's queens accompanied their pharaoh to the afterlife in their own pyramids. The access road became a monumental causeway, and the mortuary temples had large pillared courtyards leading to offering chapels and sanctuaries. During the reign of Khafre, the cult buildings underwent a development that

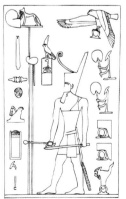

ABOVE
Reconstruction of a classic 6th dynasty pyramid complex.
(Franck Monnier)

had significant influence on the architecture of the Old Kingdom. The valley temple and the mortuary temple were built with monolithic masonry, and each contained a pillared hall or courtyard surrounded by a complex of rooms and corridors that allowed the cult priests to perform the daily ceremonies, and store

paraphernalia and sacred cult objects. Dozens of finely made statues of the pharaoh were also positioned inside the funerary temples, showing him standing alongside gods and goddesses or seated on his throne. The innermost parts of the temples typically consisted of a row of five chapels containing five statues of the

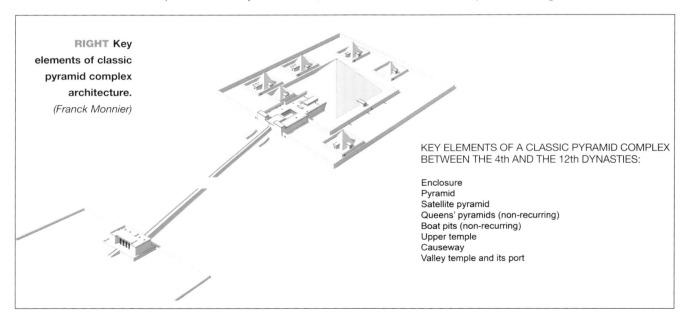

RIGHT **Key elements of classic pyramid complex architecture.**
(Franck Monnier)

KEY ELEMENTS OF A CLASSIC PYRAMID COMPLEX
BETWEEN THE 4th AND THE 12th DYNASTIES:

Enclosure
Pyramid
Satellite pyramid
Queens' pyramids (non-recurring)
Boat pits (non-recurring)
Upper temple
Causeway
Valley temple and its port

pharaoh. The layout of the mortuary temples of the 5th and 6th dynasties began with the *per-uru* or vestibule, the *wuseret* court, leading to five statue chapels, storage magazines and finally the offering hall. Inside the pyramids, the chambers and corridors built during the 4th dynasty had no mural decoration and were adorned with no inscriptions. This absence produced a monolithic environment, as opposed to the abundant offering scenes and colourful panoramas of everyday life that adorned the contemporary private tombs.

There is, however, evidence that the walls of the causeways at Giza were adorned with reliefs. Herodotus described this, and Egyptologist Selim Hassan found fragments of them near Khufu's pyramid. Relief fragments from Khufu's complex were also reused for decorating the Middle Kingdom pyramids.

Further information about the iconographic programme used for Khufu's complex can be derived by comparing the pharaonic material of the reigns that directly preceded and followed his reign. The valley temple of the Bent Pyramid, for example, contained many reliefs showing the *heb sed* ritual. The 5th dynasty pyramid of

Sahure, the 5th dynasty sun temple of Niuserre and the 6th dynasty pyramid complex of Pepi II were also adorned with *heb sed* scenes. It is thus reasonable to assume that the *heb sed* festival also played a prominent role in Khufu's reign, and would have been displayed prominently in one or both of his temples, and possibly within his causeway.

Similarly, carved decoration on contemporary royal statues and royal furniture can provide significant supplementary information about the traditions that were considered important around Khufu's reign. Only one surviving statue of Khufu, fragments of several others and a few relief fragments have survived from Khufu's own reign, but by studying the funerary furniture, statues and reliefs of adjacent reigns, for example those artefacts that belonged to his father Snefru and his mother Hetepheres, and comparing these to the statues of Khafre and Menkaure that have also survived, it is reasonable to conclude that common elements such as Horus with the *shen* ring and the cartouche were also prominent during Khufu's reign. Horus the falcon appears on the side of his mother's wooden throne, and also embraces the head of the important statue known as 'Khafre enthroned'. The *sema-tawi* unification motif is also found displayed prominently on the sides of Khafre's throne, as well as on the sides of Menkaure's throne, shown in a statue now in the Boston Museum of Fine Arts (MFA). Khufu's

BELOW The principal 4th dynasty pharaonic symbolism depicted on the sides of the throne of pharaoh Menkaure, now in the MFA, Boston. *(David Ian Lightbody)*

enthroned statues were probably decorated with the same motif, and the throne that he actually used was likely also decorated that way.

Entries on the Palermo Stone for the Early Dynastic and Old Kingdom periods refer to rituals associated with the *sema-tawi* motif, referred to as 'going around behind the walls, unification of the two lands'. This was the major event recorded in several regnal years during the reigns of Djer and Djoser. Many of the key rituals were concerned with possessing territory by physically walking or running around it, or something that represented it, such as the bollards in the *heb sed* courts that represented the northern and southern extents of Egypt. Egyptologist Toby Wilkinson remarks that the *heb sed* ritual fulfilled much the same function

as the circuit of the wall performed at Memphis by the pharaoh on his coronation day. Within the funerary context, the presence of the *heb sed* motif implies that the pharaoh was expected to continue to perform these rituals, and act as the force that kept Egypt stable and unified, in the afterlife.

The pharaoh Unas was the first to decorate the walls inside his burial chamber at the end of the 5th dynasty. His aim was to surround himself with the protection of the Pyramid Texts, a long succession of litanies, offering formulae, prayers and magical texts, some of which were recited only on the day of the funeral. This structured collection of ancient rites and expressions of religious doctrine introduced the cycle of the god Osiris, the god of the afterlife, who magically protected the sovereign. The Pyramid Texts constitute the oldest religious text known to humankind, and they probably recorded concepts that had until then only been documented on papyrus or learned orally. Perhaps because the pharaoh was less able to maintain an eternal cult at the time these texts were first carved, Unas was attempting to ensure his eternal survival in case his successors were unable to maintain their duties. Whatever the political situation above ground and the state of his funerary cult, the pharaoh could perpetuate his daily cycles of rebirth, carry out his celestial and chthonic rituals, and be seated beside the gods, thanks to the power of written language alone. One line from the Pyramid Texts (utterance 274, §406c) makes clear that the pharaoh was expected to travel around the skies in the afterlife, in a way that recalls the *heb sed* ritual:

iw dbn·n tti pt·wy tm·tywy pḥr·n·f idb·wy

"Teti has gone around the two skies, he had circumambulated the two banks"

According to archaeologist David Lightbody, this ritual concept may throw some light on the most enigmatic architectural features of Khufu's own pyramid, the star/air shafts. The pharaoh's primary ritual function was to unify and lay claim to the two regions of Egypt, to create one stable territory running from the southern border to the Mediterranean Sea, both in the celestial realm above and on the earth below. It is therefore notable that the star/air shafts described later in this book lead out from the pharaoh's burial chamber towards the two skies, due north and due south. Although the ancient Egyptians left no written explanation for the purpose of these shafts, he suggests that the architectural and ritual contexts outlined above indicate that the shafts may have had some connection with this territorial ideology. The shafts could have provided avenues through which the pharaoh's soul could rise to the extents of the northern and southern skies, or perhaps more appropriately, canals upon which the pharaoh's soul could voyage, to the ends of the great celestial waterway, winding across the starry heavens above.

RIGHT An Old Kingdom flint *peseshkef* knife bearing the *serekh* and cartouche of Khufu, from Menkaure's valley temple, now in the MFA, Boston. These ceremonial knives were used during the pharaoh's funeral to perform the 'opening of the mouth' ritual on the mummy of the deceased, to allow his ka to breathe, and consume ritual offerings, and so that his soul or *akh* could be released from his body. The ritual was also performed on statues of the deceased, so that they too could breathe and become vessels containing the pharaoh's soul.
(David Ian Lightbody)

Placing a pyramidal structure at the centre of the royal funeral complex was a tradition that lasted until the beginning of the New Kingdom. At that time, the prominent pyramid-shaped mountain above the Theban necropolis, known as El Qurn, 'the horn', was apparently adopted as a substitute. The tombs of the Valley of the Kings were dug under the pointed mountain overlooking the west bank of the Nile. Nearby, in the necropolis of the tomb builders at Deir el-Medina, private tombs were constructed that were surmounted by their own small pyramids. The architectural form was also later adopted by the Nubian and Sudanese cultures that reproduced them in their hundreds. Like many others who have followed, they were clearly inspired by those earlier Egyptian achievements.

BELOW The pyramid texts on the walls of Teti's tomb chamber, and its star-spangled ceiling.
(Franck Monnier)

Chapter Two

Description of the Great Pyramid

The Great Pyramid project employed all the capabilities of the 4th dynasty builders in one continuous phase of construction. Close inspection of its separate elements produces a detailed picture of a specific point in architectural history.

OPPOSITE **The western face of the Great Pyramid.**
(Franck Monnier)

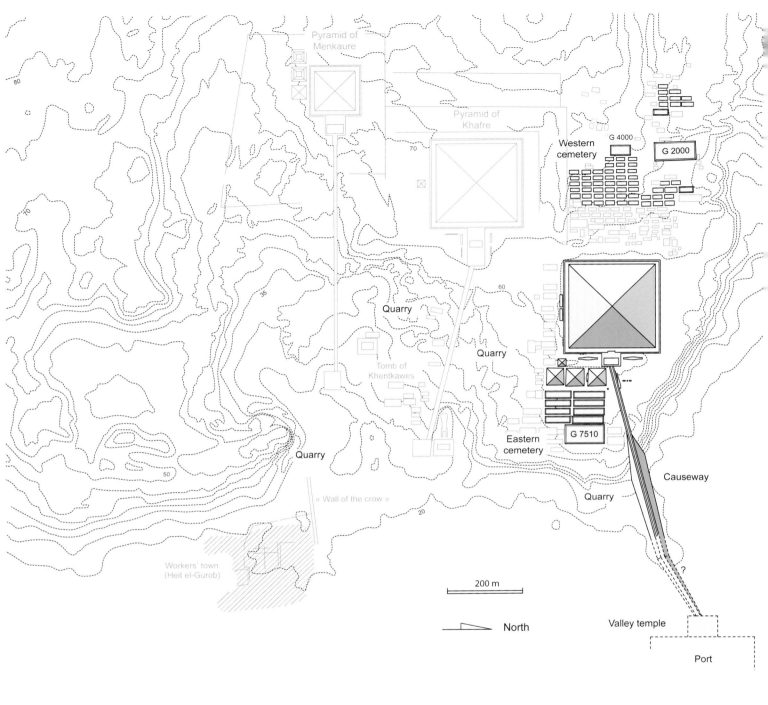

Pyramid of
Menkaure

Pyramid of
Khafre

Western
cemetery

G 4000   G 2000

Quarry

Quarry

Tomb of
Khentkawes

Eastern
cemetery

G 7510

Quarry

Causeway

« Wall of the crow »

Quarry

Workers' town
(Heit el-Gurob)

200 m

North

Valley temple

Port

ABOVE **Plan of Giza just after Khufu's Great Pyramid was completed.**
(Franck Monnier)

OPPOSITE **3D reconstruction of Khufu's complex.**
(Paul François and Franck Monnier)

The Great Pyramid presides over a vast collection of ceremonial buildings and subsidiary tombs. The majority of the burial sites belonged to senior officials, members of the court and members of Khufu's immediate family. A necropolis, a 'city of the dead', developed on two sides of the Great Pyramid in areas now known as the eastern cemetery and the western cemetery. Zones directly to the north and south of the pyramid were kept clear, as was a 130 m-wide strip close to the western side of the pyramid enclosure that now accommodates

a modern road. A humpbacked temenos wall, 3.1 m thick at the base and around 8 m high, once encircled the pyramid at a distance of 10 m. On the east side, the wall connected to the north and south sides of the mortuary temple, which was built close to that side of the pyramid. The entire ground-level surface inside this wall was paved with limestone slabs, incorporating long channels designed to remove surface rainwater. A stretch of one of the channels remains in situ, north of the surviving foundations of the mortuary temple.

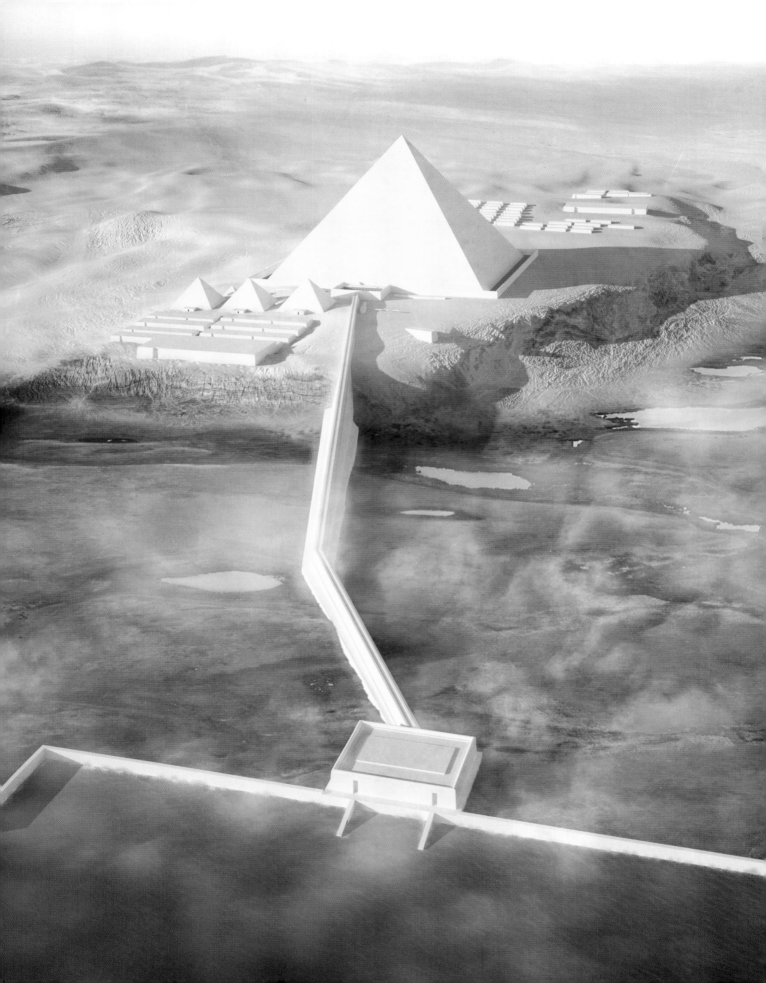

RIGHT 3D reconstruction of Khufu's mortuary temple. (Franck Monnier)

The mortuary temple

The dimensions of the Great Pyramid's mortuary temple were unprecedented, foreshadowing the gigantic temple building projects characteristic of his son Khafre's reign. Khufu's temple was reached by a long causeway that led up from the Nile floodplain and connected to the centre line of the mortuary temple, on its eastern side. From there, visitors entered a vast courtyard with granite pillars. A black basalt floor – brought from the distant quarries of Gebel Qatrani north of the Faiyum – was installed there for the first time on such a scale. The dark, opaque material that covered the entire courtyard may have symbolised the black and fertile soil that periodically covered the valley floor below, and therefore served to bring the life force of the fields right up into the desert, to the edge of

BELOW The remnants of Khufu's mortuary temple are limited to the basalt pavement and some marks in the bedrock. (Jon Bodsworth)

the pyramid itself. The walls of the temple were built with limestone, and judging from fragments discovered in the area, were covered with finely engraved and painted reliefs.

The rectangular temple building covered an area of 52.4 m by 40.3 m, or 100 cubits by 77 cubits. The courtyard occupied most of the building's ground plan, and the cloistered spaces created by the pillars that were erected around its perimeter were visible from the central space. Although the outline of the building can be traced, the inner parts of the temple, such as the vestibule, corridors, chapels and niches, are more difficult to reconstruct, and all attempts remain hypothetical. There were certainly places where ritual offerings were brought, to honour the deceased pharaoh, and where the daily rites were performed. A deep and very large well was dug here during a later period, perhaps by the Romans or Saïte period rulers. It is not known if the well was intended to be a tomb since it remained unfinished.

The causeway, the valley temple and the platform

The mortuary temple near the east side of the pyramid was formerly connected to the valley temple down on the Nile floodplain by an immense causeway structure, which was described in vivid detail by the Greek historian Herodotus when he visited Giza in the 5th century BC. The causeway was also illustrated on maps and engravings made by antiquarians John Shae Perring, Howard Vyse and Karl Richard Lepsius in the 19th century, as well as in several contemporary photographs that show significant remnants of the structure still in situ until modern times.

Growing tourism at the beginning of the 20th century and the rapid development of surrounding urban zones drove the local villagers of Nazlet el-Semman to reuse the materials they found there to build homes and hotels above the ancient foundations. The steep slopes around the plateau had driven Khufu's architects to construct foundations for the causeway that were more than 30 m high, so that an inclined path could run from the Nile valley plain, up the cliff edge to the side of the pyramid. The first Egyptologist to systematically excavate the remains of the

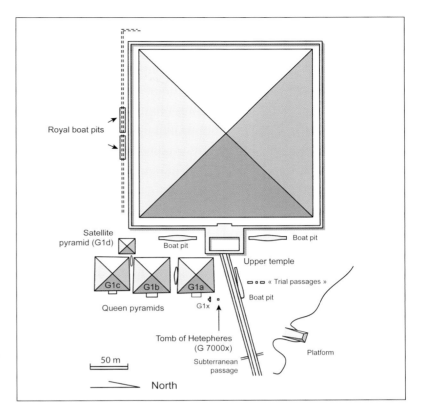

ABOVE **Plan of Khufu's complex.** *(Franck Monnier)*

BELOW **Plan of the mortuary temple.** *(Franck Monnier)*

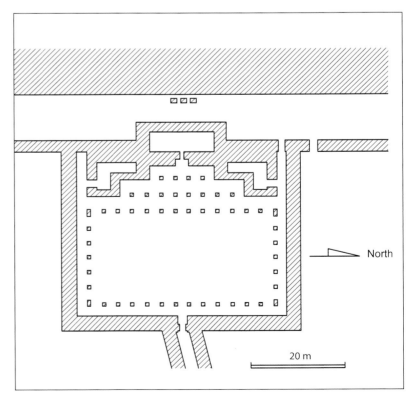

ABOVE The remains of the huge causeway were still visible in the 19th century. They were entirely dismantled during the construction of the modern town of Nazlet el-Semman. *(Robertson and Beato, 1857)*

RIGHT A tunnel was dug into the ground to allow travel from one side of the monumental causeway to the other. *(Franck Monnier)*

OPPOSITE A few stone blocks on the edge of the ridge are what remain of the huge causeway that linked the two temples of Khufu's complex. Below, the Nile floodplain is now entirely covered by the modern suburbs of Cairo. *(Franck Monnier)*

causeway, Egyptian Selim Hassan, unearthed decorated stone relief fragments that were part of the original structure. Later, French Egyptologist Georges Goyon uncovered foundation blocks and side walls from which he estimated that the ramp was almost 660 m long, with foundations 18.35 m wide and a walkway inclined at 4 or 5°. At the lower end, Goyon was also able to detect traces of the old port which was attached to the valley temple. In the 1990s, Egyptian Egyptologist Zahi Hawass established the full scale of the remains there, based on a number of core penetration samples taken across the temple and

port site, which is now covered by many metres of Nile silt that built up over the centuries. The valley temple at the bottom of the causeway has long since disappeared, but some vestiges of a long, thick port wall, extending 500 m to the east of the remains of the temple, were studied before being destroyed by real estate developers. The presence of imported basalt blocks confirm that the port was indeed built for Khufu's complex, but the sparsity of the remains prevents any significant reconstruction of the buildings, at present.

Today, there is almost nothing left of the causeway, which Herodotus estimated must have required ten years to construct, when he visited around 450 BC. He went as far as to compare the volume of work required to build the causeway to that required to build the Great Pyramid itself. Some idea of the scale of these ramps can be gained by studying the remains of the structure built by Khufu's son, the pharaoh Djedefre, for his pyramid at Abu Rawash. The causeway there has a length of nearly 1,500 m and is in fact even larger than the one that would have been built for Khufu's pyramid. Herodotus described Khufu's causeway as being richly decorated, and the structure at Giza seems to be the source of many fragments of blocks adorned with figures and hieroglyphs that were reused by Amenemhat I, a pharaoh of the 12th dynasty, to adorn his own pyramid complex, almost 50 km to the south of Giza.

ABOVE A huge platform constructed from massive masonry blocks still protrudes from the north side of the cliffs running around the edge of the plateau. Its purpose remains unclear. *(Valery Androsov)*

BELOW One of the empty boat pits on the east side of Khufu's pyramid, north of the causeway. *(Franck Monnier)*

A small passageway undercutting the causeway remains. When intact, it was possible to travel from one side of the upper section of the causeway to the other. This type of shortcut was common with such monumental structures. It made it possible for visitors to reach areas on the other side of the causeway and completely bypass the enclosed upper levels of the complex. About 40 m to the north-west of this access tunnel are the ruins of a substantially built platform made of large limestone blocks, positioned close to the edge of the plateau. The platform is 14 m by 32 m in plan. According to the scholar who first studied it in detail, Georges Goyon, this structure had a utilitarian function. It was for disposing of debris and stone offcuts from the huge construction site of the pyramid. His preliminary observations were unfortunately never followed up with further investigations, but it is worth noting that the ancient Egyptians had no real need to build such platforms to dispose of the debris, which they otherwise spread out over the ground all the way to the north of the plateau. No debris pile has ever been found below the platform, so it seems more likely that this structure, overlooking the valley below, was a location built for some particular ritual function, but the evidence currently available does not reveal what ritual this might have been.

The boat pits

Close to the exterior face of the pyramid's enclosure wall are the remains of five huge trenches. There are two along the eastern side, another running alongside the causeway and two others on the southern side. The

two southern pits are smaller but are notable because their contents remained undisturbed until the 20th century. The rectangular pits had both been closed over using an array of limestone monoliths, each weighing approximately 15 tons. A number of inscriptions bearing the royal cartouche of Djedefre indicate that it was that pharaoh, son and successor of Khufu, who was responsible for the installation of the contents and the closure of the pits. In the 1950s, shortly after its discovery, the contents of one of the pits were excavated by the Egyptian Kamal el-Mallakh, revealing hundreds of shaped wooden pieces, made of woods of various species but mainly cedar, and ropes, which were originally parts of a very large royal boat. The boat is sometimes referred to as the 'solar boat' and had been completely dismantled before it was placed into the pit, in no less than 1,224 pieces!

Excavation of the remains of a second, less well-preserved ship, lying in the second boat pit on the southern side of the pyramid, has been underway since 2011. The boat taken earlier from the easternmost of the two pits has been completely rebuilt under the direction of Egyptian Hag Ahmed Youssef Moustafa, and is now exhibited in a specially built museum situated at the foot of the south face of the pyramid, above the now-empty pit. The reconstructed vessel is approximately 43.50 m long, and it is likely that these boats were used during the lifetime of the pharaoh before being meticulously dismantled after his death and buried beside him in the funeral complex. In this way, the sovereign could enjoy travelling on these fine ships in the afterlife. Another hypothesis, put forward by Mark Lehner, sees these boats as elements used on the day of Khufu's funeral, and whose nature was so sacred that it was necessary to bury them close to the deceased pharaoh. Selim Hassan first proposed that they were 'solar boats', used to transport the soul of the pharaoh through the heavens in his manifestation as the sun god Re. This was originally proposed only as a hypothesis, but it has become accepted as fact in mainstream media. Although this point of view is not clearly supported with the texts currently available, it is nevertheless one that many Egyptologists hold today.

The subsidiary pyramids

Three pyramids that belonged to Khufu's queens (G1a, G1b and G1c) stand on the eastern periphery of the main pyramid, near the south-eastern corner of the temenos enclosure. Their partially dismantled condition reveals a three-stepped solid internal structure, covered by a masonry envelope and smooth, inclined, outer faces. Like the Great Pyramid, the cores and exteriors of these smaller pyramids were built using horizontal layers, except a few inclined casing blocks. Judging by what remains, the faces were made using fine Tura limestone, while the core structures were made of a locally sourced limestone. Their dimensions were finely set out, but for these structures the

BELOW One of the boat pits that contained a dismantled boat, located near the southern face of the Great Pyramid. This one is now situated inside the Boat Museum.
(Franck Monnier)

OPPOSITE One of the two boats that were found in pits near the southern face of the Great Pyramid. This one has been reconstructed and is now on display in the Boat Museum near the Great Pyramid. *(Franck Monnier)*

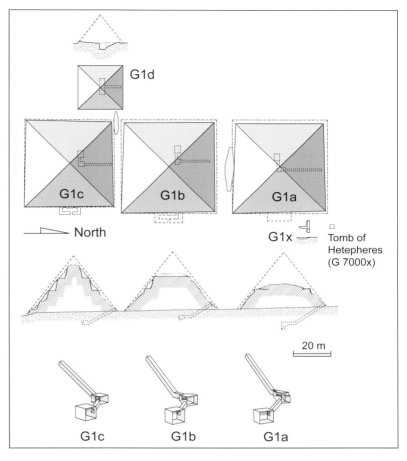

RIGHT Plans, sections and isometric views of the subsidiary pyramids situated at the east of the Great Pyramid. The tomb of Hetepheres was found at the bottom of a shaft located at the north-east corner of pyramid G1a.

(Franck Monnier)

G1d

G1c   G1b   G1a

North

G1x   Tomb of Hetepheres (G 7000x)

20 m

G1c   G1b   G1a

BELOW The queens' pyramids G1a (foreground), G1b (centre) and G1c (background).

(Franck Monnier)

71

RIGHT Queen's pyramid G1a was perhaps the burial place of Khufu's mother Hetepheres. A deep shaft (G7000x) situated near the north-east corner of the pyramid contained fine funerary furniture now on display in the Cairo Museum. A trench cut in the bedrock is visible in the foreground (G1x). This is perhaps a trace of an abandoned attempt to build the pyramid there.
(Franck Monnier)

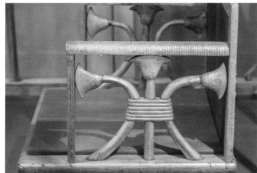

RIGHT Armchair found in shaft G7000x, now on display in Cairo Museum.
(Alain Guilleux)

RIGHT Stone vases found in shaft G7000x, and on display in Cairo Museum.
(Franck Monnier)

RIGHT Bracelets belonging to Hetepheres, on display in Cairo Museum.
(Franck Monnier)

builders adjusted the form of the first courses to account for irregularities in the natural ground surface level, instead of levelling the ground out before construction started. At ground level this process created slight variations of the positions of the edges around the structures. Each tomb contains a set of underground chambers with a similar layout, with entrances on the north side, close to the north–south axis. In each pyramid a descending passage leads due south down to an antechamber, which runs east–west, providing access to a funerary chamber whose walls were once covered with limestone slabs. All of the pyramids are bereft of inscriptions, funerary furniture and all other burial paraphernalia. Small chapels once flanked the eastern side of these tombs. G1a, located 61 m east of the Great Pyramid, was the largest, although it is now the most remote. It sits on a square base of 49.50 m each side, or approaching 100 cubits, and would have been 30.25 m high before the local quarrymen exploited its raw materials.

The queen who was buried there had the privilege of having a large boat pit set against the south side of the building, similar to those belonging to the pharaoh. Some scholars attributed this pyramid to the royal wife Meritites I, because of its proximity to the mastaba of one of her sons, Kawab. Nowadays, however, opinions tend to favour Queen Hetepheres I, mother of Khufu, whose funeral cache was found reburied in a shaft dug near the causeway, which contained a rich collection of funerary furniture (G 7000x).

Vestiges of a linear face cut in the rock (G1x), about 15 m south of the cache shaft, could be the remains of an aborted pyramid project, or could be an earlier position established for pyramid G1a before it was stopped prematurely and moved further towards the east.

The shaft containing artefacts belonging to Hetepheres was discovered and excavated by the team led by George Reisner in 1925. It is more than 27 m deep and leads down to a small burial chamber. It was here that many pieces of furniture that belonged to the queen were stored, mostly in pieces. Many of the items are now reassembled and on display at the Cairo Museum. The collection includes a bed, a canopy, an armchair, a sedan chair and fine inlaid jewellery. An alabaster sarcophagus was also placed in the chamber, and although the sarcophagus was sealed, it turned out to be empty. This treasure trove of ancient artefacts bears witness to how sophisticated daily life was for members of the pharaoh's court during the Old Kingdom, but for whatever reason, the assemblage was not accompanied by human remains.

Pyramid G1b is located about 10 m south of G1a. It rests on a square base of 49 m each side, again approaching 100 cubits, and would have risen to around 30 m when completed. It is in a poor state of preservation, having lost at least a third of its superstructure. A small boat pit is located on its south side, near the south-western corner. Regarding the possible owner of this monument, the Greek historian Herodotus recounted this fable:

Cheops moreover came, they said, to such a pitch of wickedness, that being in want of money he prostituted his own daughter, and ordered her to obtain from those who came a certain amount of money (how much it was they did not tell me); but she not only obtained the sum appointed by her father, but also formed a design for herself privately to leave behind a memorial for herself, and she requested each man who came in to her to give her one stone upon her building, and of these stones, they told me, the pyramid was built which stands in front of the Great Pyramid, in the middle of the three, each side being one hundred and fifty feet in length. (Herodotus, Histories, *book II, 126)*

This anecdote is most likely a legend created over the centuries describing the depravity of Khufu, the cruel pharaoh who would stop at nothing to satiate his pride, and so is probably not based in historical reality. In fact, almost nothing is known about the owner of this monument. Meritites I is sometimes cited as a potential candidate, while a different royal wife, of Libyan origin, has also been proposed. In reality, no document or physical evidence supports one or other of these hypotheses.

G1c is the smallest and best preserved of the three pyramids. It is less than 4 m south of G1b. Its base is a square of 46.50 m on each side, somewhat less than 100 cubits, and its original height would have been around 30 m. In a later period, a small temple of Isis was built against the walls of its chapel on the east side. In 1858 Auguste Mariette uncovered the so-called 'inventory stela' or 'king's daughter's stela' at this location, where it was installed during the 26th dynasty (Cairo Museum, JE 2091), more than 1,800 years after the rest of the funeral complex was completed. The inscriptions on the stele state that this little pyramid belonged to Princess Henutsen:

Long live the Horus Medjed, the king of Upper and Lower Egypt, Khufu, given life. He found the house of Isis, lady of the pyramid(s) next to the house of Hurun and north-west of the house of Osiris, lord of Rostau. He (re)built his pyramid next to the temple of this goddess and he (re)built the pyramid of the royal daughter, Henutsen next to this temple.

Despite the fact that it was installed long after the pyramid was built, this text may have accurately conveyed an oral or written tradition that recorded the name of the owner of the adjacent building. Apart from this one reference, almost nothing else is known about the owner of G1c.

In 1991, excavation teams led by Egyptian Egyptologist Zahi Hawass cleared a structure located 25 m east of the south-east corner of the Great Pyramid. This is now referred to as the substructure of satellite pyramid G1d. It is much smaller than the queens' pyramids described above. Very little of it survives apart from some core stones and a few of the first layer of casing blocks, made of fine Tura limestone. The square plan of the base has sides of 21.75 m in length, approximately 40 cubits. The disappearance of most of the superstructure has exposed open chambers cut into the rock below ground level. These spaces were arranged in a T-shape, with a passage descending from the north face, leading down 5.25 m to meet a rectangular room oriented east–west.

One of the most significant achievements of the Egyptian team who excavated these remains was the discovery of the remains of a pyramidion made of Tura limestone, the oldest known after that from Dahshur. The slope of its faces, 51° 40', is almost exactly the same angle as the Great Pyramid, and indicated that the height of the satellite pyramid would have been 13.80 m. The base of this apex stone, or capstone, had been cut into a convex curve, which was intended to fit into a corresponding concave form cut into the top layer of the otherwise complete pyramid. The design minimised any risk of lateral slip, which could be caused by earthquakes that hit the region episodically, or by extremely strong gusts of wind.

Discovery of this satellite pyramid invalidated an earlier hypothesis that there had been an

abandoned satellite pyramid project located east of the funerary temple, as there was typically only one satellite pyramid for each major pyramid. This proposal was based on the existence of a small set of north–south oriented underground 'trial passages' which are located about 30 m to the east of the temple, on the north side of the causeway, and which are discussed on pages 77–78.

ABOVE The exposed internal chamber and descending passage of satellite pyramid G1d, set into the bedrock. *(Franck Monnier)*

BELOW The upper casing stones and pyramidion of satellite pyramid G1d, now located north of the satellite pyramid's foundations. The pyramidion is the second-oldest known. *(Franck Monnier)*

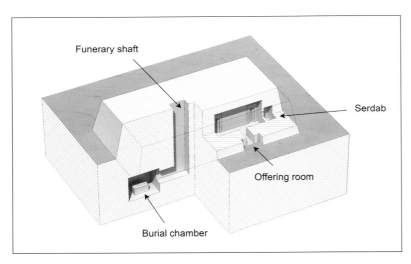

Funerary shaft

Serdab

Offering room

Burial chamber

ABOVE Isometric view of a classic Old Kingdom mastaba. (*Franck Monnier*)

BELOW A 'street' running between the large mastabas of the eastern cemetery of Khufu's complex. (*Franck Monnier*)

Cemeteries

The pyramid of Khufu is the central component of a vast necropolis which includes hundreds of associated tombs. The subsidiary pyramids for the pharaoh's queens are in close proximity to the pharaoh's eternal resting place, but the vast majority of the tombs were mastabas (bench tombs), which varied in size according to the status of their owners. These were located in one of two distinct zones: the western cemetery and the eastern cemetery, whereas the cemetery located south of the main pyramid dates to the 5th and 6th dynasties. The study and excavation of the 4th dynasty mastabas was mainly carried out at the beginning of the 20th century by several archaeological missions, the most notable of which were led by George Reisner, Hermann Junker and Selim Hassan.

The eastern cemetery, called the G7000 cemetery, is a field of mastabas clustered to the east of the queens' pyramids. Most of the tombs there belonged to princes and princesses who were members of Khufu's family. Their kinship with Khufu is proved by inscriptions found in the mastabas. Among these were the names of Djedefhor (G7210–7220), Kawab and Hetepheres II (G7110–7120), Khufukhaf and Neferetkau (G7130–7140), and Meresankh II and Horbaef (G7410–7420). These were overshadowed by a huge mastaba established at the edge of the plateau, mastaba G7510, 100 m long and 50 m wide. Its owner was Khufu's brother, the famous Ankhhaf, vizier and overseer of all works for the pharaoh, as described on the now famous Wadi al-Jarf papyrus. His name was already known, because his burial contained artefacts and inscriptions, and a fine painted bust of the man himself was recovered and is now preserved in the Museum of Fine Arts in Boston (MFA 27.442).

The western cemetery is composed of several distinct subsections. The westernmost section is referred to as G1200 and the largest mastaba in that area belonged to Wepemnefret (G1201), master of the scribes. A huge mastaba, G2000, whose dimensions equal those of the vizier Ankhhaf, sat a little further east. Unfortunately, no text has ever been discovered that identifies its owner.

ABOVE Ascending passage of the 'trial passages', now blocked with a steel door. The upper section would equate to the lower part of the Grand Gallery. *(Franck Monnier)*

ABOVE Descending passage of the 'trial passages'. *(Franck Monnier)*

Cemetery G4000 is dominated by the grand mastaba of vizier Hemiunu, also famous for his fine seated statue which was discovered in the *serdab* (an offering chamber near the entrance of his tomb), which is now preserved and displayed in the museum of Hildesheim. The titles of Hemiunu reveal that he was overseer of works for the pharaoh at the beginning of his reign. It is therefore legitimate to consider that he was the first architect of the Great Pyramid. Many other mastabas, most of which remained unfinished, were built in a very orderly fashion in this western burial ground, but a large undeveloped area west of the Khufu pyramid was left clear of burials. Hundreds of tombs were added to the cemetery through the dynasties and reigns that followed, making this necropolis one of the largest in the country.

The 'trial passages'

This set of connected tunnels, excavated from the bedrock, is located on the north side of the causeway near Khufu's mortuary temple. It comprises a small group of inclined passages and a vertical shaft, which are approximately 22 m in length horizontally and reach down to a depth of 10 m. Howard Vyse and Flinders Petrie surveyed and drew plans for these passages, revealing a layout that

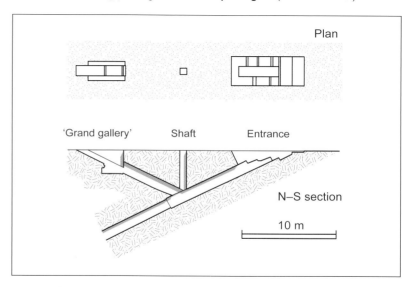

ABOVE Plan and section of the 'trial passages'. *(Franck Monnier)*

LEFT The vertical shaft leading down to the 'trial passages'. It may have provided access to view the interfaces of the plugging blocks. *(Franck Monnier)*

Petrie believed to be some sort of replica or trial version of the internal passages within the Great Pyramid. Parts of the configuration of the trial passages do resemble the Great Pyramid's descending passage where it meets the junction containing plugging blocks, which connects to the ascending passage, and parts also resemble the bottom of the Grand Gallery with its side benches. There is no parallel in the trial passages for the 'service shaft', however, and the part equating to a horizontal corridor is very short. In addition, a vertical shaft, square in section, rising above the junction between the ascending and descending passages has no equivalent in Khufu's pyramid.

It seems unlikely that these passages were intended to be covered by a scaled-down replica of the Great Pyramid, as some have suggested, both in view of the unusual location of the passages, and the lack of a close parallel in any other funerary complex. If it is assumed that it was a replica model of part of the Great Pyramid, then it must also be assumed that the construction of the internal arrangement of Khufu's pyramid was carried out according to a predetermined plan. Such a hypothesis has not yet been demonstrated and does not seem to agree with several features observed in the finished structure. No traces of foundations for a superstructure have been found, and no burial chamber has been excavated in the area. The sections and inclinations are nevertheless

similar to those of the Great Pyramid, and while the lengths are considerably reduced in scale, the parts that correspond seem to be associated with the elements designed to close the monument upon its completion. French scholar Franck Monnier therefore considers it likely that the passages were a prototype to test the closing system in the ascending passage, using a line of blocks intended to plug the access route into the monument at the junction of the two main passages. The vertical shaft may have provided access allowing observation of the point where the first closing blocks would become stuck in the narrowing corridors. A tightening of the section of the descending passage here suggests that the builders planned to introduce blocks to plug the entrance at that location, and supports the proposal that the structure as a whole was associated with the final closure of the Great Pyramid.

Scottish archaeologist David Lightbody suggests an additional use for the trial passages. According to his reconstruction, the north-facing inclined shaft could have been used for carrying out the stellar observations that determined the external cardinal alignment of the Great Pyramid. In this scenario, the additional central vertical shaft could have been created as a containment for dropping a long plumb bob line, a device that is necessary for taking precise linear and angular measurements using rudimentary stellar observation methods.

BELOW The Great Sphinx. Its identity has been discussed in recent decades. It is normally associated with Khafre, son of Khufu. However, some Egyptologists believe it was carved during the reign of Khufu.
(Franck Monnier)

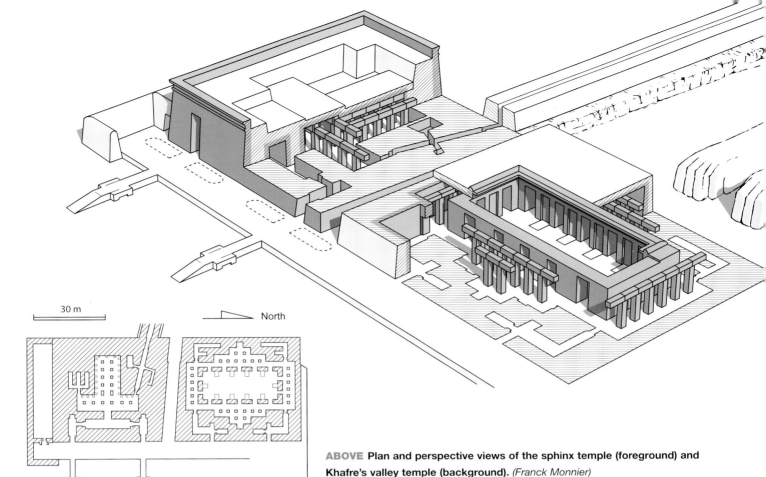

ABOVE Plan and perspective views of the sphinx temple (foreground) and Khafre's valley temple (background). *(Franck Monnier)*

30 m

North

Was the Great Sphinx and its temple a part of Khufu's tomb complex?

In 1926, Emile Baraize uncovered the remains of a temple built in front of the Great Sphinx at Giza. It is situated just to the east of the sphinx, is oriented to the cardinal directions, and has two entrances which both open to the east. Its south wall runs close to the north wall of Khafre's valley temple, with a separation of only a few metres, and the rear and front faces of the two temples were built in alignment. Like Khafre's valley temple, but to a lesser extent, the sphinx temple contained huge blocks of local limestone, filling the thickest sections of its walls.

The construction of the sphinx temple was, however, interrupted, most likely due to the death of the pharaoh who commissioned it. This left the building devoid of its red granite exterior cladding, except for around the frames of the doorways. The coping on top of the walls and the roofing of the interior spaces

were also never completed. Red granite was, however, used to dress the interior walls, and a beautiful cream-white alabaster pavement also covered the interior floor space. The internal ground plan was elaborate and is an outstanding example of rigorous axial symmetry. The layout is arranged around a large central courtyard which constitutes the principal design element of the temple, and it is very similar to the courtyard of Khafre's mortuary temple close to his pyramid. Based on the rectangular holes cut in the pavement, ten statues sat at the feet of the pillars and looked into the courtyard from all sides, except at the corners. There are fourteen openings around the perimeter of the open courtyard that give access to four pillared rooms, one in each cardinal direction.

Two gateways in the east façade provided access to enter the building, first into vestibules with rooms on one side and wide transverse galleries on the other. Right-angled bends then open into ambulatory corridors that eventually lead to the corners of the courtyard. Opposite these, on the far, west side of the courtyard, are the entrances to two pairs of corridors, but they soon terminate in dead ends. The elements of the monument were therefore arranged so that there was no direct access to the area behind it in which the sphinx sits. Access was only possible via the passage separating the two temples. Based on the available evidence, and despite its proximity to the statue, it is still not clear if this temple was dedicated to the worship of the sphinx or a related solar cult.

Due to the proximity of the monumental statue and Khafre's complex, and in particular, its valley temple and its causeway, they are often treated as elements of a single funerary ensemble dedicated to Khafre. In recent years,

however, some scholars have questioned when the sphinx was created and who created it. The temple that stands in front of its paws has been drawn into the same discussions. The prevailing view until the 1980s was that the gigantic sculpture sported the features of Khafre, who supposedly commissioned the work. A comparative stylistic study led by Rainer Stadelmann, however, set him against the mainstream when he proposed Khufu as the most probable candidate. Others, more boldly but less seriously, went so far as to revise its dating backwards by several millennia.

The sphinx lacks inscriptions or iconography, but there are characteristics of the sphinx temple that closely resemble Khafre's funerary temples, including the courtyards with statues, ambulatory corridors, the materials used, the rough-cut blocks and the two entry portals. Together they constitute a significant body of circumstantial evidence to demonstrate that the sphinx temple should also be attributed to Khafre, and not to Khufu, whose mortuary temple does not withstand such a comparison. The so-called 'dream stela' (Cairo Museum, JE 59460), which stands between the legs of the sphinx, was erected a thousand years later by order of Thutmose IV. Its text is the oldest that refers to Khafre in connection with the gigantic statue; however, the date of its installation was so long after the creation of the monuments that it cannot be taken as irrefutable proof, and it is notable that another stele erected in this location, by Amenhotep II, names Khufu and Khafre together, as if the author of that text had also found it difficult to decide who was responsible for creating the sphinx.

The various stylistic analyses carried out on the head of the sphinx by scholars involved in the debate have led to conclusions so discordant that they only seem to have proved how unproductive this line of enquiry is. One of the arguments raised by Rainer Stadelmann

relied on the sphinx's beard, which he suggested was created after the Old Kingdom. Representations of Khafre and Djedefre do wear a beard, unlike those of Khufu. Further research conducted in the 1980s, however, uncovered a fragment near the sphinx's paws that is apparently the result of a restoration of an older beard, so the arguments based on the beard also proved to be weak.

Archaeologists and geologists who have studied the Giza Plateau and the quarries on its western side have noted that Khafre's causeway does not run directly down to the valley by the most direct route, but follows a straight path heading slightly towards the south, perhaps to avoid the sphinx or an older structure at the same location. This would suggest that the causeway was built after the structure found at that location. On the other hand, it has also been noted that a channel running along the north side of the causeway was interrupted by the excavation works that created the sphinx. This seems to suggest that Khafre was responsible for building the sphinx at the end of his reign, after the causeway had been created. Another significant observation, made by Mark Lehner, is that the roughly hewn blocks used to construct the sphinx temple come from the quarrying

works that exposed the sphinx's body, which is part of the bedrock. Therefore, the sphinx and the sphinx temple were created simultaneously, and both therefore date to Khafre's reign.

The controversy regarding who was responsible for creating the sphinx divides Egyptology, yet nobody has been able to provide a decisive argument one way or another. It seems most likely, however, that the temple attached to the sphinx was the work of Khafre's architects, and that the conclusions of Mark Lehner, which indicate that the sphinx was also created during Khafre's reign, are based on relatively solid facts.

The Great Pyramid

Giza has been described as the most intensively surveyed piece of real estate on the planet, and it is the Great Pyramid itself that is the most carefully surveyed part of the Giza necropolis. The base of the pyramid is almost perfectly square and was set out with a precision only approached by Khafre's surveyors. This technical feat has no other equivalent in the ancient world. When the casing stones were still in place the sides measured on average 230.36 m, with overall variations of

RIGHT Local nummulitic limestone used for the core blocks of Khufu's pyramid. *(Franck Monnier)*

RIGHT Local limestone used for the backing stones (upper layer) and Tura limestone used for the casing stones (lower layer). *(Franck Monnier)*

RIGHT Red Aswan granite used to construct the uppermost chambers of Khufu's pyramid. *(Franck Monnier)*

OPPOSITE The remaining casing stones and pavement at the base of the northern face of the pyramid. *(Franck Monnier)*

of the casing stones and several blocks at the summit were stripped off by quarrymen during the Middle Ages and in the 19th century, and only a few huge casing stones now remain on the lowest level on the north side.

The casing was made of fine limestone blocks brought from the Tura quarries across the Nile. Each element was cut, dressed and smoothed with extreme care. Flinders Petrie was amazed by the quality of the joints between the surviving casing stones, the widths of which rarely exceed half a millimetre. To obtain this level of precision with stones of up to 15 tons is truly impressive. Once moved into place, the joints were also filled with a liquid gypsum mortar to close the gaps completely. This extraordinary level of precision was not, however, the rule for the entire monument. The outer casing and the structured masonry of the internal chambers was made using fine limestone from the Tura quarries, but this was quite different to the majority of the stones used for the bulk of the core. The great majority of the masonry is a filling of local nummulitic limestone blocks (so-called in reference to the great abundance of fossilised, single-cell marine organisms called nummulites found in the sedimentary rock), roughly squared, and with roughly hewn faces and interface joints.

The forced entry passage excavated through the core blocks, as well as the 'service shaft' and the hole excavated in the wall of the Queen's Chamber, revealed gaps between core blocks as large as 10 cm. They were often filled with mortar consisting of gypsum, sand and limestone chips. The horizontal courses of core blocks were nevertheless sufficiently solid to provide good flat surfaces on which each subsequent layer of construction could be set. Red Aswan granite was used to build the funerary chambers in and around the King's Chamber, just as it had been used in Djoser's Step Pyramid at Saqqara. This rock was much more difficult to extract and shape than the limestone, and it was brought from quarries located more than 800 km to the south. Its prolific use carried enormous symbolic value, and it served to protect the burial place from the efforts of tomb robbers, as well as from massive structural forces resulting from the superstructure overhead.

less than 10 cm on all four sides. The corners were almost perfect right angles, deviating by less than one-fifteenth of a single degree, and the base of the entire first course of the pyramid varies in height by less than 2.1 cm from a perfectly horizontal plane. The sides are oriented to the four cardinal directions, N-S-E-W, with an average deviation again less than one-fifteenth of a single degree. The architects chose an inclination for the faces of 51° 50', identical to that of the Meidum Pyramid and at least one of the queens' pyramids nearby This is a *seked*-like slope ratio of 5½ palms or 5 palms and 2 digits (for a discussion of the symbolic value of this slope, see Chapter 3). When completed, the building rose to 146.5 m, making it the tallest building on the planet at that time. Nowadays, its height has been reduced to 138.7 m. Most

DESCRIPTION OF THE GREAT PYRAMID

RIGHT Graph
highlighting the
different heights of
the core layers of the
Great Pyramid.
(Franck Monnier)

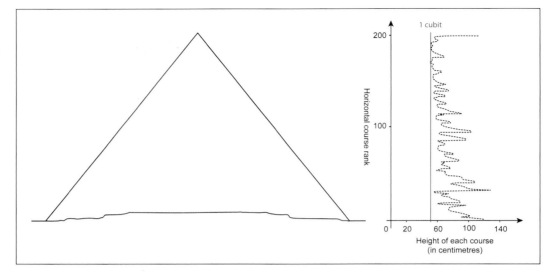

Flinders Petrie's measurements revealed a very slight concavity, or fold, running down the centre of the faces of the pyramid. This is noticeable only when the sunlight grazes over them at a very low angle. The purpose or the reason for the existence of these indentations remains unknown, but they may be artefacts of the surveying and setting out methods used by the overseers, or the result of the stone quarrying methods used to remove the casing stones from the monument in the Middle Ages.

Another anomaly is a small platform up on the north-east corner's lateral edge. A hole in the blocks at the 106th course gives access to an open, cave-like chamber, a few cubic metres in volume. It is not known if this was built into the original structure or if it is a recent development, added so that someone could monitor the surrounding landscape. This feature was already known in the 19th century and would have served as an excellent lookout or guard post. Most recently, the ScanPyramids mission reported results that may indicate the existence of a similar cavity a few tens of metres above it, although there is no conclusive evidence of such a void space inside the structure at this time.

Geochemical and geomorphological analyses have made it possible to match the core construction materials used to build the pyramid with materials found in specific local quarries. These quarries are located a few hundred metres to the south and east of the Great Pyramid and may have provided the required materials. The various visible gaps extending into the core reveal that the blocks were laid in horizontal layers, and not in inclined planes, as was occasionally the case in other pyramid structures.

According to the various surveys, the Great Pyramid would have had between 201 and 203

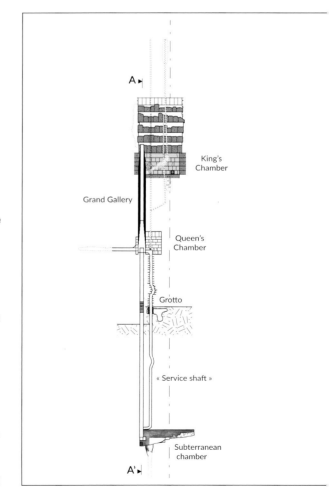

horizontal courses when completed. Although the average height of each layer is 0.69 m, their height decreases upwards, but not continuously as it fluctuates rather irregularly, between 1.50 and 0.51 m. Towards the top, however, the builders reduced the height of each layer down to a more consistent and more controllable layer height of 0.52 m, or 1 cubit in height. This is also a feature of the upper parts of Khafre's pyramid.

Based on its geometry, the theoretical volume of stone used to construct the pyramid was 2.6 million m³. In fact, the volume was significantly less, since Khufu's architects took advantage of a large, low outcrop of bedrock to reduce the building volume required. This is verified by observations made at several locations in the building, including at the level of the bedrock visible in the descending passage, in the 'service shaft', and at the north-eastern and north-western outer corners.

Measurements indicate that this outcrop does not rise much above 7 m.

The internal spaces of Khufu's pyramid are unusually arranged in a single vertical plane. The passages and chambers are positioned on this plain which is oriented north–south, and cuts through the structure close to the centre line of the pyramid. The first chamber above ground level, and the uppermost chamber, are designated the Queen's Chamber and the King's Chamber, according to an oral tradition already used by the savants of the Napoleonic Egyptian expedition. In fact, no remains of a king or queen have ever been found in the Great Pyramid, and it is likely that only the upper chamber was ever used for a burial; undoubtedly Khufu's.

The original entrance was 17 m above ground level on the north face of the pyramid. When complete, the entrance was covered by a huge vault consisting of two stacked sets of apexed stone beams, rectangular in section and

BELOW Sections showing the chambers and passages of the Great Pyramid, looking west (below) and looking due south through the centre of the pyramid (opposite). *(Franck Monnier)*

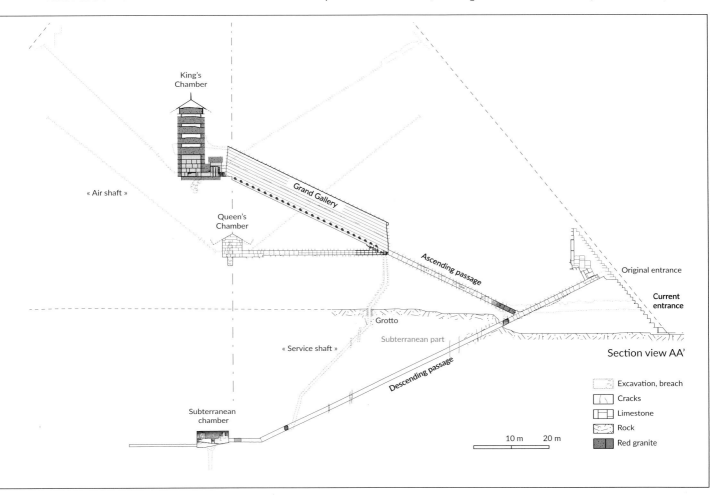

King's Chamber

« Air shaft »

Grand Gallery

Queen's Chamber

Ascending passage

Original entrance

Current entrance

Grotto

Subterranean part

« Service shaft »

Section view AA'

Descending passage

Subterranean chamber

	Excavation, breach
	Cracks
	Limestone
	Rock
	Red granite

10 m   20 m

The exposed joints in the masonry beside the vault, and all the lower abutment wall interfaces, seem to show that the vault does not extend further into the pyramid, and originally only covered the descending passage for at most 5.4 m, or around 10 cubits, from the outer entrance into the pyramid.

The thickness of the stone beams is 80 cm with only slight variations. If it is assumed that the vault was completely hidden by the surrounding masonry and the outer casing stones of the pyramid, calculations show that there were originally seven pairs of beams in the lower set and four pairs of beams in the upper set, which was set further back.

A long hieroglyphic inscription adorns the western face of the upper set. Rather than being ancient, it was actually inscribed in the early 19th century by the German explorer Karl Richard Lepsius as a tribute to his Kaiser, Frederick William IV, King of Prussia (1840–61).

The existence of the vault poses something of a problem for archaeologists, as it is apparently useless in this location. There is no real need for such a huge structure to protect the ascending passage, which was only 2 cubits in width, or just over 1 m. Did the vault

ABOVE Original entrance of the Great Pyramid. The huge blocks of the gable vault were removed in the ancient past for reuse. A long hieroglyphic inscription on the right upper monolith of the arch (just visible here) was created by German Egyptologist Karl Richard Lepsius.
(Franck Monnier)

leaning against each other at the top, in pairs. Today only one pair on each level remains, as well as two broken-off beams that are still embedded in their supporting abutment walls on the east side.

RIGHT Isometric view of the original entrance. The gable vault has been reconstructed to show its original arrangement.
(Franck Monnier)

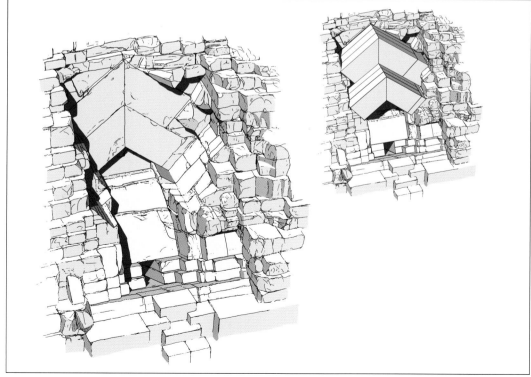

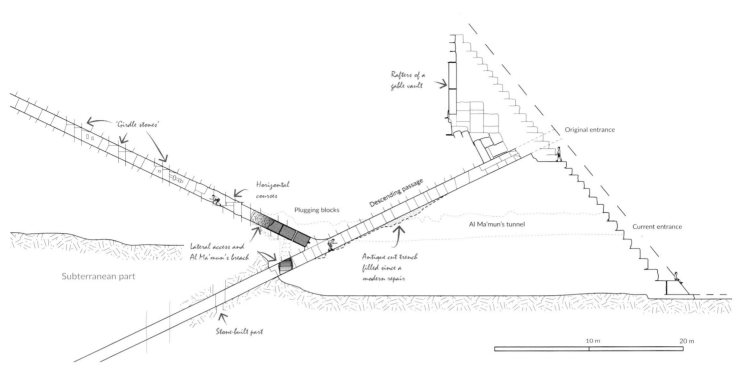

ABOVE Detailed sectional view of the lower internal arrangement of the Great Pyramid, including its entrances.
(Franck Monnier)

Within the diagram:

Rafters of a gable vault

'Girdle stones'

Horizontal courses

Plugging blocks

Descending passage

Original entrance

Current entrance

Al Ma'mun's tunnel

Lateral access and Al Ma'mun's breach

Antique cut trench filled since a modern repair

Subterranean part

Stone-built part

10 m   20 m

---

carry some symbolic significance, or was it primarily functional? Was it only intended to reduce stresses on the access corridor leading to the inner chambers? Whatever its purpose, the elaborate structure created an imposing entrance to the pharaonic tomb.

The muon detection scans carried out in 2016–17 by the international ScanPyramids team seemed to detect some signs of a void space or low-density area behind the vault. However, no additional tests have been carried out so far that might confirm these preliminary conclusions. The scans have so far yielded nothing that helps to clarify what the symbolic or functional value of the vault was.

Although there are no definitive answers at this time, there is architectural evidence from the Old Kingdom that suggests that the vaults carried some symbolic meaning (see below in the section discussing the King's Chamber and its 'relieving chambers').

Under this impressive vault, the entrance opens into a very long, straight, descending passage, 1.20 m high by 1.05 m wide, inclined at an angle of 26° 27' to the horizontal. These dimensions are 2 cubits and 2 palms tall by 2 cubits wide in section and this seems to have been the normal size for extended passages in the pyramid. The angle is an inclination or gradient of 50%, or 1:2, or a *seked*-like *ratio* of 2 cubits.

At a distance of 25 m down the passage, the rectangular underside of a red granite block is visible, flush with the ceiling. It reveals the existence of an ascending corridor that departs upwards from that point, but it completely blocks off all access to the passage. A few metres further down the descending passage from this junction is the opening to a vertical tunnel excavated by ancient explorers. This tunnel was designed to circumvent the granite closing system, to connect to the lower passages from those above that had already been accessed. Continuing downwards, more than 90 m from the entrance and 7 m before the lower end of the descending section is an opening to another tunnel, the so-called 'service shaft'. This irregularly formed tunnel leads upwards for about 60 m, eventually reaching the lower end of the Grand Gallery far above. Unlike the robber tunnels, this shaft was created by the pyramid's builders and connects the lower and upper chambers, but the reason for its construction is still debated (see below).

At the lower end of the long descending passage, the corridor levels out into a horizontal passage with a smaller section of 0.80 m x 0.90 m. After 8.9 m it opens into a large,

irregular, underground chamber known as the subterranean chamber. Before the chamber, in the western wall of the passage, there is a small box-shaped recess that still contains the fragment of a block of granite, most likely parts of one of three portcullises that protected the King's Chamber, which were destroyed and carried away by looters. The incomplete state of the underground chamber is evident, and it seems that just over half of the planned volume was ever excavated from the bedrock. Its plan is rectangular, 14.05 m long from east to west by 8.25 m wide from north to south. Its height reaches 5 m at its tallest point. An excavation carried out in the eastern end of the chamber to a depth of 1.5 m was extended to 3 m in depth at the beginning of the 19th century, by Giovanni Battista Caviglia, exceeding the depth reached by the builders. The Greek historian Herodotus reported that the sarcophagus of Khufu once rested in the subterranean chamber, on an island surrounded by water from the Nile which entered by means of canals. English explorer Howard Vyse tried to find confirmation for this testimony and had a deep well dug at the bottom of Caviglia's excavation, but after 11.50 m it did not, evidently, lead anywhere. John Shae Perring noticed Greek and Roman inscriptions, which were created with smoking oil lamps on the ceiling of the chamber, proving that the subterranean space had been visited a long time before its entrance passage was filled in with sand.

An additional passage opens in the south wall of the subterranean chamber, opposite the place where the entrance corridor arrives, but at a lower level. It finishes in a dead end after 16 m. This collection of underground spaces appears to be a set of unfinished funerary chambers that were part of an abandoned project. However, some Egyptologists, including I.E.S. Edwards, Mark Lehner and Zahi Hawass, suggest that the chamber may have had a ritual function. It could represent a place to connect with the chthonian underworld of the afterlife. In this scenario, the underground chamber was completed and conceived of as just one part of the complexed final system of passages and chambers.

The whole descending passage below the junction with the ascending corridor, and the excavated chambers, were still obstructed by debris and sand when Danish explorer Frederic Louis Norden visited in 1737–38. Henri Salt and Giovanni Battista Caviglia cleared the spaces out in 1817, as well as clearing out the lower section of the 'service shaft'. They were the first modern explorers to reach and enter the subterranean chamber.

Closer to the main exterior entrance to the pyramid, above the junction closed off by the granite block, are some deep gashes cut into the floor slabs of the passage. They led John Shae Perring to consider if the entire first section of the descending passage had originally been closed off with blocks that were forcibly removed by looters. The marks were very roughly cut to a depth of some 40 cm, but became less evident towards the entrance of the pyramid. They were still visible in the 1950s but were subsequently closed over with cement during restoration.

The granite block visible in the ceiling of the descending passage is the first in a set of three that remain in situ. The first two weigh approximately 5 tons, while the third is now fragmented. It is likely that they were first stored in the Grand Gallery above before being slid into their current position. Today, it is possible to circumvent them and enter the upper part of the ascending corridor by means of a tunnel, probably dug by al-Ma'mun's workers in the 9th century. Those excavations arrive near the top of the set of three blocks, exposing the western face of the blocking system, which remains in place from the point where the ascending passage meets the descending passage, up to the top of the set of three granite blocks. Although circumvented, they still block the

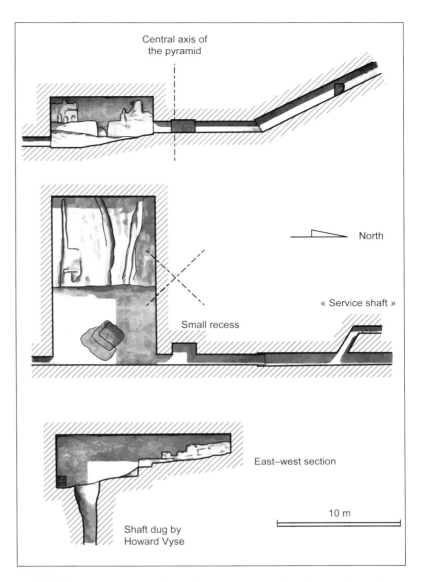

ABOVE Plan and sections of the subterranean chamber. *(Franck Monnier)*

BELOW The subterranean chamber as it looks today with a railing protecting the entrance to the well dug in the 19th century. *(Jon Bodsworth)*

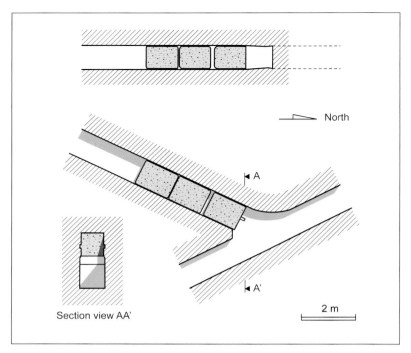

ABOVE Plan and sections reconstructing the original plugging block system at the lower end of the ascending passage.
(Franck Monnier)

ABOVE RIGHT Al-Ma'mun's breach bypassing the plugging blocks. *(The Edgar brothers, 1910)*

original access route to the upper chambers of the pyramid.

The lower end of the ascending passage is 97 cm wide, which is less than the 105 cm/2 cubits width in the passage sections above it. This meant that the blocks became lodged in place when they were slid down the passage. The masonry surrounding the ascending passage where it begins is composed of the horizontal core block layers, while most of the rest of the ascending passage above is constructed from elements that are arranged parallel to the incline. The stones surrounding the first section are squared and dressed, but not finely finished or finely grouted like those of the rest of the structure above. Ludwig Borchardt noted that the lower surrounding masonry layers must have been placed first, then dug through to create the junction between the two inclined passages, and this seems to be indicative of a change of plan during construction.

The ascending corridor is inclined at 26° 6' and is 39.27 m long. Again, this slope is close to being a regular gradient of 1:2, or 50%, or a *seked*-like ratio of 2 cubits using the ancient Egyptian system. It varies less than half a degree from the incline of the descending passage, although it slopes in the opposite direction. The walls suffer from significant erosion and are heavily fractured due to atmospheric effects and the use of relatively low-quality limestone. The walls have a very coarse appearance and it is no longer possible to trace out the various joints between the separate blocks. Detailed drawings of the walls above the granite plugs were, however, made in the past, and describe sets of joints that caught the attention of Ludwig Borchardt. These vertical joints in the side walls flank special blocks called girdle stones, where the floor and the lower parts of the side walls were formed from solid blocks cut in a 'U' shape. The floor of the corridor at these points is inclined, but the joints on the side walls run vertically, in contrast to the other joints in the corridor which have joints that run perpendicular to the inclined floor of the passage. There are three sets of these blocks, separated by approximately 4.35 m. Borchardt believed that these 'girdle stones' were located at the junctions between inclined layers of an internal Step Pyramid structure. This opinion, however, was not shared by the Italian architects Vito Maragioglio and Celeste Rinaldi, who noted firstly that the joints were vertical and not inclined, and secondly, that they appeared three times in this ascending passage and nowhere else in the pyramid. Borchardt's hypothesis could be valid if the girdle blocks appeared at other locations through the whole

internal structure of the pyramid, but that is not the case. In addition, the Meidum Pyramid, dating to Snefru's reign, was built with an internal step structure, but revealed nothing comparable within its passages.

More recently, Gilles Dormion proposed that the three sets of girdle blocks were installed to replace a sliding gate system that the architects had abandoned. Although possible, this hypothesis is problematic. If the system consisted of consecutive sets of sliding closing blocks held in side chambers at each level in the corridor, then the closure systems must have been completed with the sliding blocks installed in the waiting position. If the system was subsequently abandoned, it must have been after the ascending corridor had been constructed to a level higher than the uppermost girdle block, or else that girdle block would never have been installed. The question, then, is how the sliding blocks were removed without removing the girdle blocks. It is equally difficult to believe that the girdle blocks were installed after each of the devices was removed or closed off, given that the walls and floor formed by the girdle blocks is one solid stone. It seems that it would have been impossible to install them once the passage was completed, as these blocks are much wider than the passage. In conclusion, they could not have been fitted retrospectively, and must have been part of the original structure.

The ascending corridor leads up to a wide landing at the northern, lower end of the Grand Gallery. A horizontal corridor leads south from there and connects to the Queen's Chamber, while a sloping incline, also leading south, ascends to the King's Chamber above. The narrow 'service shaft' also connects this part of the passage system down to the subterranean chamber. It opens onto this landing on the west side.

The Grand Gallery of the Great Pyramid is certainly its most majestic architectural feature, and the one that arouses the greatest admiration among visitors. Its various elements have intrigued researchers for centuries. Some have found explanations for the various

BELOW **Detailed plan of the masonry joints in the ascending passage showing the 'girdle stones'. It now seems that only the first three constitute special structural systems, while the fourth and fifth are simply horizontal stones that the builders dug through to create the passage.** *(The Edgar brothers, 1910)*

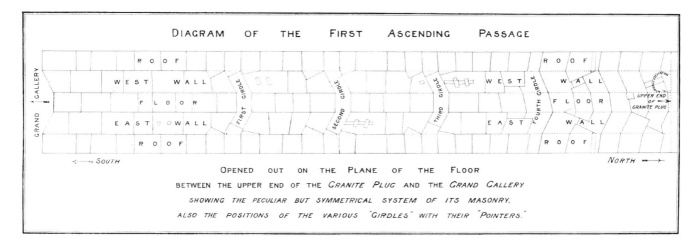

DIAGRAM OF THE FIRST ASCENDING PASSAGE

OPENED OUT ON THE PLANE OF THE FLOOR
BETWEEN THE UPPER END OF THE *GRANITE PLUG* AND THE *GRAND GALLERY*
SHOWING THE PECULIAR BUT SYMMETRICAL SYSTEM OF ITS MASONRY,
ALSO THE POSITIONS OF THE VARIOUS "GIRDLES" WITH THEIR "POINTERS."

ABOVE **The Grand Gallery looking south.**
(Jon Bodsworth)

The reason for this colouration remains unclear, but American geologist James Harrell concluded that the walls were originally finished with a reddish paint applied over a type of undercoat. Moisture from the breath of tourists, as well as iron content in the stone itself may subsequently have caused oxidation of the surface finish to produce the patina that is visible today.

The gallery is inclined at an angle of 26° 10', more or less continuing the slope of the ascending corridor below, which inclines at 26° 6'. The corbelled space is more than 47.84 m in length and is 8.6 m high throughout. At its base the gallery is 2.10 m wide, which is 4 cubits. Moving towards the ceiling, the width narrows over a succession of 7 steps, or corbels, until it reduces to approximately 1.05 m, or 2 cubits, at the top. At the floor level, two side benches, 52 cm or 1 cubit in width and height, reduce the width of the corridor to form a central channel of 1.05 m, or 2 cubits, the same width as the ascending corridor below. A thin groove runs along both sides of the gallery at the level of the third corbel.

Most scholars agree that the plugging blocks in the ascending passage were originally stored in the Grand Gallery. A system of notches aligned on either side of the landing of the gallery seem to indicate that the sloped floor of the Grand Gallery was designed as an extension of the ascending corridor's closing system. The arrangement of these notches suggests that a temporary structure was built onto beams embedded in the walls, perhaps to facilitate access for the funerary procession who brought the pharaoh to his eternal resting place, but also to help convey the granite blocks down to their final position during the closure of the tomb. But the question remains, was the gallery primarily designed for the storage and installation of the closing system, or was it originally planned as a majestic entrance hall, into which a closing system was subsequently added?

Construction details that have caused extensive debate are a set of 54 notches or slots arranged on the side benches and in the side walls of the gallery, in pairs opposite each other. The slots have been modified and resized by the builders, which makes their original purpose

'anomalies' visible in its design by postulating the existence of hidden chambers, or by resorting to even more unlikely explanations. The lack of a clear understanding of how the structure originally functioned has, unfortunately, led to a proliferation of alternative theories. More serious scholars have also developed hypotheses concerning the original function of the Grand Gallery, based on detailed studies of the features visible within the structure. Some are more convincing than others, but the limited evidence available means that it remains difficult to reach any definitive conclusions about why such an enormous structure was considered necessary.

The Grand Gallery was most probably made from Tura limestone, but the stone is no longer grey-white as it would have appeared when newly quarried. The surfaces are smooth and light-brown in colour, with a slightly reddish tint.

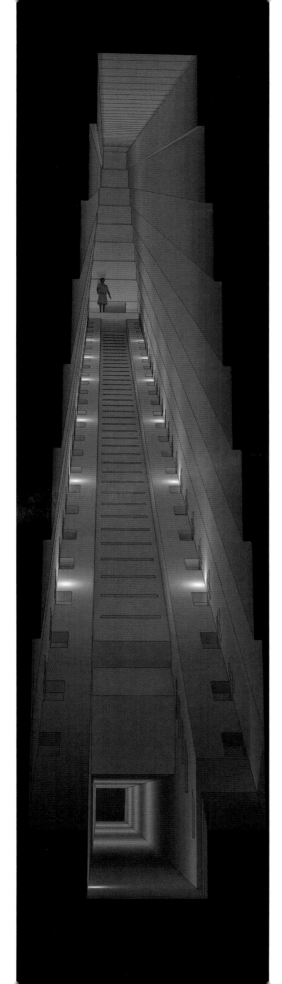

FAR LEFT 3D reconstruction of the Grand Gallery and the horizontal passage, looking south.
(Franck Monnier)

LEFT One of the 54 notches arranged on the side benches of the Grand Gallery.
(Jon Bodsworth)

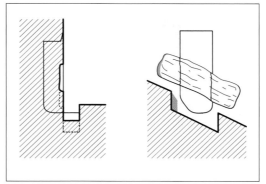

LEFT Section and frontal view of the notches in the Grand Gallery.
(Franck Monnier)

particularly difficult to determine. Several researchers have put forward hypotheses regarding their function. Ludwig Borchardt and Georges Goyon proposed a system for storing closing blocks. Jean-Philippe Lauer envisaged a framework that allowed the builders to repurpose approximately 20 granite closing blocks that were originally to be used to fill the ascending corridor, but were finally employed in the construction of the King's Chamber.

Vito Maragioglio and Celeste Rinaldi rejected Ludwig Borchardt's system as technically infeasible, and Georges Goyon's system as based on poor observations. The Italian architects, however, did not propose a more plausible explanation. Jean-Philippe Lauer's hypothesis seems unconvincing and difficult to verify, while Gilles Dormion, who originally proposed a system associated with a hidden passage, recently offered a more technical

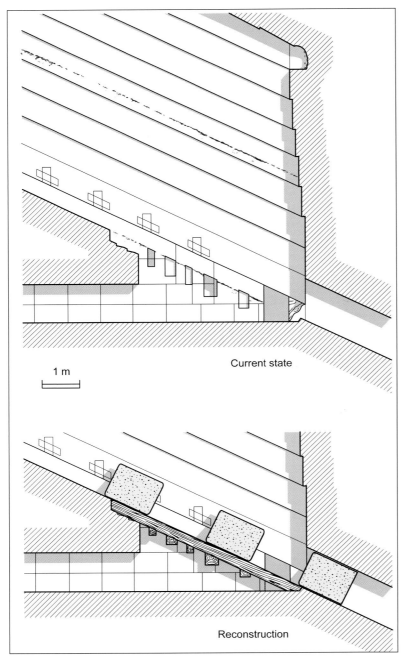

1 m

Current state

Reconstruction

ABOVE

Reconstruction of the landing junction during the sealing of the ascending passage.
(Franck Monnier)

analysis that also draws on a study by Mark Lehner. According to Dormion, the notches were made to receive the feet of a scaffolding structure installed along the entire length of the gallery, with cross beams and incorporating several platforms. He also concluded that the holes were closed off following the disassembly of the structure. The rest of his analysis is even more conjectural. It was the appearance of cracks in the King's Chamber (see below) that led the ancient builders to consolidate

the Grand Gallery with this substantial shoring structure. The slots dug in the upper faces of the side benches, therefore, testify to the addition of improvised reinforcements on either side of the gallery. This reconstruction is problematic, as longitudinal beams fastened against the walls would have been subject to bending and would have offered little resistance to possible lateral stresses. Only horizontal bracing beams stretching across the gallery might have been of use in this situation.

When the evidence is taken together, it does seem likely that the 54 holes were cut to hold poles that formed a large wooden framework, but one that was used during the construction of the gallery, and which allowed the corbels to be created gradually as the stones were set in place. Most of the blocks were installed in an inclined position, which must have made such a wooden bracing structure essential, particularly as the masonry structure of the Grand Gallery eventually reached over 20 m in height. It is likely that the wooden structure was intended to remain in place until the construction of the pyramid was nearly complete, a process that would have taken several years, and perhaps more than a decade. There is evidence of similar reinforcement structures in other pyramids, notably the Bent Pyramid of Dahshur-South and the pyramid of Meidum, so there is every reason to believe that the Grand Gallery contained a similar framework.

The groove cut along the third set of corbels on either side may have been used to help secure a raised working platform at mid-height, but the reason that some of the slots on the side benches were closed off, and others were then recut at a later date remains enigmatic. In conclusion, it seems that the mortises cut in the sides of the gallery held a structure to prop up the vault, but that does not preclude the possibility that they were also used to support a block closure system. Jean-Philippe Lauer and Georges Goyon concluded that the design of the lower parts of the Grand Gallery was closely related to the ascending corridor below it, and the slope and width of the gallery's central trench was intended to be identical to that of the ascending corridor. It also seems likely that the benches on either side of the Grand Gallery were designed to allow the blocks to be slid into place more easily during their final installation. A sliding block closure system had already been implemented before the reign of Khufu, in the satellite pyramid beside the Bent Pyramid at Dahshur-South, and in a corridor of similar dimensions. Unfortunately, it proved to be a faulty system since the blocking stones remained stuck in their waiting position and were never successfully installed to close the passage. This may explain why Khufu's architects chose to design a wider gallery covered with a tall vault, so that they could better control the closing of the tomb and avoid repeating an unfortunate construction failure.

A horizontal corridor leads directly south from the landing at the bottom of the Grand Gallery, towards the Queen's Chamber, a distance of 33.60 m. The passage is 1.05 m wide by 1.17 m high. The floor slopes very slightly, dropping

8 cm from the northern end to the southern end, probably due to a slight compacting of the masonry towards the centre of the pyramid. An unusual arrangement of joints is visible between the blocks on the walls. They are aligned vertically with each other rather than being offset, and this arrangement covers just over half the length of the side walls. These attracted the attention of Gilles Dormion and Jean-Patrice Goidin who believed that they indicated the presence of concealed cavities that had been closed off. In the 1980s they decided to drill holes in the walls, which they did after receiving the appropriate permissions. Their experiments attracted a great deal of media attention, but the holes revealed nothing more than very fine sand filling gaps in the masonry. Investigations undertaken by a Japanese team also proposed the existence of hidden corridors in the vicinity. To date, no hidden

BELOW The inner arrangement of the Great Pyramid from the upper end of the ascending corridor to the Queen's Chamber and the King's Chamber. *(Franck Monnier)*

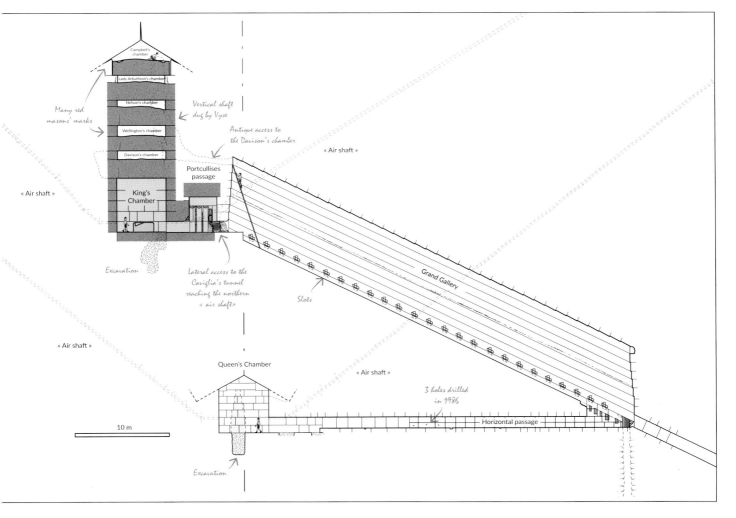

corridors have been found, but the evidence available does seem to indicate that the corridor underwent some profound modifications during construction, which led to its unusual architectural characteristics. The rows of identical and directly superimposed blocks may have been installed to hide a feature that the Egyptians abandoned and it has been proposed that they hide rows of storage magazines such as were found in the pharaonic tombs of the 3rd dynasty, but such features have never been found in any of the pyramids that followed Khufu's, at least in the arrangements suggested. Although nothing has been found, the idea of a change of design during construction is nevertheless plausible.

Like the Grand Gallery, the Queen's Chamber is an impressive structure and it was also most likely made from Tura limestone. The chamber's floor is nearly 21 m above the level of the

BELOW The east wall and the corbelled niche of the Queen's Chamber.
(Jon Bodsworth)

pavement outside the pyramid. It measures 5.23 m from north to south (or 10 cubits) by 5.76 m from east to west (or 11 cubits) and is covered by a massive solid gabled or apexed stone roof with opposing internal faces angled at just over 30° from the horizontal. The roof beams are propped up against each other along a centre ridge-line that runs east to west, and which is almost exactly equidistant from the north and south faces of the pyramid. The chamber's height ranges from 4.69 m above the floor at the south wall, to the highest point of the gable roof at 6.26 m (nearly 12 cubits) above the floor level. The chamber is also very close to being equidistant from the east and west sides of the pyramid, but is actually shifted slightly towards the east.

The pavement within the chamber was completely dismantled sometime in the distant past, and by the 18th century the remaining paving blocks were described as being in disarray. This left a step up to the floor level in the entrance corridor, which remained in place. A hole dug in the floor at the eastern end of the chamber was the work of ancient explorers. According to Flinders Petrie's measurements, the east and west walls are very slightly sloping inwards, while the north and south walls both lean slightly towards the north. The deviations from vertical are between 1 and 2.5 cm, which is far too small to cause any structural problems. In fact, it demonstrates the remarkable quality of the construction. A hole dug by Colonel Howard Vyse through the north wall, at the north-west corner, located the ends of the beams, and revealed that while the exposed internal slope length of the roof was approximately 3.05 m, the beams continued into the walls for a further 3.09 m, giving a total internal side beam length of 6.14 m. This means that the centre of gravity of these beams lies inside the walls, rather than above the open space. Petrie thought that this may have been of use during the installation process, and it could also have been of some use during their transportation to the site, but recent reconstructions by Franck Monnier suggest that the beams were moved into place slowly, over mounds of supporting materials, and were never left free standing, or hoisted into place using a crane structure. Only once the whole

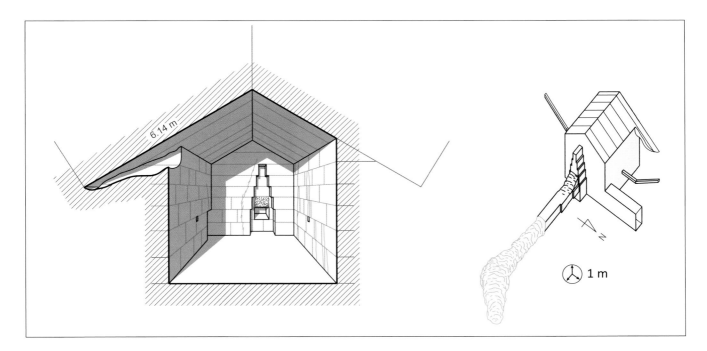

ABOVE Perspective view of the Queen's Chamber looking east. The cracks are shown in red. On the right is an isometric view of the Queen's Chamber with the horizontal access passage, shafts, niche and robbers' tunnel. *(Franck Monnier)*

RIGHT The west wall of the Queen's Chamber. *(Jon Bodsworth)*

roof was in place with the beams propped up against each other was the supporting structure and material below removed.

This room is the first in recorded history to be covered with a stone gable roof, and a structural analysis of the chamber is very informative. In addition to the slight deformations and inclinations mentioned above, there are many cracks on the walls, particularly on the south and east walls, which may have been made during construction. In later pyramids, the gable roof burial chambers are devoid of such cracks, which may be related to the fact that the north and south walls in later examples are not structural elements and bear no weight from above. The sloped beams pass directly over the chamber walls and are supported on abutment walls hidden deep within the masonry behind them. A space was left just above the tops of the vertical side walls to separate them from the underside or intrados

of the gable roof beams passing over them.

In the case of the Queen's Chamber, however, it seems that Khufu's architects had not yet realised the importance of separating the beams from the vertical walls, and the danger of directly laying beams over the walls while also supporting them on abutments. As the vertical chamber walls impinge on the roof beams at approximately their mid-points, this would have created high stresses at those locations, and could have resulted in cracks propagating from those points. It seems that this danger was not foreseen before the construction of this chamber, which surely represents one of the first attempts at creating this type of roofed space. The subsequent addition of clearance spaces over the side walls was a major improvement in this roofing technique. However, it is worth noting that the beams of the Queen's Chamber are all still intact.

In the eastern wall of the chamber is the so-called 'niche', which is a tall corbelled alcove cut into the wall. It is positioned off-centre to the south with respect to the central axis of the chamber. The cavity is 1.05 m (or 2 cubits) deep by 1.57 m (or 3 cubits) wide at the bottom. It is cut in the form of a corbelled vault, which reduces in four steps as it ascends, down to a minimum width of 0.52 m (or 1 cubit)

at the top. The steps decrease in half cubit intervals from the widest at the bottom to the narrowest at the top, i.e. 3, 2½, 2, 1½ and 1 cubits, so that the step width of each individual corbel is a quarter of a cubit.

The height of the first corbel is 1.70 m, followed by 0.81 m, 0.72 m, 0.74 m and 0.70 m, which forms an irregular sequence with no apparent symbolic or structural meaning. The total height of the niche is 4.69 m, somewhat less than 9 cubits. The geometric properties of the recess have inspired speculation about its symbolic meaning and purpose, and the discovery of fragments of diorite in the vicinity suggests that it was built to house a statue. Ancient explorers, no doubt intrigued by this niche, and also by a stone block located in the centre of it, removed the stone to uncover what seemed to be a tunnel that had been filled in with loosely packed masonry. Hoping to uncover a secret chamber, they excavated the tunnel for around 6 m, and then reached masonry that appeared to be made up of regular pyramid core blocks. They extended their tunnelling into this solid core of blocks for a further 9 m, before accepting that their work was futile and giving up.

The presence of a tunnel that was apparently carefully concealed is at first sight very intriguing, but the fact that the blocks of its walls were neither aligned nor carefully cut indicates that it was only intended for temporary use during construction, and was not part of the planned final system of passages and chambers. Its purpose was therefore not necessarily linked to that of the niche, and the corbels of that feature do not continue into the masonry behind it. The stonework of the niche is made of fine limestone, carefully squared and finely jointed, whereas the stones surrounding the tunnel beyond are irregular construction blocks with rough interface joints. This qualitative difference shows that the level of care taken to construct the Queen's Chamber was not considered necessary for the bulk of the pyramid's construction elements or core. The tunnel from the niche also suggests that the structures of the chambers and the permanent passages must have been installed, at least for the Queen's Chamber and its corridor, before the core block layers were raised around them, otherwise the tunnel would not pass through two different types of masonry, in addition to the finely cut masonry of the chamber's walls.

According to Franck Monnier, rather than indicating the presence of a hidden room as some believed, this backfilled tunnel is more likely to be the remains of an old construction tunnel, which allowed workers to enter the Queen's Chamber after the roof was in place in order to dismantle the temporary structure that would have been installed to support the roof beams during their installation. The temporary structure could have been either a powerful wooden shoring framework or a mass of small and medium-sized chunks of stone. The secondary access system would have saved them from having to remove the temporary material via the corridors leading all the way back to the main entrance. The backfilled tunnel was not covered with a protective roof and it was blocked off after it was used, whereas the niche was not. This strongly suggests that the tunnel and niche were not functionally linked, even though the precise purpose of the niche remains unclear.

The Queen's Chamber was probably not built for a queen, and there are several plausible hypotheses that attempt to explain its purpose. It could originally have been planned as the main burial chamber, which was subsequently abandoned in favour of the King's Chamber. It has long star or air shafts that lead to the north and south, like the King's Chamber, but for the Queen's Chamber they were never completed and were closed off. According to some researchers including Mark Lehner and Zahi Hawass, it was intended to be a *serdab*; a room with a statue containing the ka of the pharaoh where offerings could be made. The Step Pyramid complex belonging to Djoser had a room of this type near its north face, although located outside the pyramid. This was a place where regular offerings could be made to the deceased pharaoh. However, as all the access routes into the Great Pyramid were blocked off after it was completed, this hypothesis does not seem to make good sense.

The star or air shafts are long narrow channels with square cross sections of 21 cm by 21 cm. They start from holes in the north and south walls of the Queen's Chamber at a height of approximately 1.50 m above the floor level, then run up and out towards the north and south faces of the pyramid. The one in the north wall runs horizontally due north for a distance of 1.93 m, then angles up towards the north face of the pyramid. On the way through the solid core of the pyramid it also takes a turn to the west to avoid the Grand Gallery. It then climbs at an angle of inclination of approximately 39°, which means that it runs almost perpendicularly towards the outer face of the monument, but it terminates before it reaches the surface. The second shaft starts from a hole in the south wall of the Queen's Chamber, directly opposite the first, and runs due south for a distance of 1.96 m before climbing up towards the southern face at approximately the same angle, 39°, as the northern shaft. The lower entrances to the shafts in the Queen's Chamber were originally closed off with a thin layer of stone when construction was completed. The holes that are visible today were discovered in 1872 by the well-known Scottish doctor James Grant (Bey) who worked in Cairo at the time. They were then opened up by a worker brought in by English engineer Waynman Dixon, who was also carrying out research at the pyramid for the Astronomer Royal for Scotland, Charles Piazzi Smyth. Once the holes were cut into the walls, they found shafts perfectly preserved behind their limestone covers. They discovered objects concealed in the northern shaft, presumably left there by the builders, which are now known as the Dixon artefacts. They consist of a small copper hook (BM EA 67819), a dolerite stone ball (BM EA 67818) and a small piece of wood that was preserved in the collection of the Marischal Museum in Aberdeen, Grant Bey's home town.

LEFT **The opening of one of the shafts into the Queen's Chamber. They were originally hidden by the masonry. Grant Bey and Waynman Dixon cut into the walls and discovered them in 1872.** *(Jon Bodsworth)*

According to the late Egyptologist Alexander Badawy who studied the shafts in some detail, the conduits were originally referred to as ventilation shafts because when Vyse and Perring unblocked a similar set of shafts in the King's Chamber, they noticed a flow of air coming from the exterior. Flinders Petrie followed suit and called them all ventilation ducts, despite the fact that this could not have been their function since those of the Queen's Chamber never reached the outer surface. They were closed off completely and deliberately, well short of the outer surface.

In the 1990s and 2000s, the Queen's Chamber's star/air shafts were the focus of the most publicised investigative project that had ever taken place in the Great Pyramid. A team of German engineers led by Rudolf Gantenbrink conducted exploratory campaigns between 1992 and 1993, dubbed Upuaut Projects 1 and 2, using a small robot equipped with caterpillar tracks and a camera. The label Upuaut was derived from the name of the ancient Egyptian wolf god who was believed to lead the pharaoh and his armies through the afterlife.

With the cameras rolling, the miniature robot rover was fed into the shafts to discover what lay at its ends. The north shaft proved to be too sinuous and could not be followed after the first few metres, but the southern conduit was explored for a distance of 63.50 m, until the robot reached a limestone closing block embedded with two copper protrusions. The block was dubbed the 'door', and its discovery led to another two missions, overseen by Minister of Antiquities Zahi Hawass, to investigate what it might be. The team developed a new robot that they named the Pyramid Rover, and the first of the new missions was carried out in 2002 in collaboration with the National Geographic TV channel. The Pyramid Rover successfully travelled up to the door and, using an impact-echo probe, was able to establish that the door was only a few centimetres thick. It then used a drill to cut through the block. Putting a probe with a small camera through the hole revealed an enclosed space behind the door, which was effectively an extension of the shaft by around 19 cm. Unfortunately, very little detail could be seen, as

RIGHT The objects discovered in the northern shaft of the Queen's Chamber by Grant and Dixon, now on display in the British Museum. Small copper hook and dolerite stone ball. *(Jon Bodsworth)*

BELOW Objects discovered in the northern shaft of the Queen's Chamber by Grant and Dixon, and reproduced in the *Harper's Weekly* journal in 1873.

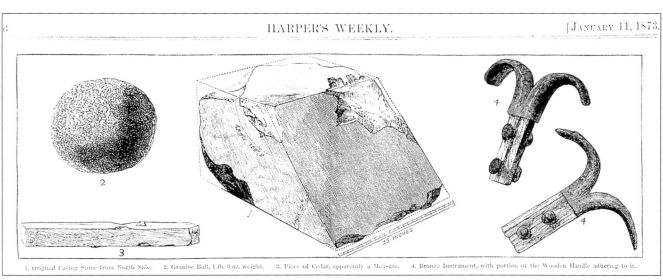

HARPER'S WEEKLY. [JANUARY 11, 1873.

1. Original Casing Stone from North Side.   2. Granite Ball, 1 lb. 3 oz. weight.   3. Piece of Cedar, apparently a Measure.   4. Bronze Instrument, with portion of the Wooden Handle adhering to it.

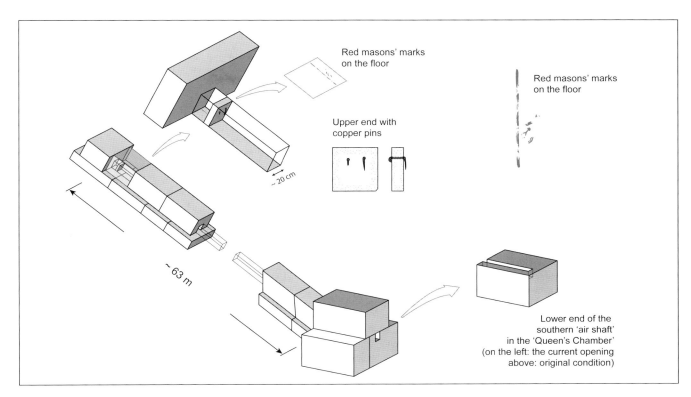

Red masons' marks on the floor

Upper end with copper pins

~ 20 cm

~ 63 m

Red masons' marks on the floor

Lower end of the southern 'air shaft' in the 'Queen's Chamber' (on the left: the current opening above: original condition)

the camera could only look straight ahead, did not have a wide-angle lens and was illuminated by a low-power light source.

After winning permission to continue the investigations, a team led by the University of Leeds took a robot to Giza in 2010. Their machine was dubbed the Djedi Rover after the ancient Egyptian magician described in the Westcar papyrus. It was able to negotiate the tight turns in the northern shaft and revealed that it also terminates after approximately 63 m, ending in the same way as the southern channel, in a 'door' with two copper protrusions.

The Djedi robot also returned to the 'door' in the southern shaft, and by putting a new camera through the existing hole it was able to observe more details within the previously discovered space. There was little to be found there, other than some construction marks left behind by the builders; numbers made with the same red ochre paint used elsewhere in the Great Pyramid, most notably within the relieving spaces above the King's Chamber. Some researchers have suggested the marks are the numbers 100, 20 and 1 in Egyptian hieroglyphs, summing to 121 in the Egyptian numbering system, and have speculated that it indicates a number of cubits in length. It has also been

noted that this number is 11 x 11 and that the number 11 is also found in the principal dimensions of the other shafts leading from the King's Chamber, when measurements are converted to cubits. If the shafts had a symbolic purpose, then it is not inconceivable that the numbers chosen to define their lengths and inclinations may also have been imbibed with symbolic meaning.

Each of the limestone blocking stones has a pair of copper protrusions but their purpose remains enigmatic. The block on the south is around 5 cm thick, and it is likely that the one on the north is similar.

The media hype surrounding this door, and the associated expenditure of time and money, was motivated by a desire to discover a hidden room within the pyramid, behind one of the small closing slabs. In the end, these doors led to nothing but the ends of abandoned projects. Despite the fact that the shafts in the Queen's Chamber lead nowhere, there are various hypotheses about the original purpose of the conduits, which must have required substantial effort to construct, and which do not appear in any of the other pyramids.

As the shafts in the King's Chamber point towards the sky, due north as well as due south

ABOVE The northern shaft in the Queen's Chamber. Several modern exploratory missions employing robots revealed it was 63 m long. The upper end is sealed with a block that covered a small cavity. It seems to be a dead end.
(Franck Monnier)

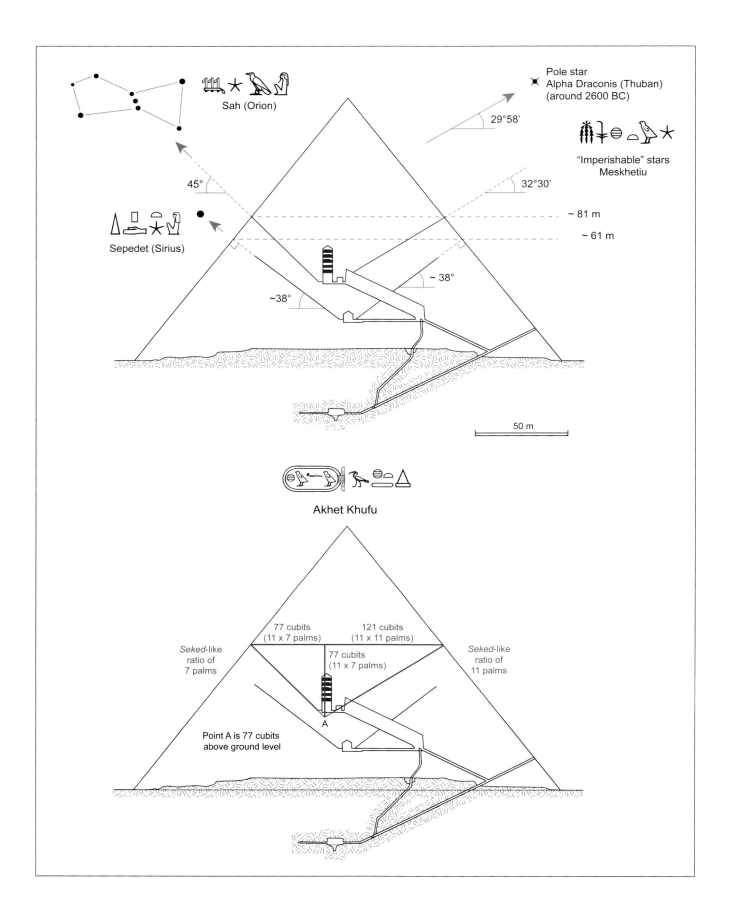

Sah (Orion)

Pole star
Alpha Draconis (Thuban)
(around 2600 BC)

29°58'

"Imperishable" stars
Meskhetiu

32°30'

~ 81 m

~ 61 m

45°

Sepedet (Sirius)

~ 38°

~38°

50 m

Akhet Khufu

77 cubits
(11 x 7 palms)

121 cubits
(11 x 11 palms)

Seked-like
ratio of
7 palms

77 cubits
(11 x 7 palms)

Seked-like
ratio of
11 palms

Point A is 77 cubits
above ground level

A

where the sun passes, many scholars have suggested that they are targeted at certain stars, or certain areas of the night sky that had specific meanings for the ancient Egyptians. The shafts in the Queen's Chamber are now closed off, but the ones exiting in the King's Chamber climb all the way to the exterior faces of the pyramid. The first stellar theory seems to have originated in the world of freemasonry, in a treatise written at the end of the 19th century by Albert Churchward. He proposed that the Great Pyramid was a Masonic temple, and that the two southern shafts (falsely considered to be parallel) were symbolically oriented towards the star Sirius, considered to be the 'light of the grand orient'. This type of association was later addressed by the scientific community, most notably by the Egyptologist Alexander Badawy, who considered the shafts with respect to the Pyramid Texts of the later Old Kingdom in which this star Sirius holds a principal place. The Egyptian Egyptologist proposed that the southern shaft of the King's Chamber allowed the soul of the pharaoh to begin a pilgrimage to the constellation of Orion, while the northern shaft led to the 'eternal' stars of the polar region, which never 'set' below the horizon. This archaeo-astronomical line of enquiry was later elaborated by Robert Bauval, who proposed that the whole Giza complex was intended to resemble the form of the three prominent stars of Orion's belt.

Most of these theories are difficult to accept wholesale, as they propose a shaft system logic or layout that was pre-planned as a coherent whole, despite many signs that there were changes made during construction. It seems particularly difficult to reconcile the termination of the shafts from the Queen's Chamber with a master plan. These features are unique to the Great Pyramid, so it is also difficult to understand what would have motivated the designers to adopt such an elaborate architectural expression of a religious concept, only to abandon it quite suddenly afterwards. It remains difficult to fully understand the links between the orientation of the shafts and objects in the night sky; however, it does seem likely that they had a symbolic purpose related to the afterlife of the pharaoh and the heavens above, as was discussed in the opening chapter.

The precise measurements made during the exploratory missions initiated by Rudolf Gantenbrink established the lengths and inclinations of the shafts. Further study of the geometry of the features also revealed that each pair of shafts opens or terminates at the same level; approximately 69 m above ground level for those leading from the Queen's Chamber, and approximately 81 m above ground level for those leading out of the King's Chamber. Although they terminate, the Queen's Chamber shafts climb almost perpendicularly towards the external faces, which would be the shortest path to reach the exterior. Those leading from the King's Chamber, however, have inclinations that are clearly not intended to be perpendicular to the external faces.

The positions of the shafts leading from the King's Chamber were evidently defined by a more complex set of rules; ones able to compensate for the fact that the King's Chamber was significantly off-centre in the north–south axis. Despite this complication, the King's Chamber's shafts still exited the pyramid at the same level and may also have been imbibed with symbolic meaning.

At the top of the ascending corridor, on the west side of the landing at the bottom of the Grand Gallery, is the opening to a narrow, irregularly sloped, excavated tunnel that connects the upper chambers and corridor system within the pyramid's superstructure with the lower section of the descending passage,

ABOVE The shaft and the grotto photographed in 1910. *(The Edgar brothers, 1910)*

OPPOSITE Two theories explaining characteristics of the air/star shafts in the Great Pyramid. *(Franck Monnier)*

and which leads down to the subterranean chamber. Although it is irregular in places, the direct path taken by this 'service shaft' suggests it was the work of the builders rather than looters, as some researchers believed until recently. The entrance at the top of the tunnel is about 70 cm wide. It runs west for about 1.40 m, before suddenly plunging vertically down into the core masonry of the monument for more than 7 m. It then slopes steeply towards the south. After another 8 m it arrives at what is commonly called the 'grotto' of the Great Pyramid. In reality, the grotto is a small cave with a deep hole in the floor filled with sand, gravel and clay. The cave is cut into the natural bedrock mound that rises up into the body of the pyramid in this area, approximately 7 to 8 m above the peripheral pavement level

surrounding the monument. The core layers were raised around and over the rock mound, and the grotto was left behind near the centre of the pyramid's base. A vertical masonry structure passes through the north side of the grotto. It is made of cut blocks of medium size, grouted with mortar, and it extends the 'service shaft' channel vertically through the grotto. The shaft then continues down through the natural bedrock, before veering onto a steep southward descent for 26 m, eventually descending more steeply for approximately 10 m until it arrives at a short horizontal tunnel. This opens into the west side of the descending passage, 7 m uphill from the bottom end of the long sloping entrance corridor.

This plunging 'service shaft', almost 60 m deep and with a cross section that never exceeds 70 cm square, could only have been worked by one stonemason at a time, and its excavation must have been extremely difficult to accomplish. Lower down, the most challenging sections passing through the bedrock were tackled by cutting a sloping shaft through the stone. Near the top where the shaft is almost vertical, small lateral notches were cut into the side of the shaft for the excavator's feet. No matter which end the passage was cut from, the workers must have been constantly exposed to falling debris resulting from the excavation work, either due to the removal of waste stone via the passage above them as the hole was cut downwards, or from falling chunks of stone from above as the passage was cut out overhead.

Recently, Gilles Dormion convincingly reconstructed the probable sequence of tasks undertaken by the workers digging out this passage. His argument is as follows: If the purpose of the shaft was only to connect the Grand Gallery to the descending passage, then the Egyptians would probably have opted for a shorter and more direct route that would have emerged at a much higher point in the descending passage than is the case. Instead, he argues the evidence indicates the lower part of the shaft was dug earlier on to provide access to the subterranean chamber during the early stages of construction. This would have facilitated the excavation of the descending passage, which reached down 30 m below ground level, and more than 72 m from the

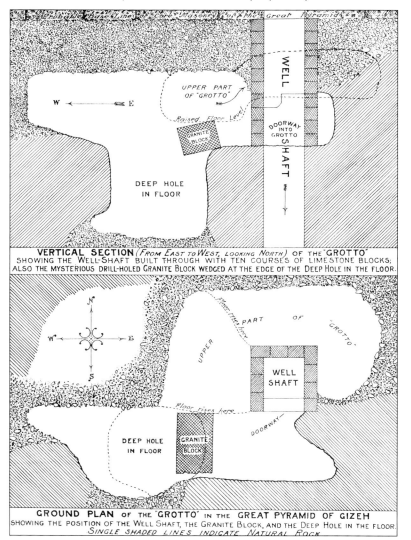

VERTICAL SECTION *(From East to West, Looking North)* OF THE 'GROTTO' SHOWING THE WELL-SHAFT BUILT THROUGH WITH TEN COURSES OF LIMESTONE BLOCKS; ALSO THE MYSTERIOUS DRILL-HOLED GRANITE BLOCK WEDGED AT THE EDGE OF THE DEEP HOLE IN THE FLOOR.

GROUND PLAN OF THE 'GROTTO' IN THE GREAT PYRAMID OF GIZEH SHOWING THE POSITION OF THE WELL SHAFT, THE GRANITE BLOCK, AND THE DEEP HOLE IN THE FLOOR. *SINGLE SHADED LINES INDICATE NATURAL ROCK.*

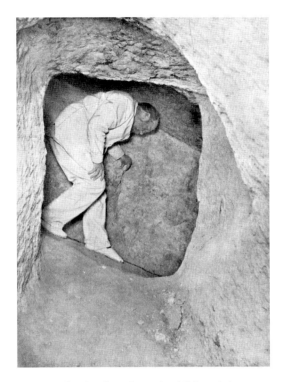 

entrance by the time it reached this point. Accessing this distant location and removing material from the same entrance passage must have significantly slowed the progress of the work, and so it seems that the Egyptians decided to build a second access route from the place where the workers had reached by that time, up to ground level. This would have improved the flow of oxygen down to such a depth, and would have provided an alternative evacuation route that could also be used for removing excavated rock chippings. This shaft was therefore dug down from the bedrock above, first taking advantage of a depression already excavated in the natural bedrock; the current 'grotto'. When the architects later abandoned the underground subterranean chamber project in favour of a set of passages and chambers up in the superstructure of the pyramid, they first filled the grotto in with sand, gravel and clay, before building the core block layers over it. Later, when the design of the ascending passage granite plugging block system demanded a secondary escape route, the shaft was dug from the Grand Gallery's lower landing down to, and then through, the grotto. This was when the masonry structure that passes through the grotto was erected, protecting the escape route from any potential

collapse of the cave, and finally connecting the two parts of the pyramid. Reopening this rudimentary tunnel let the last workers activate the plugging block system from the inside, before escaping down through the 'service shaft', and finally emerging outside at the top of the so-called descending passage.

Many questions remain regarding this theory about the construction of the 'service shaft', and it is undoubtedly a complex explanation. Some Egyptologists and researchers consider it incoherent, and have not accepted it. In the words of Georges Goyon, to 'barricade a door and then leave the window open' at first seems difficult to accept, but it is worth considering that if the descending passage was to be closed off at its entrance, and if a portcullis system was being added in front of the King's Chamber, then the windows were not really being left open. It is even possible that the lower end of the descending passage, and hence the lower entrance to the 'service shaft', was to be closed off with another row of blocks, but there is no evidence that the process was ever actually put into operation. Perhaps once the antechamber portcullis system was installed in front of the King's Chamber, it was considered unnecessary to further restrict access to the upper levels from below. Finally,

ABOVE Lower end of the 'service shaft' where it opens at the bottom of the descending passage. Left photo taken from inside the shaft entrance. Photographed in 1910. *(The Edgar brothers, 1910)*

FAR RIGHT The remains of one of the portcullis stones that sealed the antechamber. This one was removed by the robbers. Four other fragments were found in the grotto, the descending passage and in the recess of the small horizontal passage leading to the subterranean chamber.
(Jon Bodsworth)

BELOW
Reconstruction of the portcullis system sealing the access to the King's Chamber.
(Franck Monnier)

it is worth remembering that a near vertical ascent of the narrow 'service shaft' would be a significant challenge by any measure.

At the top of the Grand Gallery is a huge rectilinear block of limestone often referred to as 'the great step'. It forms a high platform giving access to the uppermost level of the pyramid's internal funerary chamber system. Its upper surface reaches the highest floor level in the pyramid, 43 m above the pavement outside. Visitors pass from the top of the tall Grand Gallery through a small doorway on the step that leads into a short passage with a section 1.12 m high by 1.05 m wide. This is 2 cubits and 1 palm high, by 2 cubits wide (the same

dimensions as the ascending and descending passages far below). The passage leads to a small antechamber room, barely wider than the corridor, but approximately 3.79 m tall. The purpose of this chamber was to block access to the burial chamber beyond. Except at the north end towards the gallery, this room was mainly constructed using blocks of red Aswan granite, a stone that is very difficult to cut and shape, and extremely hard to penetrate for anyone trying to break through it.

A series of granite portcullis stones once filled the space but they have now been broken out and removed. Nevertheless, the antechamber retains some elements that have

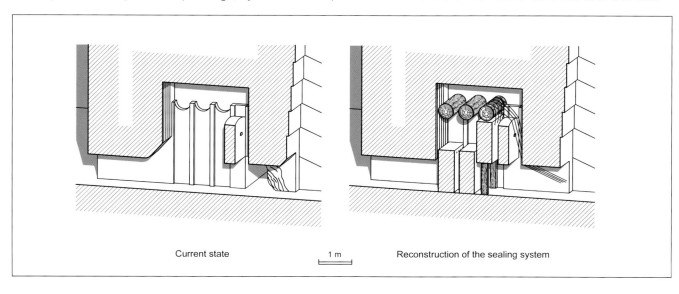

Current state   1 m   Reconstruction of the sealing system

allowed archaeologists to virtually recreate and understand the original closing mechanism. The inside face of the north wall above the entrance from the Grand Gallery is made of limestone and is undecorated, while the inside wall on the south face, above the entrance into the King's Chamber, is adorned with four tall narrow vertical grooves, 8 to 9 cm wide and spaced 17 cm apart. On the walls on either side of the antechamber room, to the east and west, are three large vertical grooves, 0.52 cm (or 1 cubit) wide. Three huge granite portcullis slabs once spanned the spaces between these grooves, while a fourth block known as the granite leaf, which was not intended to drop down, guarded the space in front of these blocks near the entrance. Several pieces of granite were found broken and abandoned by looters in various parts of the pyramid, and of these pieces, three most likely belonged to a granite portcullis. Two of them have pairs of holes approximately 7 cm wide and 19 cm apart, which appear to match up with the narrow vertical grooves on the south wall. The reconstructions indicate that the three granite portcullis slabs slid down inside the large lateral grooves until they blocked the passage. When first installed they were held up in a waiting position using wooden wedges pressed against the walls. Semi-cylindrical recesses cut at the top of the wall grooves accommodated heavy wooden logs around which ropes were wrapped. The ropes were then connected to the portcullis slabs and also served to support them. Once the pharaoh had been laid to rest, the

workers would remove the wedges, then lower the portcullis blocks using the ropes, which were controlled from a position near the great step. The holes in the portcullis blocks would have served as tie points for the ropes, to facilitate their lowering and control them as they slipped down into their final, closed positions.

Despite the massive strength of this structure, it was penetrated by looters who forced through the rock above the granite leaf, passed over the top of the closing system and tunnelled down into the ceiling of the passage leading into the King's Chamber. At some point after the passage was first forced, the portcullis slabs were broken up and the pieces were removed from the pyramid. Despite the fact that it was ultimately breached, this closing system, with three vertical portcullis slabs, was the first of its kind. The design was apparently considered effective since similar systems were adopted for many of the pharaonic burials of the Old Kingdom, especially during the 6th dynasty.

At the end of the short corridor leading from the antechamber is the most imposing structure of the whole pyramid, the so-called King's Chamber where Khufu was laid to rest. The large chamber is a magnificent elongated box, made entirely from finely worked red granite blocks, and so completely void of all decoration that it recalls modern, minimalist architecture. Its floor is on the same level as the antechamber and the great step, and it stands on the vertical plane that cuts through the centre of the pyramid from north to south. Unlike the Queen's Chamber, however, the

BELOW Three classic techniques that were used to seal passages during the Old and Middle Kingdoms. The left one was first used in the Great Pyramid. It was reused during the 5th and the 6th dynasties.
(Franck Monnier)

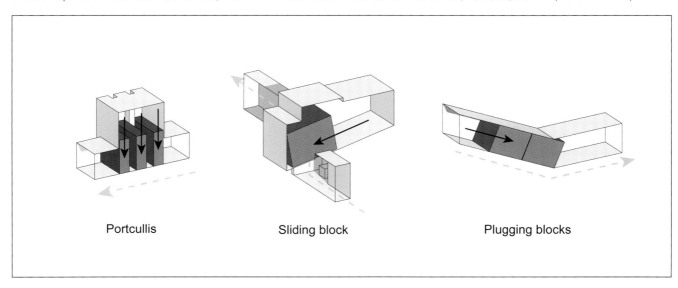

Portcullis   Sliding block   Plugging blocks

RIGHT View of the
King's Chamber
towards the west. The
sarcophagus lies in the
western part.
(Jon Bodsworth)

BELOW View of
the King's Chamber
towards the east. The
entrance is on the
northern side.
(Jon Bodsworth)

King's Chamber is located well south of the east–west centre line. The dimensions of the room are 10.47 m by 5.24 m in ground plan, and 5.84 m in height, which is precisely 20 cubits by 10 cubits in plan, by 11 cubits and 1 palm high. The long axis runs east to west. The cut stonemasonry of the whole room, including the paving, walls and ceiling, is composed entirely of red granite brought from Aswan, finished so that the surface of the blocks is smooth to the touch.

The inside surface of the ceiling is flat and consists of nine long monoliths running north–south, arranged side-by-side and resting on the north and south walls of the burial chamber. Above the chamber, the upper faces of these stones are left roughly finished, unlike the other three sides that are cut flat so that they can sit side-by-side to form a continuous ceiling with no gaps. The ends of the beams are embedded in the walls to the north and south and cannot be observed. Above this first layer are no fewer than four more layers of these huge granite monoliths, with each layer separated from the last by intervening voids around 1 m in height. These interstitial spaces are created by stubby granite walls around the sides of the chambers, finished on their internal faces, apart from the fourth and fifth relieving spaces near the top, which have no granite wall blocks. The uppermost layer of granite roof beams sits on large limestone blocks on the north and south sides. Those also support limestone blocks at the ends of the granite beams, which in turn help support the gable roof above. Above the top layer is a larger space that sits under a large limestone gable roof formed by pairs of sloped beams, similar in arrangement to those of the Queen's Chamber far below. It is not known if the apexed gable roof is double-layered like the vault over the main entrance to the pyramid, or even triple-layered, as found in pyramids of the 5th and 6th dynasties.

The total volume of granite used to build the structure of the King's Chamber, including the monoliths forming the relieving spaces above it, is approximately 1,100 m³. This equates to a total mass of approximately 3,000 tons of red granite, all of which was transported 800 km down the Nile from Aswan by wooden ship.

Following the colonial and nationalist fashion of the period, English explorers Howard Vyse and John Shae Perring, who dug through the side walls between these spaces, named them after English people they wanted to commemorate. This is why, from top to bottom, they are today known as Campbell's Chamber, Lady Arbuthnot's Chamber, Nelson's Chamber and Wellington's Chamber. The chamber at the bottom is known as Davison's Chamber after the person who first discovered it.

When these chambers were first accessed in the 19th century, many red ochre construction marks and hieroglyphic inscriptions could still be seen in Campbell's Chamber, including the names of Khufu written in sketched-out cartouches. Other information noted included numbers and levelling marks, providing valuable written evidence of the technical work of the pyramid builders. While some of the marks are still visible today, most of them have been covered over by a rash of modern graffiti, including the names of visitors written out using candle soot. Nevertheless, the surviving information and

RIGHT Isometric drawing of the King's Chamber and its surroundings. The gable vault is shown here with one layer of beams, but there are likely to be two or three layers. *(Franck Monnier)*

BELOW Builder's marks and inscriptions left in the 'relieving chambers'. *(Howard Vyse, 1840)*

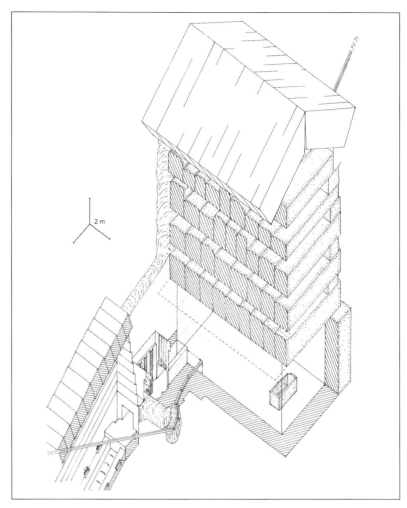

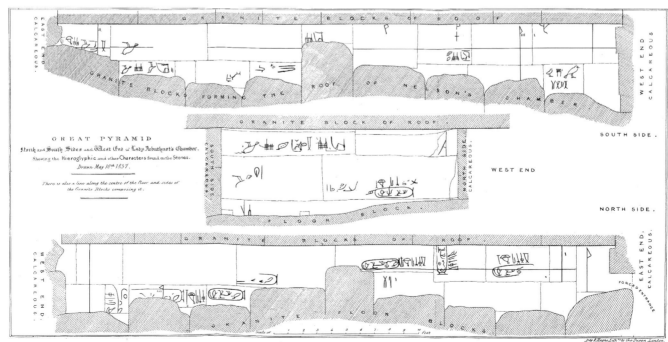

GREAT PYRAMID
North and South Sides and West End of Lady Arbuthnot's Chamber.
Showing the Hieroglyphic and other Characters found in the Stones.
Drawn May 10th 1837.

There is also a line along the centre of the floor and sides of the Granite Blocks composing it.

numbers that remain on the faces of the rafters demonstrate that they were cut and prepared elsewhere before being installed in the pyramid in a pre-established order.

This hybrid design of these 'relieving chambers' covered at the top by a gable roof is not seen anywhere else. The purpose of the succession of heavy monolithic roofs, acting mechanically as fixed-end horizontal beams, was possibly to raise the gabled vault overhead so that it did not interfere with or affect the structure of the Grand Gallery. The use of a gable vault may have carried a symbolic value as it replaced the more traditional corbelled vaults used in the pyramids from the beginning of the 4th dynasty, but it also appears that the architects were keen to discard the older design of vault and attempt something new, and there may have been more compelling structural reasons for this change. Franck Monnier recently investigated the possible reasons for the evolution of the gable vault design, and the replacement of the corbelled ceilings. From a practical point of view, the change seems curious, since corbelled vaults were relatively easy to build and were mechanically efficient. Monnier argues, however, that practical reasons were not the only factors being considered. The symbolic value of gable roofs is clearly visible from the end of the 5th dynasty onwards, when they were decorated with patterns of stars representing the celestial vault above. In this respect, it is notable that the profile of a step pyramid resembles the form of a corbelled vault,

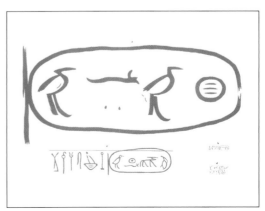

while the profile of a gable roof mirrors that of the smooth-sided pyramids. The outer faces of the true pyramids face up towards the sky, while the internal ceilings of the gable-roofed burial chambers perhaps reflected the sky and the pyramid above, via a subtle inversion process. The pharaonic tomb is also a gateway to the other-world, and it is possible that the two sloping sides of the gable roof symbolised a door with two half-open panels, like the 'double doors of heaven' mentioned several times in the Pyramid Texts.

Down in the King's Chamber, below the 'relieving chambers', a pair of star or ventilation shafts open in the north and south walls, in the eastern half of the space. The openings are 0.93 m above floor level and have rectangular sections approximately 21 cm by 14 cm (similar to those in the Queen's Chamber and probably equating to 3 palms by 2 palms). The King's Chamber's shafts, however, were originally left open, and the shafts continue all the way up to the north and south faces of the pyramid on the outside. The channels attached to the Queen's Chamber, on the other hand, were closed off at the chamber walls and before they reached the outside faces. On the north and south sides of the King's Chamber, both shafts first run horizontally for a short distance of 1.50 m, then slope upwards and outwards, before reaching the outer faces of the pyramid, 77.55 m above the exterior pavement on the south side, and 78.43 m above the pavement on the north side. External masonry where the shafts exit has been removed in these locations, but calculations indicate that both shafts would originally have continued until they exited the pyramid at approximately 80.6 m (154 cubits) above the pavement, when the casing stone faces were completed. On the north side, the shaft deviates slightly to the west on its journey, to avoid the structure of the Grand Gallery, which rises to the north of the King's Chamber. Like the Queen's Chamber shafts, they were thoroughly explored by the Upuaut robot project in the 1990s and were fully cleared out. They now serve to supply air to the upper chambers via a modern ventilation system, giving them the function formerly, and perhaps mistakenly, attributed to them.

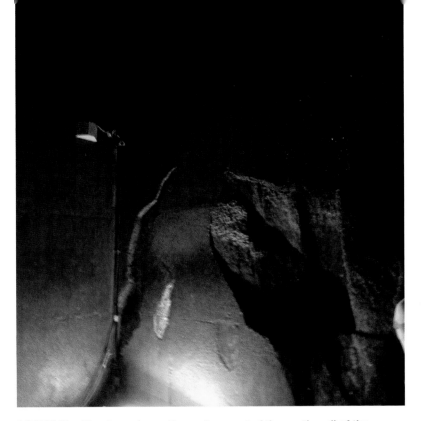

ABOVE Significant cracks on the eastern part of the south wall of the King's Chamber. The entrance to the air/star shaft is badly broken. *(Michel Sancho)*

BELOW Isometric reconstruction of the sarcophagus of the King's Chamber with the precise measurements made by Flinders Petrie. *(Franck Monnier)*

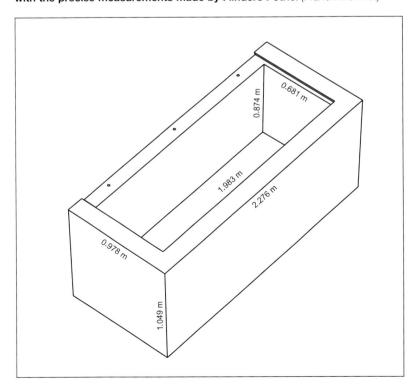

A monolithic red granite sarcophagus, cut from a single piece of stone, sits in the western part of the chamber, demonstrating the sepulchral function of the space. Flinders Petrie measured the sarcophagus in minute detail, and from its dimensions he determined that it must have been brought into the chamber before construction was complete. Ancient tomb robbers broke off the lid and fractured the edges of the coffer. However, enough details have survived so that its original closing mechanism has been reconstructed with some degree of confidence. The lid was moved into place using a sliding system, then locked in place by means of three small cylindrical stone pins. They sat in cylindrical holes under the edge of the lid and dropped into place into holes in the upper face of the edges of the coffer as it was finally closed.

There are several indications that the King's Chamber suffered from a partial structural failure during construction, despite its enormous mass and the strong materials used to build it. The floor across the centre of the King's Chamber drops more than 5 cm from the north side to the south side, although this value diminishes towards the east and west walls. Some vertical wall joints are displaced by a few millimetres, while larger fractures and displacements distort the south wall, particularly around the ventilation shaft exit. The edges around the outlet of this star/ventilation shaft are chipped away, while the ceiling beams are all fractured across their undersides

in a line running close to the southern wall. A similar situation is visible in the three 'relieving chambers' directly above the King's Chamber. The beams of Campbell's Chamber, however, which rest freely on their supports, were not affected by the incident which caused these cracks. Only the joint separating them from the north wall opened by 3 cm. The beams of the gabled ceiling where they meet at the top are also separated by approximately 3 to 5 cm along the centre line.

In 1765, the English diplomat Nathaniel Davison first discovered the opening at the top of the Grand Gallery, carved into the stonework. He followed the conduit there for several metres along a route that deliberately bypassed the granite blocks below until it led directly into the first 'relieving chamber' space. The chamber, which is directly above the King's Chamber, bears his name today. The channel leading directly to it also demonstrates that the people who excavated it knew how to avoid the granite blocks above the King's Chamber. All this evidence seems to indicate that an incident occurred during construction, after the superstructure had been completed. The overseer of works then created this improvised tunnel to examine the damage above the King's Chamber. Apparently, the ancient workers were satisfied by examining only this first 'relieving chamber', as they did not extend their investigations further upwards. The vertical tunnel, which today bypasses the ceilings on the east side providing access to the upper relieving chambers, was the work of English explorers Howard Vyse and John Shae Perring, 44 centuries later.

Brown marks on the ceiling of the King's Chamber, close to the north and south walls, may indicate that the architects also installed a wooden shoring framework when they became concerned that the roof was unstable. The marks there are more than one metre long and all run down the middle of the monoliths near their ends. Two smaller rectangular marks are located further away from the walls. The chamber is 5.84 m high, so to build a support structure would have required planks of significant length, and these would have been either brought into the pyramid via the descending and ascending passages or been recycled from an existing structure which was still inside the pyramid. Calculations suggest that planks of adequate length could have been manoeuvred through the junction between the descending and ascending passages, and in fact a bevel cut on the upper edge of the junction there could have been made to facilitate such logistical manoeuvres. Another possibility is that the marks in the King's Chamber were caused by supports used during the transportation of the monoliths from the quarry, located more than 800 km to the south, and that they are not related to the structural problems encountered on site at all. However, comparison with the relieving spaces above seems to indicate that the marks are particular to the King's Chamber, and the most likely hypothesis remains that they are related to a consolidation project.

Flinders Petrie noticed the cracks in his survey of 1882, but accurate measurement and recording of further structural movement only began in the 1980s, with a controversial study led by Gilles Dormion and Jean-Patrice Goidin. The research methods and the technologies they used were innovative for the time, but the team's belief in the existence of a secret chamber undermined the value of their conclusions. The different hypotheses they put forward to explain the mechanical behaviour of the structure were all based on the existence of a contiguous cavity located close to the King's Chamber. The study was inconclusive and reported only that the use of different types of masonry could be a possible cause of the distortions and fissures observed. Jean Kérisel, a civil engineer associated with the study, elaborated on the discussion, proposing that the material behind the south wall must be irregularly arranged, because only this could cause such variations in the stone structure that the resulting shearing forces would crack the cantilevered granite monoliths above. Whatever the cause, the cracks are consistent with a disaster occurring towards the end of construction, after the superstructure was in place. Flinders Petrie suggested that this could have been the result of an external phenomenon such as an earthquake, but there is no clear evidence to support that hypothesis at this stage.

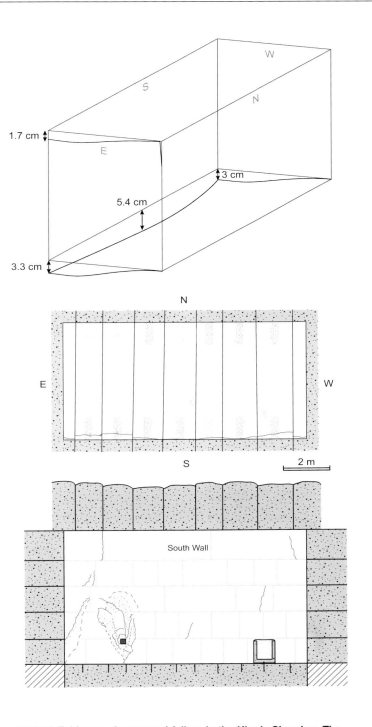

ABOVE Evidence of structural failure in the King's Chamber. The uppermost drawing shows the extents of the movement of the walls. The drawings below outline the brown marks and cracks on the ceiling, as well as the cracks on the southern wall.
(Franck Monnier)

Were changes made to the planned project during construction?

The lower section of the ascending passage and the upper part of the 'service shaft' were dug through completed layers of core blocks. The fact that these changes were incorporated into the design led Flinders Petrie and Ludwig Borchardt to wonder if the pyramid's original plans had been changed during construction. Other features of the pyramid indicate that changes were made to plans, such as the two different and quite independent upper chamber systems, as well as the fact that the Queen's Chamber's star/air shafts were closed off before they reached the exterior.

On the other hand, some researchers including Rainer Stadelmann do not concur with this point of view. According to Stadelmann, the Egyptian tomb architects constructed pharaonic tombs with a three-chamber layout from the Early Dynastic Period onwards, for symbolic or religious reasons. Such a tradition could explain the internal arrangement of the pyramid of Khufu and prove that there was no change of plan during construction. The 'three-chamber system' theory is, however, far less certain than its author maintained, and it is necessary to

manipulate the various tomb layouts to support the theory that all the royal monuments of the period followed such a system.

The assumption that the Great Pyramid must have been built with a single coherent plan reflects a longstanding and widely held perception that the construction of the Great Pyramid was carried out without any degree of uncertainty or any errors being made during the process. This viewpoint is more like a belief system, and it does not provide a clear view of the evidence or an objective interpretation of the facts. A major failure clearly occurred in the King's Chamber, but many researchers still cannot accept that the Great Pyramid, one of the wonders of the ancient world, built with a superstructure whose geometry is almost perfect, could have been left with any imperfections. The problem with this exceptional status is that it removes the monument from its historical context and out of its developmental sequence, which was underway before, and continued after, its construction. The pyramids erected between Djoser and Khafre's reigns did incorporate many traditional elements, but the designs were constantly evolving, and the Great Pyramid's designs were no exception in this respect.

On the other hand, attributing all changes to errors or failures that occurred during

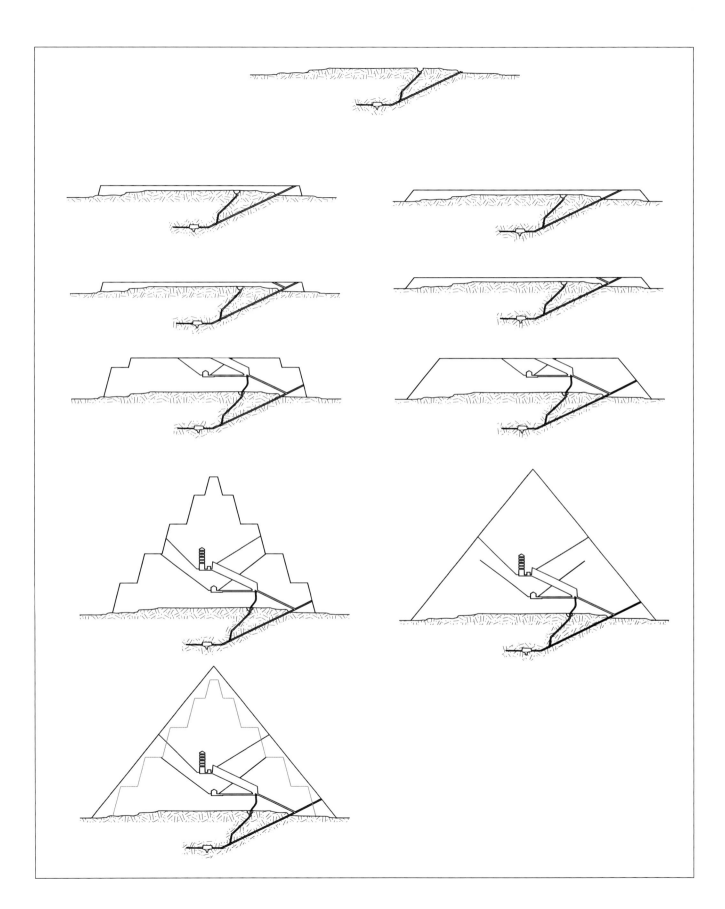

construction could be to misunderstand the nature of the observed changes. A modification occurring during construction was not necessarily the result of a fault, or of an accident or negligence, but could be the result of an innovation, an improvement or a simple change of mind. As these construction projects took several decades to complete, it would not be surprising if the project's overseers made decisions later on that differed from those made at the beginning of the pharaoh's reign, perhaps after several years of deliberation. The skill and power of the Egyptian architects resided in their ability to create novel monuments and develop new construction technologies in order to complete ambitious new projects for the pharaoh.

Since it was built in one vertical plane running north–south, the peculiar internal arrangement of the Great Pyramid is often depicted in a vertical section, looking from the east side closest to the Nile, and this holds for the other pyramids of the 4th dynasty. A comparative study based on these vertical sections will most likely conclude that the Great Pyramid was unique. A plan view, however, reveals a layout that became a classic pattern for similar monuments. Firstly, the entrance is on the north side. Secondly, the corridor leading to the sarcophagus chamber runs due south and is blocked by three portcullis slabs. The burial chamber is oriented east to west and is covered with a gable vault, and it houses a sarcophagus, which is placed at its western end.

As well as introducing several important innovations, the multiple pyramid projects commissioned by Khufu's father Snefru demonstrate that trial and error was customary during the construction of the royal tombs. It seems, in fact, that it was only during Khufu's reign that the funerary architecture eventually consolidated into something approaching a coherent internal layout, albeit after the lower sets of chambers and passages had been superseded or abandoned.

The funerary ideology was finally represented in the tomb chambers at a schematic level. The daily course of the solar star, rising to the east into the world of the living and passing over to the domain of the dead where it set above

the western desert, was manifested in the rectangular tomb chamber, twice as long in the east to west axis as it was in the north to south direction. The sarcophagus was placed close to the western end. The orientation of the entrance passage was aimed towards the Imperishable Stars in the northern sky, through which the pharaoh was thought to travel to the afterlife.

The upper layout of the Great Pyramid represents the results of a developmental sequence that subsequently underwent very few changes, until it became the classical pharaonic tomb arrangement during the 5th and 6th dynasties. Taken as a whole, the Great Pyramid's internal layout is a palimpsest, with the classic upper arrangement overlying the Queen's Chamber and the subterranean chamber, which were the imprints of abandoned projects.

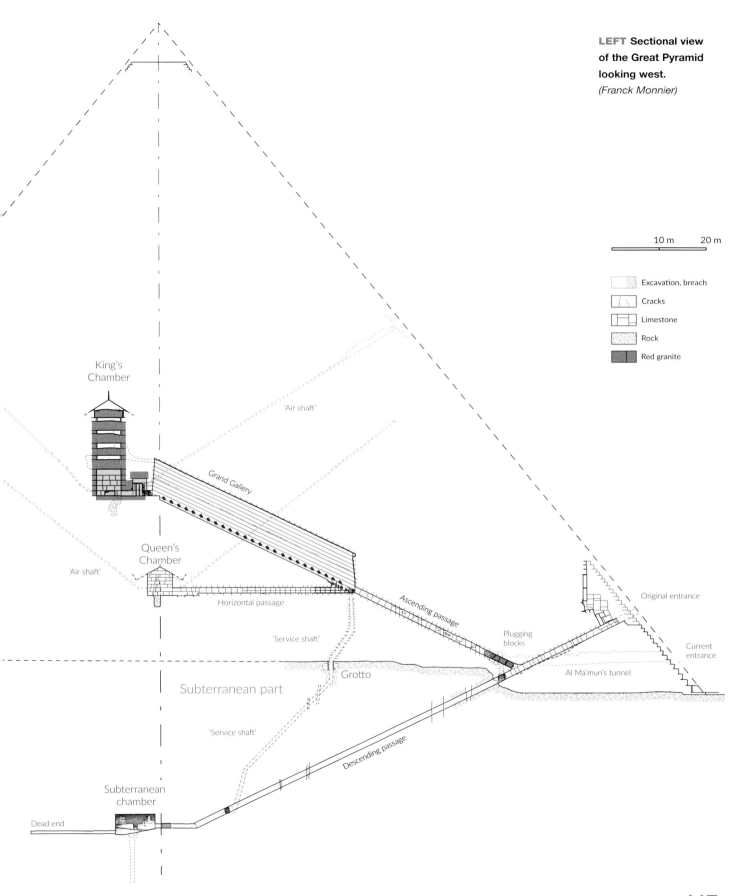

10 m   20 m

Excavation, breach

Cracks

Limestone

Rock

Red granite

King's
Chamber

'Air shaft'

Grand Gallery

Queen's
Chamber

'Air shaft'

Horizontal passage

Ascending passage

Plugging
blocks

Original entrance

Current
entrance

'Service shaft'

Grotto

Al Ma'mun's tunnel

Subterranean part

'Service shaft'

Descending passage

Subterranean
chamber

Dead end

Chapter Three

Building the Great Pyramid

Despite centuries of destruction and erosion, evidence survives of Egyptian construction methods and the identities of some of the builders are now known. The majority of the labourers left no written history behind, but the overseers of the teams and the architects of these great monuments did leave fragments of information. Their papyri, reliefs, tombs and statues reveal aspects of the lives and works of the Great Pyramid builders.

OPPOSITE Remains of a quarry at the foot of Khafre's pyramid. The Great Pyramid is in the upper left corner. *(Franck Monnier)*

Who built the Great Pyramid?

The people who built the prestigious monuments at Giza came from a variety of backgrounds and worked in a number of different roles. High-ranking officials joined forces with heavy load haulers; learned scribes worked with experienced artisans; meticulous administrators teamed up with expert surveyors. The majority of the manual workers were arranged into teams for quarrying, transporting and finishing the stonework, but there were a multitude of supporting roles for those who organised food, small beer and water supplies. They came together on this great project to immortalise their leader and gain their own immortality as a result. Unfortunately, information regarding the vast majority of these workers is limited. A few high officials left details about their lives in their mastaba tombs, but the majority of the construction workers did not leave records of their daily activities behind, only noting their roles within teams or their areas of responsibility. Almost nothing can be said about their contribution to the evolving design of the pyramid, or in planning out the construction work.

BELOW Statue of vizier Ankhhaf, now on display in the MFA museum in Boston. *(Alain Guilleux)*

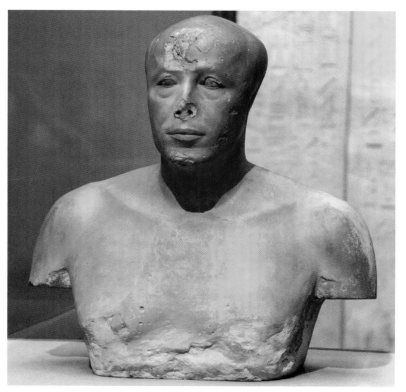

Funerary and religious inscriptions make no reference to architectural trials or preliminary designs. To do so would have risked undermining the message that these sacred monuments were created by divine inspiration. Evidence from the New Kingdom shows that work on the sites was carried out according to plans directed by Ma'at, to ensure that all would run smoothly. The goddess Ma'at embodied the concepts of accuracy, harmony and the fine balance that governed the universe. It is likely that the same concepts were applied during the Old Kingdom. Khufu's own father was called Snefru, 'He who makes things perfect, Horus, lord of Ma'at'.

Nevertheless, several forgotten ostraca (limestone and pottery sherds used as sketch pads on construction sites) have been found that carry working architectural drawings. From these, it is possible to reconstruct some of the engineering issues being considered by the architects during the planning phases for monuments. This type of drawing was prepared by scribe-draftsmen referred to as 'scribes of forms' (*sesh-qedu*).

The most well-known individual who played a role in the design and construction of pyramids was Imhotep. He was famed as the most learned of men; an architect, artisan and sculptor for the pharaoh Djoser, and as the person who first used cut stone to create large buildings. His name has echoed down through the ages. He was worshipped as a deity during the New Kingdom and his reputation spread throughout the Mediterranean basin. He was revered by the Greeks and Romans as a great physician, and eventually became an important figure in the alchemical and Masonic rites of the Renaissance. There is, however, only sparse evidence of this great man from his own time. Only a single contemporary inscription is known, carved on the base of a statue, but it does verify his existence and his extensive responsibilities during the reign of Djoser:

The Chancellor of the King of Lower Egypt, the first after the King of Upper Egypt, the Administrator of the Grand Palace, the hereditary noble, the High Priest of Heliopolis, Imhotep; carpenter-builder, sculptor-engraver, manufacturer of vases. (Imhotep Museum of Saqqara, JE 49889)

The Egyptians of later periods considered him to be a universal genius, on the basis of oral tradition and written records. Inscriptions in the temple of Edfu recognised the scholar as the source of an instruction guide detailing how to build the perfect temple. The documents allow a vague glimpse into the great deeds of this famous character. His titles mention the different offices and trades he was involved in, and it seems that he was in charge of the great funerary complex of Djoser. There is no mention, however, of him being a 'Master of Works', a title that became common in later Egyptian history. It referred to those in charge of supervising the building sites on behalf of the pharaoh, and who worked alongside the ruler during the foundation rituals for establishing the ground plans of new temples.

Hemiunu is generally regarded as the architect and Master of Works for Khufu's pyramid. He was the son of Nefermaat, the vizier who had supervised the earlier funerary projects of the reign of Snefru, father of Khufu. The papyri recently found at Wadi al-Jarf on the Red Sea coast prove that a man called Ankhhaf also supervised the construction of the pyramid of Khufu. He was Khufu's brother and would have served in this role during the final years of the pharaoh's reign. Statues of both of these officials have survived and are among the most admirable works of art from the Old Kingdom. They reveal two very different characters. Hemiunu is authoritative, poised, but rather stout. Ankhhaf's features are more defined and depict an alert character who has faced many tests. He looks assertive, but his face is tinged with a little weariness.

There was no title that corresponds precisely to the modern term 'architect', and the title 'Master of Works' undoubtedly covered a broader range of roles, from the simple site manager to the project director in today's terminology. The vizier, the pharaoh's second-in-command for the affairs of state usually also held this position, but the number of activities the vizier was responsible for surely meant that he would have had little time to execute construction plans, or to advance the construction techniques used during the 3rd or the beginning of the 4th dynasty.

To accomplish the most ambitious projects, the pharaoh relied on his vizier to surround himself with the most competent technicians and managers, the people most able to carry out the required tasks. A sequence of titanic 4th dynasty projects were carried out from the reign of Snefru until the reign of Menkaure, and all of these were completed within a single century. They could not have been created without a policy of talent development and a system in which the best candidates were promoted. The biographies of officials often emphasised that they had distinguished themselves in their conduct, had won the recognition of the pharaoh, and had been rewarded for their services. As far as the pharaoh was concerned, it must have been important to motivate the tens of thousands

ABOVE Statue of vizier Hemiunu, now on display in the Hildesheim museum.
(Alain Guilleux)

of workers, because his time on earth was
always running out. The names adopted by
teams usually referred to as 'phyles' or 'phylai'
indicate that competition was one of their
motivations. The 'vigorous team' and 'enduring
team' suggest physical prowess was valued,
while the team 'powerful is the white crown of
Khnum-Khufu' may have expressed their pride
in their Upper Egyptian roots, as the white
crown was the crown of that region.

The labourers were organised into a
hierarchy. Divisions consisted of a total of 2,000
workers. Each division was divided into two
groups of 1,000 (*aperu*), composed of 5 phyles
of 200 workers (*sa*). Each phyle was divided
into teams of 20. According to Mark Lehner's
calculations, in order for the Great Pyramid to
be completed in the required time, each team
had to transport and set at least five blocks
in place every day, which meant one block
every two hours. Overall, it would have been
necessary to employ 1,360 workers for the
transportation of the blocks. As each group was
composed of only 1,000 men, it is likely that an
entire division of 2,000 workers was assigned
to this task. Since the construction inscriptions
found in the 'relieving chambers' above the
burial chamber in Khufu's pyramid relate to
three different groups, it appears that more than
one division was involved in the transportation
of building elements, at least temporarily when
complex structural elements had to be raised
at the same time as the core block layers
were being installed. A further 1,000 men were
assigned to cut and finish the stone blocks.

The artisans who manufactured and repaired
the tools must be added to this total, as well
as the quarrymen and the personnel in charge
of feeding and supplying this army of workers,
leading to a total workforce estimated by Mark
Lehner to have comprised at least 20,000
people, although the majority of these would
have worked on a seasonal basis, during
the inundation season when their fields were
flooded over.

To manage such an enormous workforce,
the Egyptians had to create systems of
logistical management, supported by rigorous
administration and accounting. This enormous
group lodged not far from the construction
site, at Heit el-Ghurab, where excavations led
by Mark Lehner as part of the Giza Mapping
Project have unearthed the remains of a
workers' town dating back to the reigns of
Khafre and Menkaure. It was located on the
edge of the valley floodplain. The periphery
of the town, where it met the lower edge of
the necropolis, was defined by a powerful
defensive wall known as the 'wall of the crow'.
The excavations of the workers' town revealed
a sequence of long covered galleries. Each of
them seems to have had a second floor and
could shelter from 40 to 50 individuals. One
room housed a guard, and there was kitchen
and storage space. It seems that no fewer than
2,000 workers were permanently employed and
supported by the state and supervised from an
administration quarter not far from the town.
The workers' town dating back to the reign of
Khufu is still to be uncovered.

RIGHT **Entrances to ancient quarry galleries in the limestone cliffs at Maasara.**
(Somers Clarke and Reginald Engelbach, 1930)

RIGHT **Entrances to ancient quarry galleries in the limestone cliffs at Maasara.**
(Somers Clarke and Reginald Engelbach, 1930)

Raw material sources

Long-time specialists in the study of Egyptian rocks, Dietrich and Rosemarie Klemm, conducted research that provided details of the origins of the stones used to build the Old Kingdom pyramids of Egypt. Working with the Egyptian department of antiquities (now the Ministry of State for Antiquities), the German geologists collected nearly 1,500 samples from the monuments for analysis using geochemical and petrographic methods. The study of the microstructure of the stones has made it possible to compare fragments from numerous quarries and suspected resource extraction sites. Their conclusions demonstrated that the great majority of the materials used to build the pyramids came from local sources. The availability of limestone may also have been a factor influencing the choice of where to build a pyramid, and while it may not have been the first issue considered, it might have been the one that was ultimately the most important.

Some of the quarries are clearly visible around the Giza Plateau in the south-eastern areas and close to Khafre's pyramid. They are also evident at the nearby pyramid site of Abu Rawash in Gabal el-Madawarah.

Higher quality rocks for tomb chambers and temples were also sought out, and surveyors and quarrymen undertook expeditions to the distant corners of the Egyptian world to find good materials. Fine limestone was used to clad the faces of the pyramids, but that type of material was rare. Since the reign of Snefru, it had been sourced from the other side of the river, the eastern bank, in the quarries of Mokattam East, Tura and Maasara, all now located in the suburbs south of Cairo.

The fragments of papyri recently discovered near the port of Wadi al-Jarf recorded

RIGHT **Map showing the location of quarries and mines worked during Khufu's reign.**
(Franck Monnier)

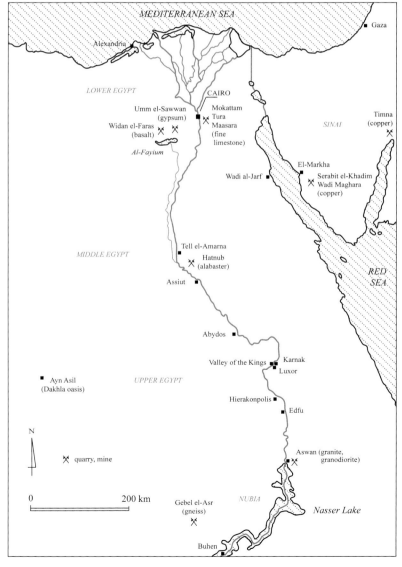

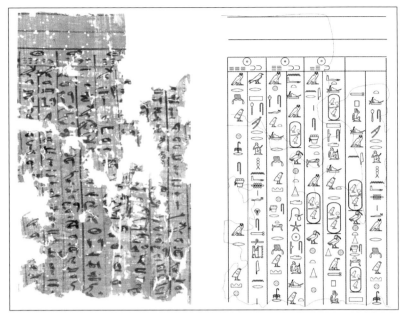

the transport of stones from Tura to the construction site of the new pyramid of Khufu, which was referred to using its ancient Egyptian name, the Horizon of Khufu:

Day 26. Inspector Merer sailed with his team from Tura [south]; loaded with stones for the Horizon of Khufu; passed the night at the Lake of Khufu.
Day 27. Sailed from the Lake of Khufu; navigated to the Horizon of Khufu, loaded with stones; passed the night at the Horizon of Khufu.
Day 28. Sailed from the Horizon of Khufu in the morning; navigated back up the river to Tura [south].
Day 29. Inspector Merer spent the day with his team collecting stones in Tura south; passed the night at Tura south.

The harder rocks of red granite and granodiorite were mined in the vast Aswan quarries, more than 800 km south of the Memphite Necropolis, which includes Giza. Although some architectural elements made from granite were already used in the Early Dynastic tombs at Abydos, it was first used in quantity in the pyramid of Djoser. Granite gained considerable importance during the reign of Khufu, until it was extracted on a very large scale during the reign of Khafre.

Reliefs on the causeway of the pyramid of Unas dating to the 5th dynasty illustrate the transportation by river of monolithic granite columns, as well as cornices, destined to be used in his mortuary temple. The associated hieroglyphic text states that they came from Abu, the ancient Egyptian name for Elephantine, present-day Aswan. Elsewhere, inscriptions on a stele taken from the funerary chapel of a 6th dynasty official called Weni, also now in the Cairo Museum, describe the loading of granite architectural elements and a greywacke sarcophagus intended for the pyramid of the pharaoh:

His majesty sent me to Ibhat to bring back the sarcophagus 'Chest of the Living' and its lid, as well as a costly and noble pyramidion for the pyramid of Merenre, my mistress.

His majesty sent me to Elephantine to bring back a granite false door and its lintel as well as [other] doors and associated elements of granite, and also to bring back a granite doorway and lintels, for the upper chamber of the pyramid of Merenre, my mistress. In [just] one expedition consisting of six barges, three transport ships and three eight-oared/ribbed boats did I travel north with [them] to the pyramid of Merenre. [...]

His majesty sent me to Hatnub to bring back a great offering table of Hatnub alabaster, and I organised that this offering table was brought down [after] seventeen days of quarrying at Hatnub. I had it travel north in a barge; I made for it [this] barge from acacia wood 60 cubits long and 30 cubits wide, assembled in seventeen days in the third month of the Shemu *season. Despite there being no water on the sandbanks, I moored successfully at the pyramid of Merenre. Everything in my charge had come to pass exactly in accordance with the order of the majesty of my lord. His majesty sent [me] to excavate five canals in Upper Egypt and to make three barges and four transport ships from acacia wood of Wawat, for which the rulers of those foreign lands of Irtjet, Wawat, Iam and Medja cut down the wood. I completed this task in the space of one year, including filling [them] with water, and the loading of large amounts of granite intended for the pyramid of Merenre.*
(Based on the translation by Nigel Strudwick, Texts from the Pyramid Age, n° 256)

This text states that the alabaster came from Hatnub, a place south-east of the present-day Tell el-Amarna in Middle Egypt. A rock at the entrance to the quarry there retains an inscription with the name of Khufu. The alabaster sarcophagi of Pharaoh Sekhemkhet and Queen Hetepheres I, mother of Khufu, were also extracted from there.

Gypsum, a raw material used to make mortar during the Old Kingdom, was extracted from an area in north-eastern Faiyum at Umm el-Sawwan. Its proximity to Giza suggests that it may have been one of the main resources providing the estimated 500,000 tons required for the Great Pyramid alone.

The dark green/gneiss stone used to make the statues for Khafre's valley temple was brought from the southern part of Nubia, from an area in the western desert 65 km north-west of Abu Simbel known as 'Khafre's quarries'. An engraved stele from the site includes Khufu's cartouche and testifies to its exploitation during his reign.

The black basalt used to pave the floor of Khufu's mortuary temple was probably taken from Widan el-Faras (Gebel Qatrani), north of the Faiyum. An old road paved with stones there connected the quarry to the former shore of the lake. The stone would then have been loaded onto boats for transport to Giza.

These building materials could never have been mined or shaped without copper. This valuable metal was used to make thousands of tools for the stonecutters and carpenters. Its ore was mined in the Sinai region far to the east of Giza, at the mines of Serabit el-Khadim, not far from the shores of the Red Sea, and

ABOVE LEFT Gneiss rock quarry at Gebel el-Asr. *(James Harrell)*

ABOVE Stele carved with Khufu's name at the gneiss quarry of Gebel el-Asr. *(Reginald Engelbach, 1938)*

BELOW Panoramic view of the basalt quarries of Widan el-Faras.
(Franck Monnier)

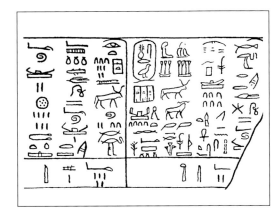

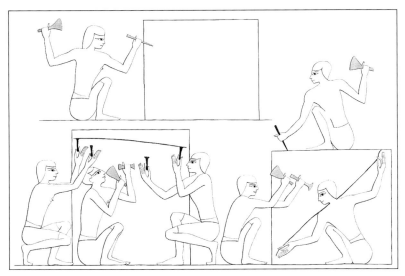

ABOVE Depiction of workers cutting and dressing blocks of stone in the tomb of Rekhmire.
(Ippolito Rosellini, 1834)

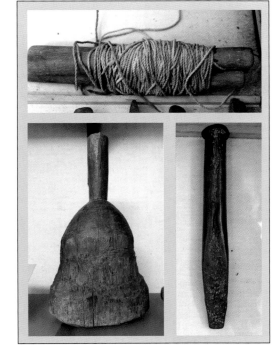

RIGHT Original tools used by the ancient Egyptians, now on display in the Cairo Museum. Measuring rope, a wooden mallet and a copper chisel.
(Franck Monnier)

probably also at Timna, now in Israel. Snefru and Khufu's teams left their names engraved in the rock faces at Serabit el-Khadim along with texts celebrating punitive actions undertaken against the Bedouins who threatened Egyptian activities in the region. It is easy to imagine the strategic value of such production sites, and it is no surprise that the Egyptians established fortifications in the nearby coastal plain of El-Markha, facing back over the Red Sea to the port of Wadi al-Jarf, located on the opposite shore. This port was a key link for importing the products back to the Memphite region via the Wadi Araba and Middle Egypt.

In addition, it was necessary to obtain an immense quantity of wood. Local species such as palms and sycamore were used to reinforce the ramps and the causeways. Acacia, jujube and doum palms were used to build the ships that transported people and materials from one end of Egypt to the other. Exotic woods were imported from the mountains and ports of Lebanon, such as conifers and most notably, cedar. The long planks produced by the tall cedars growing in the mountains of Lebanon were suitable for manufacturing large scaffolding structures and powerful levers. Cedar was also used extensively for building vessels such as Khufu's 'solar boat'.

The yearly records on the Palermo Stone state that cedar was procured for the construction of two boats, 100 cubits (52.4 m) long, during the reign of Snefru. Also mentioned are 40 boats loaded with conifers. Most of the wood resources were derived from local sources, but it is clear that such a large construction site had special requirements that could only be satisfied from beyond the borders of Egypt.

Raw material processing

Since the publication of several studies that synthesised all that is known about ancient Egyptian quarrying and stoneworking, it is no longer a subject shrouded in mystery. The multitude of traces and notches left by the quarrymen and stonemasons made it possible to determine the main methods used. Only a deep misunderstanding of the subject still leads some writers to claim that the achievements of the ancient Egyptian stoneworkers were

impossible during their era. Many writers have sought alternative explanations to account for the unprecedented achievements observed, and have proposed, for example, that the blocks were in fact a type of concrete mixed on site. However, once the methods and tools are better understood, the feasibility of undertaking such a giant project becomes more understandable.

Many stoneworking tools have been uncovered during excavations. The Egyptians used bronze tools from the Middle Kingdom onwards, but mostly used copper to carve the softer stones such as sandstone and limestone throughout the dynastic era. Local limestone blocks of Menkaure's mortuary temple at Giza, dating to the 4th dynasty, display many large tool marks made by copper chisels struck with a mallet. The harder stones such as granite, granodiorite and quartzite forced them to adopt other methods. The copper chisels could not easily penetrate these types of rocks. The most common tool adopted was a striking stone (usually dolerite) in spherical or ovoid form. Many of these have been found on the ground in the ancient Aswan red granite quarries, but also during excavations in the Memphite Necropolis, especially near the pyramid of Djoser and at Giza. One particularly well-known specimen was found inside a star/air shaft in Khufu's pyramid.

Scenes from the 18th dynasty tomb of vizier Rekhmire on the west bank at Luxor illustrate the use of striking stones for making limestone sphinxes and colossal granite statues. Some of these pounders had side handles for a better grasp and their weight could vary from a few kilograms to several tens of kilograms. Studies carried out by Clarke and Engelbach highlighted the role of these tools for quarrying the famous unfinished obelisk of Aswan, which dates to the 18th dynasty. That ancient project, albeit a failure, demonstrates the audacity of the ancient Egyptian builders. The obelisk would have been approximately 42 m high, almost a third of the height of the Great Pyramid, with a

ABOVE Relief from the mastaba of Kaemrehu depicting sculptors and the tools they used to carve and polish stone statues. *(Cairo Museum, photo: Franck Monnier)*

BELOW LEFT Dolerite balls at Aswan, used to carve hard stones like granite. *(James Harrell)*

BELOW Stone axe tool kept in the Cairo Museum. *(Franck Monnier)*

weight approaching 1,000 tons. Unfortunately, a massive crack appeared during the quarrying work, forcing the workers to abandon their titanic project. Although it was undertaken 1,000 years after the great pyramid era, the extraction method used is a good illustration of what the Egyptians of the Old Kingdom were capable of, since we know that obelisks were already being erected at that time, as evidenced by the inscription in the 6th dynasty tomb of Sabn at Qubbet el-Hawa near Aswan:

The majesty of my lord sent me to construct two great barges in Wawat so as to ship two great obelisks north to Heliopolis. (Translation from Nigel Strudwick, Texts from the Pyramid Age, *n°244)*

There is an obvious continuity in the techniques used. The huge obelisk is still attached to the bedrock, and it is possible to see countless marks left during its excavation. The monolith was at first separated from the bedrock on either side by a slow and laborious excavation process, carried out by nearly 140 individuals. The workers struck the ground regularly with spheres of dolerite, pounding the granite surface away at an imperceptible rate. The balls did not cut or crack the rock but pulverised the surface

using percussion and compression. The concave furrows on the faces of the obelisk, on the opposing faces and at the bottom of the trench, show that the workers moved side to side in a very confined space. The work was laborious. According to a recent study, each worker was allocated an area of approximately half a square metre and would only pound away 1.5 cm in 12 hours of uninterrupted work. At this rate, the extraction of the obelisk would have required 11.5 months. This is probably a realistic estimate, since according to these same calculations, Hatshepsut's two 18th dynasty obelisks, which flanked the 5th pylon in the temple of Karnak, would have required seven months to produce. This correlates with the information contained in inscriptions from that time.

The percussion-based stoneworking method was not restricted to the quarry. Most of the granite blocks were sent to the construction site in a roughly finished state. Raised bosses were left protruding from the faces of the stones to provide attachment points for the many ropes used during transportation. Only once the elements were set in place was the finishing work carried out, and it was necessary to use the striking stones once again to complete this final stage.

Very fine longitudinal cut marks left on some

RIGHT The 'unfinished obelisk' abandoned in the Aswan granite quarries. Traces left by the dolerite balls are visible along the sides of the excavated monolith.
(James Harrell)

FAR RIGHT
Archaeological artefacts showing traces left by tubular copper saws.
(Flinders Petrie, 1883)

blocks and statues seem, at first glance, to prove that toothed saws were also used. The problem is that the copper-toothed tools that could have been available to the Egyptians of the Old Kingdom would have been too soft to cut the hardest stones in this way. Nevertheless, many fine vases were carved in a variety of stone types already during the predynastic and Early Dynastic periods, and even more impressive are the thousands of fine stone vases found stored and piled up in the galleries of the pyramid of Djoser. These demonstrate that a high level of expertise and advanced stoneworking techniques were indeed known to the artisans of the early Old Kingdom.

The mystery of the methods used to cut stone was solved thanks to the discovery of several pieces that were abandoned before the work was complete. Exterior shaping and polishing was done using flint blades and flakes. The cutting out of the interior of the vases sometimes left a cylindrical void with a finely lined internal face. Unfinished pieces reveal that the space was made with a rotating, tubular copper saw that cut around the outside of a central core. The core was occasionally found left attached at the bottom. This technique was brilliantly explained by Flinders Petrie, and later verified by experimental archaeologist

ABOVE AND LEFT
Experimental archaeology carried out by Alexander Sokolov (Antropogenez. ru Project), Nikolai Vasiutin, Oleg Kruglyakov and Valery Senmuth Androsov (ISIDA Project) to demonstrate how tubular copper saws could have been used for drilling out granite cores. Their experiments left marks similar to those found on stone vases discovered in Egypt.
(photos: Valery Senmuth Androsov)

Denys Stocks, who combined a wooden drill shaft with a copper cylinder stuck over its end. The entire tool was rotated using a bow with a cord wrapped around the shaft, similar to the drill bows used by carpenters that are often illustrated in Egyptian tomb scenes. To apply further pressure, weights could be hung from the top of the shaft, which would swing round as the tool rotated. The cutting surface was not, however, serrated with teeth, but was a flat edge. The cutting action was achieved by the addition of abrasive sand into the cutting slot. The friction and cutting were caused by the cylindrical copper blade moving quartz sand over the stone, causing the assembly to act as a cylindrical saw. A 6th dynasty scene from the tomb of Ibi includes a rare representation of the method in action. In that case the shaft is devoid of the bow advocated by Denys A. Stocks.

This method explains the presence of the fine slots in the blocks and statues mentioned above. It was possible to use cylindrical or long flat-edged copper blades and abrasive sand to produce the same results as hard-toothed blades. Although it was a prolonged process, it was possible to cut large blocks in half using this method much more rapidly than could be achieved with striking tools. Nevertheless, the copper blades and sand could only be used in cases where long blocks were already fully or partially detached from the rock and were waiting to be cut into several pieces. The advantage of using this new method was two-fold. Firstly, the amount of material lost by cutting was far less than that lost by percussion.

Secondly, once sawn, the elements could be rearranged side-by-side in the final building and be almost perfectly joined together.

Stocks estimated that the sawing, cutting out and finishing of Khufu's sarcophagus required approximately 28,000 hours of work to complete, or nearly two years if three artisans were assigned to the task and worked on it for 12 hours every day. Several rotating teams working night and day could have reduced this duration to one year. These estimates relate to the working of the hardest stone, red granite, but the same method could have been applied to limestone, especially the softest type of limestone, which constitutes the greater part of the core of the pyramids. Even a toothed copper saw could have been used to cut the core blocks. The enormous sloped casing stones of the first level of the south and east faces of Khafre's pyramid have extremely fine interface joints, and the stones have a remarkable continuity of grain patterning. All have notches to insert large levers.

On the other side of the pyramid, the north-west corner sits on steps cut into the bedrock to receive the 'backing stones' and finally the 'casing stones' that have now disappeared. These steps have the same notches on their outer faces. It appears then that by cutting steps into the bedrock to receive the masonry in one location, it was possible to take advantage of the extracted materials to lay foundations in other locations where they were lacking.

The near-perfect arrangement of the relocated stones proves that they retained the same relative positions that they occupied when they were still embedded in the bedrock. This would have reduced the work of cutting and polishing to finish the joint faces. It is quite possible that the builders of Khufu's pyramid also employed this approach.

The work required to shape granite blocks must have taken a toll in terms of time, workers and other resources. The surviving casing blocks nevertheless show that the Egyptians optimised the tasks to be done by organising them in very rational ways in order to complete their huge projects with a minimum of effort. Granite or basalt facing stones were finished only on their adjoining or exterior faces. It was preferable to adjust and reshape the limestone

BELOW Egyptian scene from the tomb of Ibi (Deir el Gebrawy, 6th dynasty) describing the use of tubular tools. *(Norman de Garies Davies, 1902)*

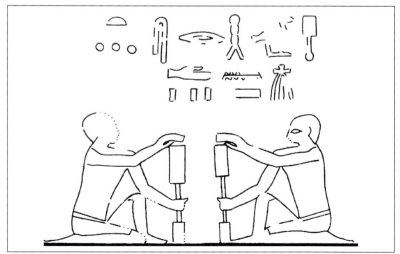

backing stones against which harder stones were to be placed, and then, if necessary, fill any remaining spaces in joints with mortar and chips of limestone.

The transportation of small construction elements from their places of production or extraction to the building site is not difficult to understand. Bricks and stones of small dimensions could easily be carried by hand or on shoulders, or on stretchers carried between pairs of workers. Many scenes from the private tombs of ancient Egyptians illustrate these activities very well. When navigable waterways were not available, transportation over longer distances could be achieved using the normal method for carrying goods around Egypt over land, which was to use pack animals, and in particular donkeys. The main difficulty lies in explaining how larger blocks were moved, whose masses varied from a few tons to several hundred tons, some of which had to be transported over very long distances.

Transport by waterway

The river was most effective for carrying the larger stone blocks and many of the routes took advantage of the Nile currents. Once the barges were pushed out into the river they would be carried away with their cargo towards the north. Going back upstream was done using sails, which were filled whenever favourable winds blew in the opposite direction to the current. Although there are only a few depictions of the transportation networks, the logistical operations that are depicted were usually linked to the waterways, and the Nile was the main artery of this system. The river was shown teeming with ships sailing upstream (sails raised) and downstream (all sails folded), laden with fine limestone from Tura or red granite from the distant quarries of Aswan.

The most explicit scenes showing the transportation of construction elements are engraved on blocks from the causeway of the 5th dynasty pyramid of Unas at Saqqara. These show two cornices with grooves and two pairs of palmiform granite columns being transported by ship for delivery to the pyramid complex: 'Arrival from Elephantine with granite columns for the pyramid' and 'Arrival from

ABOVE AND BELOW Lower layers of Khafre's pyramid indicate that huge blocks were extracted from this side to be reused in the same order elsewhere. *(Franck Monnier)*

BELOW Masonry from Menkaure's mortuary temple at Giza. *(Franck Monnier)*

Elephantine loaded with granite cornices for the pyramid called "Beautiful are the places of the son of Re, Unas".'

At Giza, the 5th dynasty mastaba tomb (G 2370) of the vizier and head of all the royal works Senedjemib Inti contains reliefs depicting a ship loaded with a sarcophagus and its lid, both intended for use by the tomb's owner. The accompanying text tells that his son Senedjemib Mehi obtained permission from the pharaoh to bury his father in a fine Tura limestone sarcophagus:

I begged from my lord that a sarcophagus be [brought] for him from Tura. The majesty of my lord had an overseer of troops together with an overseer of officials ferry over in order to bring this sarcophagus from Tura in a great cargo vessel of the residence. [...] Everything was done for these troops, just like that which had been commanded in the residence. This sarcophagus was

brought together with its lid to the necropolis of the pyramid 'Horizon of Khufu', and was placed in his tomb, it having been conveyed by water from Tura and placed in its bed during five [or seven?] days in transit. (Based on the translation by Edward Brovarski in Giza Mastabas 7)

This scene is rare in that it describes the transportation of a block quarried on the eastern side of the Nile valley, via inland waterways, over to Giza on the west side of the valley. The depictions provide a valuable illustration of the texts that accompany the scene, and also elaborate a few other rare texts from the Old Kingdom. The ship's name is *Isesi, great of power* and it is designated as a cargo vessel. It is shown devoid of sails, being carried away by the currents and steered by two men at the stern. According to the legend that accompanies the scene, the three men at the front of the ship are the overseers of ten (men),

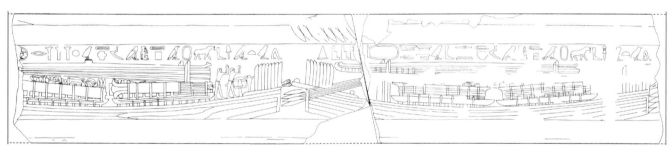

the chief navigator and the first mate of the ship. The captain is at the stern.

The Wadi al-Jarf papyrus discovered in 2013 contained the journal of 'inspector' Merer. He recorded several similar journeys that his team completed, carrying casing stones from Tura to Giza. This travel by waterways must have been the most time-consuming part of the transportation of blocks to the construction site at Giza. According to the reports, the team took only one day to travel upstream to Tura on their journey to collect more materials, but once they had their precious cargo on board the troop required twice as much time to return to the construction site, even though it was located 15 km downstream.

The fact that a 13th biannual cattle count is recorded on one of the fragments indicates that the events took place towards the end of Khufu's reign, in his 26th or 27th year, and so it is possible that the team were carrying casing stones for the completion of the pyramid complex at that time. The evidence indicates that transportation between the two sites was entirely carried out by waterways and that there was probably a structured network of named canals. The precise route used is difficult to identify, as the Nile river bed has experienced significant displacement across the valley since the Old Kingdom. The heavy cargo alone does not explain why the troop required twice as much time to transport downstream as was necessary to return to Tura with an unladen ship, despite the favourable currents. The papyrus mentions a stopover at 'the entry of the lake of Khufu' (Ro-She-khufu). That was the administrative centre of operations directed by Ankhhaf, which allowed the expedition to rest at the halfway point of the journey and spend the night in safety, waiting to complete the mission the following morning.

French Egyptologist Pierre Tallet originally thought this corresponded with a place located directly opposite the quarries, close to the west bank of the valley near Abusir. It is 8 km across the valley from the quarries, and the ships could have travelled directly west across the river to this location before they turned north to travel another 11 km to Giza, to complete their journey the following day. His most recent research, however, has concluded that this location was

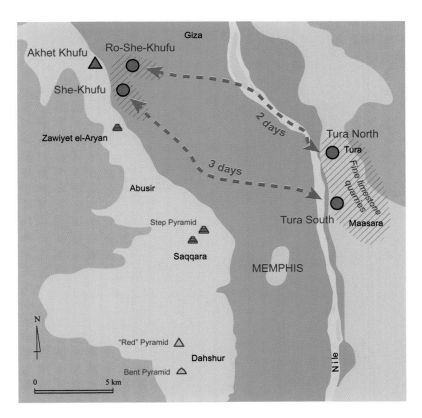

ABOVE Journey taken by inspector Merer and his team to transport limestone from Tura to Giza. The route has been reconstructed based on Merer's journals that were recovered from Wadi al-Jarf. *(Franck Monnier after Pierre Tallet)*

BELOW Scene from the tomb of Senedjemib Inti at Giza showing the transportation of a limestone sarcophagus and its lid from Tura to Giza. *(Edward Brovarski)*

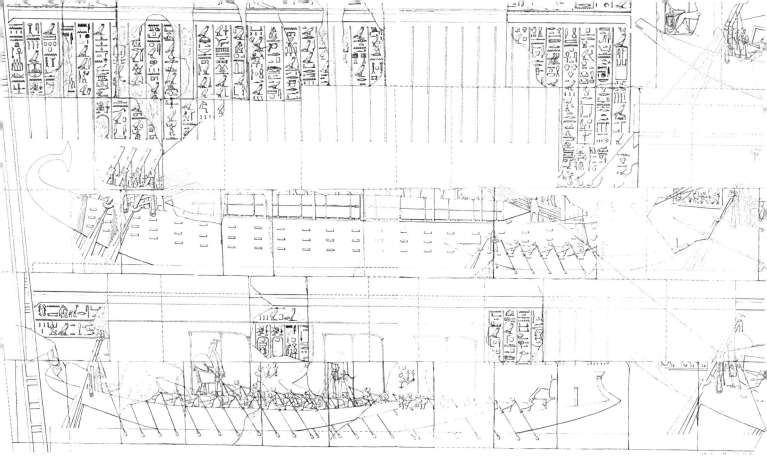

ABOVE Monumental
scene from
Hatshepsut's temple
at Deir el-Bahari (18th
dynasty) showing two
huge obelisks being
transported by ships.
(Édouard Naville, 1908)

probably closer to Giza. It may even have been near the entrance to the main basin at Giza. Crossing the river with its strong currents in a convoy of heavily laden boats must have been a very delicate operation, possibly explaining why it took a whole day to arrive at the 'Lake of Khufu'.

The additional duration of travel to the pyramid is difficult to explain, but the answer may lie in the arrangements of the waterways during the Old Kingdom, the details of which remain obscure. It is known, however, that during the 4th dynasty it was possible to dock boats at the valley temples of the pyramids, and this implies they could be reached by a river channel or via a canal leading from such river channels. Either way, the currents were most likely reduced in that area given the distance from the main river channel. If the 'Lake of Khufu' was also near the west side of the valley, the intermediate and final points of the journey must effectively have been connected by a canal isolated from the main stream. It may even have been necessary to pull the ships for this last part of the journey. This method is depicted in a scene from the 5th dynasty mastaba of Ptahhotep at Saqqara. Boats with rowers are shown working with haulers manoeuvring on

the shore to tow a barge carrying a small stone chapel. One of the upper registers reveals another barge pulled only by haulers.

An inscription from the 6th dynasty tomb of Weni the Elder at Abydos described in detail the number of boats he had built and canals he had dug to bring granite construction elements from Aswan. The fleet comprised three vessels 42 m long, a large raft 31 m long and 16 m wide, and other boats to assist them. A few centuries later in the 18th dynasty of the New Kingdom, a scene showed the transport of two huge granite obelisks. The relief in Hatshepsut's Deir el-Bahari temple depicts the huge barge towed by a flotilla of smaller boats. This scene, with its copious details and its large scale constitutes the most brilliant record of this type of convoy. The length of the main vessel has been estimated at as much as 80 m, and the obelisks it carried were up to 28 m tall, among the largest ever erected. Another scene from the New Kingdom, in the tomb of the architect Ineni, recorded the construction of a single 63 m by 21 m barge to carry a pair of obelisks for Thutmose I. Two intact surviving obelisks at the temple of Karnak, both 20 m tall and weighing 260 tons, demonstrate the skills of those who designed and manufactured wooden structures sufficiently strong to move and float these huge pieces of solid stone over long distances, without breaking them due to their enormous masses. Furthermore, an obelisk described in a mathematical problem recorded by Hori the scribe in the 19th dynasty papyrus Anastasi I is given as 110 cubits or 57.6 m long, but it is impossible to know if the manufacture of such an enormous monument was ever actually attempted.

The granite monoliths covering the King's Chamber of Khufu's pyramid, and the Tura limestone gable-roofed burial chambers made during his reign, used dozens of stones weighing more than 50 tons each, and it must have been necessary to construct a fleet dedicated to their transportation. No texts record the workflow used to load, launch, move and disembark the cargoes, but many centuries later Pliny the Elder stated that the largest items were loaded onto ballasted barges moored in a dedicated channel. Once the stones were in place, the ballast was unloaded and the boats would rise up and float free. This may be the process described in the biography of Weni, where several channels were dug in order to load granite elements. Some later documents from the New Kingdom are the only ones to provide detailed information about the transport of blocks by inland waterway. These notes are on a series of ostraca that recorded the number of boats needed for the delivery of stones, for the construction of the Ramesseum, the temple of Ramesses II in Thebes. A number of blocks are described along with their precise dimensions, so that the captains knew exactly what quantities were allocated to each barge. These fleets consisted of around ten ships whose average cargo capacity was approximately 15 tons. This rigorous cargo management recalls the great logistical and administrative achievements of their ancestors during the Old Kingdom.

Overland transport

Transport over land was even more challenging. Once the boats had been unloaded, the remainder of the journey to the construction site was carried out using only muscle power. Sleds able to support enormous loads were pulled from the ports and quarries along sandy and rocky tracks. There is evidence that animals were also used to pull blocks of stone. A scene showing two cattle pulling a sled carrying a naos shrine is illustrated on the 5th dynasty mastaba tomb of Hetepherakhti, while in two other contemporary tombs, that of Idu at Giza and in the mastaba of Niankhkhnum and Khnumhotep at Saqqara, the men are shown working with the cattle to pull a chapel mounted on skids. Later inscriptions include that on the Stele of Neferperet, which dates to the early 18th dynasty and was discovered in the fine limestone quarries of Maasara. It depicts three pairs of zebu cattle pulling a large block of limestone fixed on a sled. In later times, the funerary boat was often showed being pulled on a sled hauled by cattle. Although from varied contexts, these examples show that animals could be used to supplement human muscle power when required, but it remains difficult to assess what proportion of the work was carried out in that way. Clearly, animals could help the workforce on certain occasions, but it may have been a more typical occurrence than the handful of illustrations suggest.

Whatever the source of muscle power, the transport of heavy loads secured on skids or sleds seems to have been the rule, and there are no examples showing the transport

BELOW Animal-drawn sled depicted on a stele from the Tura quarries (18th dynasty).
(Georges Daressy, 1911)

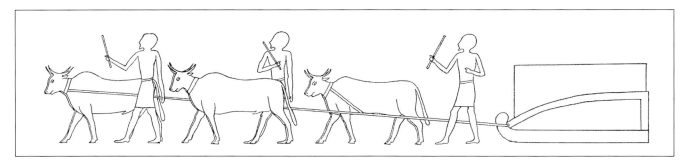

ABOVE Rope found in one of the Giza boat pits, now in the Solar Boat Museum.
(Franck Monnier)

RIGHT Wooden sled found in the pyramid complex of Senwosret III at Dahshur, now in the Cairo Museum.
(Franck Monnier)

of blocks on a wheeled vehicle. Wheels were used during the 4th or 5th dynasties for moving tall siege engines, but there is no evidence that they were ever used for transporting construction elements. The stony and sandy nature of the Egyptian soil was unsuitable for most wheeled vehicles, and the enormous weight of the monoliths being moved would have strained even the most substantial axles and wheels.

The majority of Old Kingdom scenes showing transportation depict loads mounted on sleds with rounded skids in front. These were necessary for running over the loose material that accumulated in front of the sleds as they moved. Columns, cornices, sarcophagi, door jambs and lintels, chapel shrines and even large stone vases could be moved in this way, and they remained attached to their sleds until they reached their final destinations, even when they were being transported by boat.

The package was shipped in one piece. Traction was generally produced by a team of workers, the size of which was determined according to the load being hauled. A mathematical problem on the papyrus Anastasi I demonstrates a calculation in which the volume of the obelisk being conveyed led to the determination of the number of workers required to move it. Unfortunately, as the solution does not appear on the document, the ratio applied in that case remains unknown. The French Egyptologist Simon Delvaux, however,

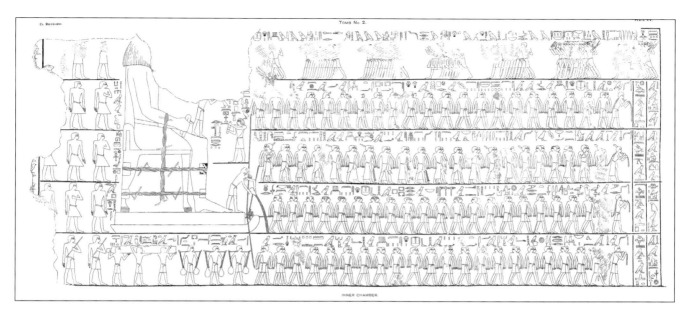

has recently argued that the surviving texts and depictions indicate that a ratio of approximately 350 kg per person was used to calculate the number of workers required to move a load over horizontal ground. Inscriptions from the Middle Kingdom left in the quarries of the Wadi Hammamat mention the transportation of huge monoliths by bands of 500 to 2,000 workers.

A famous scene from the 12th dynasty tomb of Djehutyhotep at Deir el-Bersheh shows a colossal statue of the deceased being moved, and includes details showing the method of lubricating the sled. There are also details of the mass that was moved and images of all the workers assigned to the task. The accompanying text tells that the statue measured 13 cubits (6.8 m) high, that it came from the quarry of Hatnub, and that it was being taken to the home city of the local governor or 'nomarch'. To get there, this massive statue of approximately 58 tons had to be pulled across 17 km of the desert road from Hatnub to the valley. It was then pulled another 20 km along the riverside to the city. Four rows of 172 workers, arranged in pairs, are shown. An individual pours water under the front of the skids to lubricate the track in front as the statue moves. He is accompanied by jar carriers who maintain a steady supply of liquid. Tests carried out at Karnak by the French Egyptologist Henri Chevrier established that, under optimal conditions, a single individual is able to tow a one-tonne block across flat, lubricated ground. Based on these conditions, the Egyptians apparently had more than enough workers to complete the task, although it is likely that the characteristics of the soil were usually less than favourable.

A similar system must have been used for transporting the monoliths to the pyramid complexes of the Old Kingdom. Although less detailed, a 5th dynasty relief from the causeway of Sahure's pyramid at Abusir includes a text describing a team bringing a pyramidion capstone to the site: '[Bringing] The white gold pyramidion of the pyramid "Sahure's souls shines" by the two crews of the two boats' (Translation by Tarek El Awady, *Sahure, The Pyramid Causeway*).

Only a fragment of this scene has survived, and the section showing the pyramidion unfortunately did not. This means that the only known representation showing the construction of a pyramid is missing its central element. It is, however, possible to see that the monolith was pulled by 16 men, while another poured water in front of the sled, a task that appears to have been imperative in this type of scene.

The use of lubrication makes good engineering sense, but only on tracks specially designed to facilitate sliding. The existence of such tracks has been established, and tests show that the silt of the Nile valley considerably reduces the friction between sleds and the ground when wet. On the other hand, it would have been impossible to move heavy loads

ABOVE Scene from the tomb of Djehutyhotep (12th dynasty) showing a colossal statue weighing approximately 58 tons being hauled. *(Percy Newberry and Willoughby Fraser, 1893)*

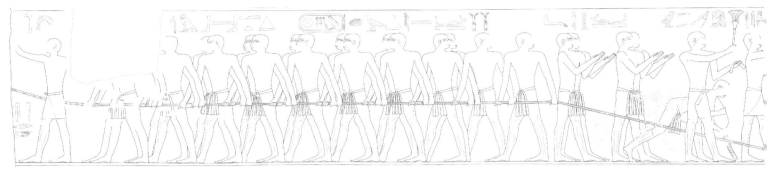

ABOVE A depiction of a pyramidion being pulled by a team, from Sahure's pyramid causeway at Abusir (5th dynasty). *(J. Malátková, © Charles University, Faculty of Arts, 2018)*

over waterlogged soil, as the load would have become bogged down rapidly. The path had to be suitable to receive the laden sleds and hauling teams without becoming seriously damaged.

A good example of such a track dating to the Middle Kingdom was found near Mirgissa fort, beyond Egypt's southern frontier. A slipway was built there so that boats could be pulled around the dangerous rapids of the Nile's second cataract. The track was originally 2 km long, although it has now disappeared under the waters of Lake Nasser. The remnants that were studied indicated that the technique described above was used there. The track was less than 4 m wide and had a concave profile to accommodate the boats, which were probably towed along on their hulls rather than tied to sleds. The track had been reinforced with multiple logs arranged transversely, embedded in silt and forming a flush surface. Rut marks in the silt indicate the use of wooden skids separated by 1.2 to 1.7 m. These marks could have been left by loads of cargo on sleds that followed the boats. The only footprints found were left by goats that crossed the track shortly after its last use, and this suggests that the haulers did not march up the track, but alongside it on dry land. Tests have shown that the slipway could support and transport a load of 9 tons using these methods.

Slipways of this type, but running over horizontal land, have also been found at the 12th dynasty Middle Kingdom sites of the pyramids of Senwosret II at Lahun, and of Senwosret I and Amenemhat I at Lisht, and there are also representations of water pourers creating lubricated tracks from the Old Kingdom. Remnants of transport tracks from the Old Kingdom have been found at Abusir, beside the Red Pyramid of Dahshur-North, near the Mastabat 'al-Fara'un' at Saqqara and beside

the quarries at Hatnub, Aswan and Gebel el-Asr, and most notably, leading from the basalt quarry at Widan el-Faras, north of the Faiyum.

Other slipways are more like ramps. One recently discovered near the south-western corner of Khufu's pyramid may have been part of a large construction track. At 4 m long and 4 m wide, the surviving stretch consisted of two parallel stone block walls with an infill of rubble between them. The original purpose or function of the track remains unclear, but there is no doubt that it was a transportation route. Although it was found near Khufu's pyramid, it is directed towards one of the mastabas of the necropolis built at the end of the 4th dynasty (G1S). At present it remains impossible to say if it was used for the construction of the Great Pyramid or another monument.

A similar but longer track, with mortar-bonded retaining walls spaced 5.7 m apart, was also found south-east of the pyramid. It started west of the sphinx and was used to take materials to the mastabas of the eastern cemetery. Clay seal imprints with Khufu's name on them were found in the rubble fill material, indicating that it was constructed during his reign or shortly thereafter. Based on the available evidence, these structures were never made of cut stone or mudbrick, but were made of mortared rubble, while the parallel retaining walls contained a filling of limestone debris.

Almost nothing is known about the surface finish of the slipways. The narrow width of these structures must have forced the engineers to abandon silt as a finishing surface. Such a soft roadway would have been hazardous for workers and would quickly have been damaged by trampling. Perhaps it is more likely that the surface was made of wooden planks arranged to form rails, which once wet would have

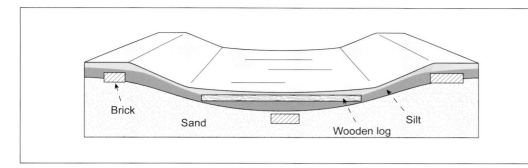

LEFT Sectional
view of the slipway
excavated at Mirgissa.
(Franck Monnier)

provided less resistance to the movement of
the sleds. Similar slipways dating to the reign of
Khufu have also been found at Wadi al-Jarf, in
warehouse galleries furnished with tracks that
were used to move closing blocks into place
when the storage spaces were not being used.

The quarries of Gebel el-Asr in Lower Nubia
were reached along tracks with characteristics
that suggest sleds may not have been the only
cargo vehicles deployed. The extraction of the
gneiss from that remote location necessitated the
development of a 65 km-long track leading to the
port where the Toshka wadi reached the Nile and
the stones were loaded onto boats. Excavations
carried out in the area of these quarries revealed
several sections of stone pavements with
walls that were raised more than 1m from the
surrounding ground level. Two parallel ruts less
than 10 m long stopped abruptly at the foot of
the structure, suggesting that they might have
been tracks for vehicles used to lift and then
place the materials to be exported onto the track.
The track is obviously not a simple pulling path,
otherwise it would have been built level with the
surrounding ground.

These remnants demonstrate the
considerable distances over which materials
were transported and suggest that the Egyptians

BELOW Remains of a
transportation route of
the Old Kingdom for
hauling basalt blocks
from Widan el-Faras
to the Faiyum lake.
(Franck Monnier)

RIGHT Construction ramps for pulling stone blocks in the pyramid complex of Senwosret II (12th dynasty) at El-Lahun. *(Flinders Petrie, 1923)*

may have developed an original transportation system as a result. Was the track only for pulling sleds along, or could the Egyptians have invented a platform with rotating wheels? The evidence currently available is insufficient to draw any firm conclusions on this matter.

Elevation of the building elements

While the transportation of loads by waterway or over land can be explained using the available archaeological and epigraphic evidence, there remains a lack of information regarding how the stones were secured to their sleds, how they were loaded onto and unloaded from boats, and how sleds were unloaded close to the work sites. Neither the iconography nor the texts give any description of these tasks. This lack of documentary evidence also makes it difficult to fully understand the systems used to move the loads to the foot of the pyramid, and to then lift the blocks into their final positions on the structure. The inability of Egyptologists to provide a comprehensive explanation for this work has opened the door to amateur researchers who have invented their own theories to try to solve this 'mystery', but only the scientifically plausible hypotheses will be reviewed here.

There are three main categories of theories put forward to explain how the blocks of the pyramids were lifted into place. The first is based on the use of lifting equipment, the second is based on the use of monumental ramps that ran up the outside of the pyramid and the third is based on the use of

construction ramps that ascended within the structure of the pyramid. Hybrid theories often draw on more than one of these approaches.

Researchers usually examine the details of the structure in order to identify the principles used in its construction. This approach is rational, and it seems logical that the order in which the different parts of the building were erected should be studied before trying to explain how each block was raised and set in place. Despite its homogeneous external appearance, a pyramid is not a simple pile of stones set down one on top of the other. The structures varied substantially and the design techniques used depended on what dynasty the pyramid was created in; in other words, during which stage of the evolution of this type of architecture it was built in. The pyramids of the 3rd dynasty all consisted of concentric steeply sloped layers leaning against a central core. The layered pyramid of Zawiyet el-Aryan has core layers that are not horizontal but curved.

The Meidum Pyramid marked a transition between the older methods of construction and those used for the next group of giant pyramids. The first phase was a series of steps built with steeply sloped layers leaning onto the central core. It was then enlarged with more steps, following the same principle, then modified a second time with masonry arranged in horizontal layers. This final envelope gave it a perfect pyramidal shape with triangular faces. Subsequently, the pyramids were always built using horizontal layers. Later pyramids demonstrate that the Egyptians continued to employ an internal stepped core structure but were built using horizontal layers. The pyramids of Khufu's queens, the pyramid of queen G3a

OPPOSITE A few different theories about construction ramps for raising stone blocks of pyramids. *(Franck Monnier)*

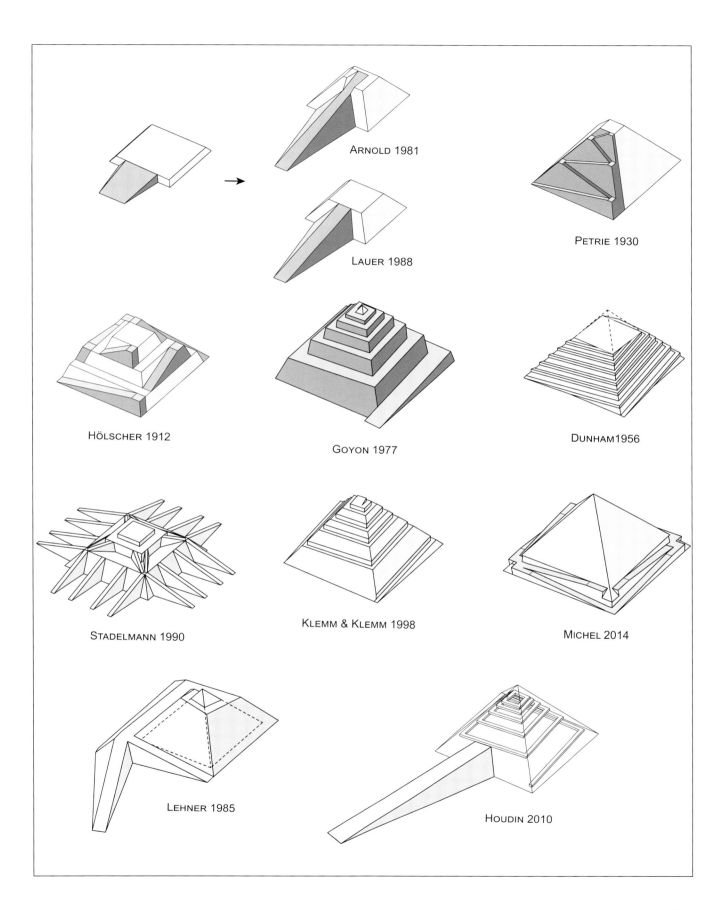

ARNOLD 1981

LAUER 1988

PETRIE 1930

HÖLSCHER 1912

GOYON 1977

DUNHAM1956

STADELMANN 1990

KLEMM & KLEMM 1998

MICHEL 2014

LEHNER 1985

HOUDIN 2010

RIGHT **Internal
stepped structure
of the pyramid of
Niuserre at Abusir
(5th dynasty).**
(Franck Monnier)

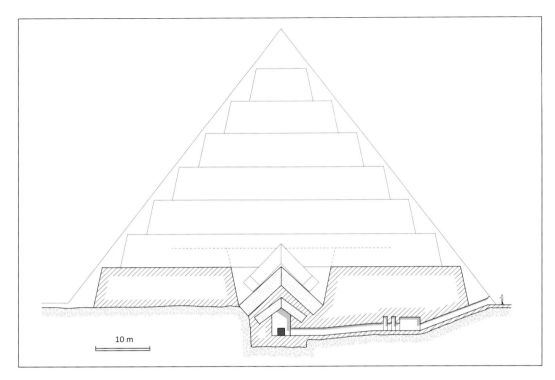

10 m

of Menkaure, that of Menkaure himself, and
all the pyramids of the 5th and 6th dynasties
at Saqqara and Abusir show evidence of this
underlying structure.

The larger pyramids at Dahshur and Giza are
too complete to reveal their internal structures;
however, the results of microgravimetric surveys
carried out in the 1980s seem to show that
the core of Khufu's pyramid is also a stepped
structure. Construction of the pyramid of
Sekhemkhet in Saqqara and the layered
pyramid at Zawiyet el-Aryan was stopped only
a few metres above ground level, but some
important aspects of the structures are visible
as a result. It is clear that the central core was
not built in advance and that the external layers
leaning against it were added at almost the
same time. The construction levels therefore
rose up across the whole area at once. The
theory formerly put forward by Karl Richard
Lepsius and reiterated by Auguste Choisy,
whereby the pyramids were built outwards,
layer by layer, from a central core that was
completed first, is therefore not supported by
the archaeological evidence, and this holds
for the 3rd dynasty as well as all subsequent
dynasties. Similarly, the abandoned 4th dynasty
pyramid construction site of the 'Great Pit'
at Zawiyet el-Aryan revealed that the outer

perimeter blocks of the first layer had already
been arranged to define a base square of
210 m (or 400 cubits) before it was abandoned.

It is difficult to explain the continued
presence of step structures within true pyramids
with triangular faces after the constructions
of the Meidum Pyramid, except by making
some assumptions. The symbolism expressed
by Djoser's Step Pyramid of the 3rd dynasty
is thought by some scholars to invoke the
concept of a staircase leading up to the
heavens, and it may be that this idea was
so fundamental to the Egyptians' funerary
beliefs that they retained it even when the
steps became invisible from the outside, once
construction was complete. On the other hand,
the internal form could be the result of a system
of construction. The modifications made to the
4th dynasty pyramids of Snefru at Meidum and
Dahshur-South, and the 5th dynasty pyramid
of Neferirkare at Abusir demonstrate that the
builders were able to lift and set blocks in
place around the whole periphery of a pre-
existing stepped monument, without requiring
completely open flat platforms to build from.
On the other hand, the unfinished tomb of
Neferefre, which was begun as a pyramid with
a stepped core and then converted into a
mastaba, seems to indicate that the pyramids

of the 5th dynasty were first built in steps, before being covered with a masonry envelope with triangular faces. Did this also apply during the late 4th dynasty, or were steps only present in the pyramids where this type of structure is now visible? It seems likely that some of the same methods were used in adjacent dynasties, although it is possible that the builders adopted different construction methods depending on the size of the projects to be completed.

At the abandoned pyramid site of the 'Great Pit' at Zawiyet el-Aryan, it is clear that the perimeter of the lowest layer was first set out around the base, despite its incomplete state, while the satellite pyramid of Dahshur-South does not show any evidence of an internal step structure. These various facts suggest that the Egyptians were armed with a wide range of construction techniques and were able to cope with the changing requirements of each pharaoh's architectural programme.

In an attempt to throw further light on the methods used, scholars often quote Herodotus from the 5th century BC. The Greek historian reported the Egyptian priests' own accounts of the construction of the pyramid of Khufu in this way:

He compelled all the Egyptians to work for him. To some, he assigned the task of dragging stones from the quarries in the Arabian mountains to the Nile; and after the stones were ferried across the river in boats, he organised others to receive and drag them to the mountains called Libyan. They worked in gangs of 100,000 men, each gang for three months. For ten years the people wore themselves out building the causeway over which the stones were dragged, a work which was in my opinion not much easier than the building of the pyramid, for the road is nearly five stadiums long [925 m] and twenty yards wide [18 m] and elevated at its highest to a height of sixteen yards [14.4 m], and it is all of stone polished and carved with figures. The aforesaid ten years went to the building of this road and of the underground chambers in the hill where the pyramids stand; these, the king meant to be burial-places for himself, and surrounded them with water, bringing in a channel from the Nile. The pyramid itself was twenty years in the making. Its base is square, each side eight hundred feet [244 m] long, and its height is the same; the whole is of stone polished and

BELOW The three queens' pyramids of Khufu's complex reveal inner stepped structures.
(Franck Monnier)

most exactly fitted; there is no block of less than thirty feet in length [9.24 m]. (Herodotus, Histories, *II, 124)*

This pyramid was made like stairs … When this, its first form, was completed, the workmen used short wooden logs as levers to raise the rest of the stones, they heaved up the blocks from the ground onto the first tier of steps, when the stone had been raised, it was set on another lever that stood on the first tier, and the lever again used to lift it from this tier to the next. It may be that there was a new lever on each tier of steps, or perhaps there was only one lever, quite portable, which they carried up to each tier in turn; I leave this uncertain, as both possibilities were mentioned. But this is certain, that the upper part of the pyramid was finished off first, then the next below it, and last of all the base and the lowest part. (Herodotus, Histories, *II, 125)*

Herodotus communicates some uncertainty regarding the methods used, and his remarks are particularly difficult to interpret because of his ancient Greek architectural vocabulary. There

BELOW The report left by Herodotus concerning the construction of the Great Pyramid with wooden levers inspired many interpretations, like this one dating from the 19th century. *(Antoine-Yves Goguet, 1820)*

was clearly some speculation on his part, as well as a lack of clarity on the part of the priests of Memphis themselves who were separated chronologically from the reign of Khufu by 2,000 years. Their claim that the work required the constant efforts of 100,000 workers seems a gross overestimation, and elsewhere they also accused Khufu of prostituting one of his daughters in order to cover the expenses of his ambitious project. It seems likely, then, that their broad approximations about the dimensions of the monuments and the construction methods used could be misleading. If there was an underlying step structure, they said nothing about how that structure itself was built.

This questionable information has generated a great deal of speculation and has supported a diversity of theories, some relating to ramps, but mostly detailing the use of hypothetical lifting machines. The vagueness of Herodotus's description has given free rein to theories that have filled the void created by the lack of facts. It is possible that the Egyptians were able to design lifting devices, but there are no descriptions or depictions of any such apparatus anywhere in the existing records from pharaonic times. This lack of evidence

CONSTRUCTION DES PYRAMIDES D'EGYPTE SELON HÉRODOTE.

ABOVE **Wall painting from the tomb of Rekhmire (18th dynasty) showing a ramp made up of brick layers.**
(Prisse d'Avennes, 1878)

means that any attempt to define the technical details of a lifting machine is difficult to support, particularly if it attempts to explain the entire construction of a pyramid.

Nevertheless, researchers continue to explore this line of enquiry. Some have envisaged machines inspired by the shaduf, an agricultural device that can lift large amounts of water from the Nile into irrigation channels using leverage. Others have advocated more simple arrangements of levers and wedges for elevating blocks. Some archaeologists and engineers have proposed anachronistic and elaborate systems employing pulleys, capstans and hinged beams. One other proposal is that small rocking sleds were used to move and lift blocks, examples of which are in fact known in the form of small models included with New Kingdom ritual foundation deposits, but it remains unclear how these were actually employed. The elevation of blocks using such machines would surely have taken more time than for pulling them up a straight ramp and would have been a precarious task if the steps were high.

Whatever method was used, a simple calculation shows that if the pyramid was built with 2.3 million blocks in approximately 26 years, then working at the rate of ten hours every day, one block was set in place every 2.7 minutes. This remains challenging to explain using any of the existing hypotheses.

A few centuries after Herodotus, the historian Diodorus of Sicily wrote about the construction of the Great Pyramid in a way that contradicted what his illustrious predecessor had said, but was more in line with the evidence currently available:

...these stones have preserved to this day their original arrangement and all their appearance. They are said to have been brought from Arabia very far, and arranged by means of terraces; for then we had not yet invented machines. (Diodorus of Sicily, Book I, sec LXIII).

Most of the authors who propose that the pyramid was built using monumental ramps theorise that the construction was carried out by setting out horizontal layers of core blocks along with casing stones positioned around the perimeter. The ramps envisaged have assumed a variety of forms and dimensions, but at least there is a body of evidence to support these hypotheses. The archaeological record from the pharaonic era is full of evidence indicating that the Egyptians used ramps to raise building blocks to the required levels. If the mathematical problem included in the New Kingdom Anastasi I papyrus is to be believed, then these ramps reached considerable dimensions: 'A ramp of 730 cubits (382 m) in length and 55 cubits (29 m) wide, containing 120 compartments filled with wood and reeds, will be built, and rising to 60 cubits (31.5 m) at the top side.' Elsewhere, the 18th dynasty tomb of Rekhmire in Thebes included a depiction of this type of ramp.

Architect-turned-Egyptologist Jean-Philippe Lauer formulated one of the most popular ramp theories of the mid-20th century. Based on a theory of the German Egyptologist Ludwig Borchardt regarding a hypothetical ramp running up the front of the Meidum Pyramid, the French Egyptologist attempted to depict

a similar but more imposing ramp at Giza, almost as wide as the pyramid at its base, but with sloping sides that decreased the size of the access track as the layers were added. Although simple and easy to understand, the proposal was problematic in several respects. Most notably, its construction would have been almost as expensive in energy and materials as the pyramid itself. In order to avoid reaching an unfeasible volume, the track would have had to be so steep that it would have been difficult to pull up blocks weighing several tens of tons. Secondly, construction work on the pyramid would have been interrupted every time it was necessary to raise the ramp up to the height of the layer under construction. Finally, if this method was used, then the casing stones of the pyramid must have been installed with finished faces that did not require any adjustments or further smoothing after they were set in position, as the ramp would have covered a very large section of these stones.

Some complete sets of casing stones have survived in situ. The pyramid of Khafre at Giza is still crowned with a large section of finely cut casing stones, as is the Bent Pyramid in Dahshur-South. The remnants of the casing of the last phase of the Meidum Pyramid is also made up using blocks of Tura limestone, although they were apparently installed in haste. The lowest layers of casing stones of the satellite pyramids of Khufu also remain in place. They have construction bosses still protruding that show it was never completed. The bosses do suggest, however, that the final dressing of the casing stone faces was done last and was carried out from the top to the bottom.

It seems that during the Old Kingdom, the finishing of the faces was carried out after the layers had been completed, and it was therefore necessary to retain some sort of temporary structure such as scaffolding or a ramp at that stage. The small provincial pyramid of El-Sinki was certainly built with frontal ramps, one against each side, but the small dimensions of that project are not comparable to the colossal construction projects carried out at Giza. It remains difficult, again, to identify one standard method. At the very least, the use of ramps can be considered as plausible for the stepped pyramids of the 3rd dynasty where the masonry blocks were more easily transportable.

The frontal ramp has been presented in many versions, but it cannot escape the weaknesses inherent to the original proposal. Variations include the semi-internal front ramp penetrating into the core of the building, the zig-zagging frontal ramp and the small radiating ramps on all four sides, all of which demand excessively steep inclinations and could not avoid disrupting the final finishing of the casing stones. It is for this reason that the spiral ramp, first proposed by Noel F. Wheeler, has gained traction. Its most obvious advantage is that it is more economical with materials than the frontal approach ramps.

The first step in constructing a spiral ramp is to envelop the building on all four faces in a masonry structure that will be dismantled after completion of the work. Inclined ramps originate at the four corners and encircle the building in a helical pattern. The first version of the theory left very little room for the movement of workers, and so it was reworked by Dows Dunham. Georges Goyon, in turn, proposed a variation with a single ramp, more colossal and able to accommodate large troops of haulers. Goyon's massive ramp certainly resolved the problem of the lack of space, and offered a more solid foundation, but it required a journey of several kilometres to reach the highest parts of the large pyramids. More seriously, this type of ramp would obscure the external faces and edges of the structure, making it almost impossible to control the geometry of the final structure or work on the casing stones while it was in place.

Egyptologist Mark Lehner undertook a comprehensive study of the geology, geomorphology and topography of the Giza Plateau in the early 1980s, which allowed him to draw up a list of important factors that could be used to reconstruct the development of the necropolis. He revealed that the quarry that produced most of the materials for the Great Pyramid was located south of it, east of the pyramid of Khafre, and concluded that the building materials had to follow a path heading straight from the quarry towards Khufu's building site to the north. By taking into account the developmental history of the field of mastabas established by George Reisner, he was able to determine what areas of necropolis were unoccupied spaces during the construction of the Great Pyramid. His study suggested that the area on the eastern side of the pyramid was being used for the construction of the satellite pyramids and the mastabas of the eastern cemetery. In the west, on the other hand, there was a clear space more than 130 m wide between the western cemetery mastaba field and the pyramid, which he could only explain by the existence of a construction area. The north and south sides were also untouched by construction. As for the debris that had accumulated over the escarpments of the plateau, there was no trace of building blocks, but mainly limestone waste.

This information led him to envisage a long stone ramp rather than a brick-built one. Its approach was initially linear, leading up from the quarry to the south up to the south-west corner

BELOW Section of finished granite casing stones near the entrance to Menkaure's pyramid. Most of these granite stones remained unfinished.
(Franck Monnier)

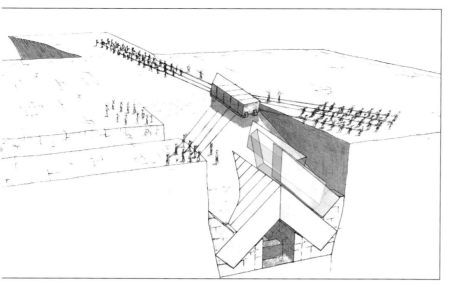

ABOVE Team of haulers installing the second layer of roof beams into a gable-roofed burial chamber, by sliding them over the finished mass of the pyramid. This method was proposed by Franck Monnier, based on evidence from the 5th and 6th dynasties. Red ochre guide lines were drawn on the west wall of the burial pit so that the huge monoliths could be positioned accurately, from east to west. *(Franck Monnier)*

BELOW Teams manoeuvring the lower layer of roof beams into their final positions after bringing them down the main construction trench incline.

(Franck Monnier)

of the pyramid. It would then have continued to rise up along the western side of the pyramid against which it was built. Eventually it would have adopted a spiral form to reach the top of the pyramid, completely enveloping the building. This innovative approach has shed new light on the site and on ways of understanding issues related to construction. A straight section of masonry ramp, 62 m in length, would fit well within the open landscape to the south and on the west side. The rest seems to be more conjectural and does not correspond well with the space available on the east side. An enveloping ramp, 30 m wide on the east side, would have covered the site of the mortuary temple and the boat pits, and the whole structure would have used as much material as the pyramid itself, a volume that all the quarries operated during Khufu's reign could not have produced. Its presence would again have prevented rigorous control of the geometry of the monument, which was required to produce the high-quality form that is still evident today.

In addition to the various problems posed by enormous enveloping ramps, there is the problem of slope angles. It would have been extremely dangerous for large troops of workers

THIS PAGE Transport of an architrave and moving of an obelisk by French archaeologist Georges Legrain's team at the beginning of the 20th century. Legrain was responsible for restoring the Great Hypostyle Hall of Karnak Temple using rudimentary reconstruction methods. This architrave weighed 42 tons and his workers were also able to move an obelisk fragment weighing 80 tons. Legrain demonstrated that inclined ramps, wooden rails, rollers and ropes were enough to explain how the Egyptians built their impressive monuments, when utilised appropriately. *(Georges Legrain)*

ABOVE **An Old Kingdom statue of a scribe, now on display in the Cairo Museum.** *(Franck Monnier)*

to drag stones weighing many tons up such long, inclined ramps.

A final aspect of these theories is the question of how such ramps might have been removed after being used. If this was done then it was clearly done so well that no vestiges of any monumental ramp has ever been detected anywhere on a site from the Old Kingdom. The German geologists Dietrich and Rosemarie Klemm were the first to approach the problem from this angle, and their conclusion was that the course of the helical ramp proposed by Georges Goyon must have been incorporated within the periphery of the structure under construction. As attractive as this theory may seem, it is still difficult to explain how there would have been sufficient width for such a route, and how the excessive length of such a route would have been manageable.

The most widely disseminated new theory of the last decade was the one formulated by the French architect Jean-Pierre Houdin, who was firmly convinced that the Great Pyramid of Khufu was built from the inside out using an internal spiral ramp. Popular though this theory was, recent investigations carried out by the

ScanPyramids mission seem to have proved it wrong, as they found no evidence of remains of such a structure in their recent muon scanning projects.

The existence of so many theories demonstrates that the problem is more complex than it first appears. This complexity is the result of the various construction methods used, the disruption and loss of the majority of the evidence in the archaeological record, and the subsequent lack of proven facts to work from. Modern scientific methods may yield more information from the recovered archaeology than is currently available, but current analyses can only work from what is known. The question of how the pyramids were built is both historical as well as technical, and the objective here is not to devise a method that could have worked, but to determine how the ancient Egyptians actually did it. In many respects, the search for answers continues.

Mathematics

The practical building and transportation methods developed by the ancient Egyptians were significant advances, but they relied on intellectual, informational and technical systems that were abstract in nature. These systems let them measure, calculate, communicate, develop and share plans between members of the administration, even if they were located in different places and employed at different times.

These systems can be referred to as information technologies. The scribes of ancient Egypt invented several such ingenious and novel systems, some of which are still used today, including the base ten number system and writing with ink on paper (originally papyrus). These methods are so familiar to us that we take them for granted, but before the ancient Egyptian scribes invented them, these fundamental systems did not exist.

Most of these systems were developed to solve specific practical problems of everyday life, most importantly of agricultural production and surplus distribution. They were then repurposed and employed to enhance the pharaoh's monumental architecture. Hieroglyphic writing is first known from around 3300 BC. The earliest evidence comes from the pharaonic necropolis at Abydos, where carved ivory tags and imprinted seals allowed the scribes to name and categorise produce and signal ownership of individual items. Once they had invented papyrus, they were able to record inventories of produce and materials, including luxury items, in large tables made up from multiple rows and columns. The 365-day calendar they developed allowed them to coordinate daily agricultural tasks to be carried out through the different seasons of the year. At Giza, writing and calendars would have helped them plan out the different phases of the huge construction projects, in coordination with the seasonal agricultural work that remained a priority. Numeracy first allowed them to count how many animals they owned. This knowledge was of vital importance because the livestock provided the nutrition that allowed them to survive. The cattle count became a major biannual event. At Giza, the number of blocks to be ordered and transported to site each day would similarly have been carefully counted and recorded.

The first standardised linear measurement system known in history was invented by the ancient Egyptians and is referred to as the cubit. It was originally used to measure everything from the size of fields to the depth of the Nile floods. It was then repurposed to define the size of the stone blocks to be quarried and shaped, and then used to set out the monumental architecture. For the first time, one system was applied and understood throughout the land. The height of the annual flood was measured in cubits, palms and digits, and was recorded for each year of the pharaoh's reign. This information was chronicled prominently on the Palermo Stone annals dating to the end of the 5th dynasty, because it allowed the administrators to estimate the annual grain yield and tax each field accordingly.

Geometry let the ancient Egyptians calculate the area of the fields to be harvested and taxed, and to measure the volume of the grain produced and stored in the cylindrical granaries. Their accounting skills then allowed them to redistribute the surplus grain to feed the workers or pay the administrators. This surplus management was particularly important in the years when the flood was low and the crop yield from the fields was poor.

LEFT The Palermo Stone, which chronicled the major events during each regnal year. The maximum height of the inundation was also recorded, in cubits, palms and digits. *(Copy of the Palermo Stone in Cairo Museum, negative photo: Franck Monnier)*

At Giza, the cubit linear measurement system was used to accurately measure the size of blocks to be cut, the height of the monuments to be built, and the dimensions of the ground plans to be set out. The use of a common measurement system let masons work in distant quarries such as Aswan and Widan el-Faras, many days' journey from Giza, yet cut blocks that were the correct sizes for the projects being carried out at the final destination. When the stones arrived at the work site, geometry applied with cubits, levels and plumb lines let the builders accurately angle the slopes of the casing stones, set the blocks in place and estimate the volume of stone brought to the site each day.

Only a few surviving examples of texts from the Old Kingdom contain technical information. Unfortunately, mathematical documents were not treated with the same reverence as religious texts or tomb biographies, which were often engraved on stone or painted on tomb walls. Most of the geometric calculations were recorded on papyrus, a perishable material that degrades quickly in the presence of moisture. Most knowledge of the subject is

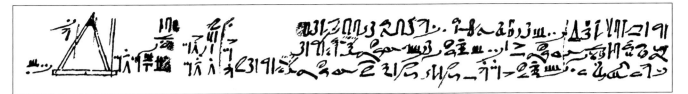

based on manuscripts dating from the end of the Middle Kingdom, such as the Rhind Mathematical Papyrus and the Moscow Mathematical Papyrus, both of which contained problems primarily concerned with accounting or geometry related to daily life, showing how to distribute food or subdivide fields. Although they date to a time long after the majority of the construction at Giza was carried out, some of the examples show how to calculate the slopes of the faces of pyramids using a system called the *seked*, whose origins are often traced back to the 4th dynasty. Problem 56 of the Rhind papyrus is one of the most widely studied. It demonstrated how to determine the *seked* slope of a pyramid 250 cubits (131 m) high by 360 cubits (188.5 m) on each side at the base.

Method to calculate a pyramid of 360 for the base, 250 for its inner height. Let me know his seked. *Then you calculate 1/2 of 360, it happens 180. Then you make sure to multiply 250 to find 180, it happens 1/2 1/5 1/50 in cubits, this cubit being equal to 7 palms. Then you make sure to multiply by 7. Its* seked: *5 1/25 palms.*

This *seked* is equivalent to an inclination of 54° 15' in modern nomenclature, using degrees and minutes.

The only pyramid with dimensions similar to the values in this problem is the lower part of the construction of the Bent Pyramid. If it had been completed in its entirety, its base of 362 cubits on each side would have been surmounted by a superstructure 260 cubits high, which would have been close to what is described on the papyrus. However, its slope was sharply reduced part way through construction and it never reached that full height. The inclination of the faces on the lower section nevertheless ranges from 54° 30' to 55°, close to what was calculated in Problem 56.

The examples on the Rhind Mathematical Papyrus indicate that in order to define the size and shape of the pyramids, the architects began by choosing the desired base and height dimensions for the pyramid, measured in cubits. They then worked out what the associated slope value was. It was not usually the *seked* that determined the base and height dimensions, and so the reasons for the choices of overall outer dimensions and proportions must be found elsewhere.

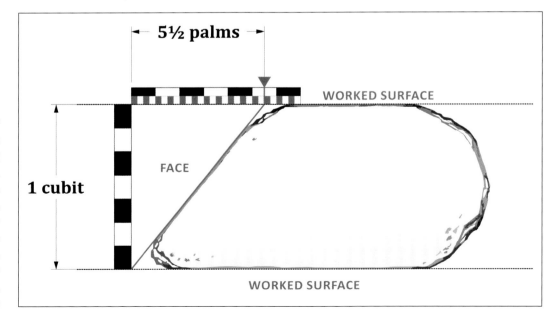

5½ palms

WORKED SURFACE

FACE

1 cubit

WORKED SURFACE

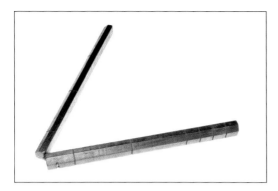

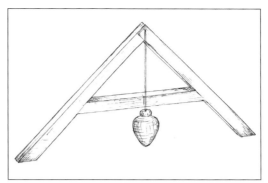

While only a few surviving examples of texts from the Old Kingdom contain technical information, it is possible to derive data regarding the architectural principles and geometric methods used during construction directly from the monuments. There is a vast literature on the geometrical properties of pyramids. New geometrical relations are regularly detected in the architecture of the Great Pyramid of Khufu, with the Golden Ratio and Pi often being key components in discussions.

Scholars do not all agree on what the real intentions of ancient Egyptians were. Did they design these gigantic buildings with such proportions, or are the observed relationships only the unintended consequences of the chosen dimensions?

In the 19th century, once the Great Pyramid's external dimensions had been established with some degree of accuracy, English scholars such as Petrie, Smyth, Agnew and Taylor all noted that the Great Pyramid's sides have the precise slope required to give the building proportions that match those of a circle's radius and circumference. The observed geometric relationship is as follows: a circle formed by using the height of the pyramid as a radius precisely equals the length of the pyramid's perimeter at ground level. This relationship only holds for a pyramid with the precise slope which is that of the Great Pyramid and of the pyramid at Meidum, which was completed at the end of Snefru's reign, not long before Khufu started his pyramid at Giza. From Petrie's survey, the relevant form of Khufu's completed building can be expressed as 1,760 cubits around by 280 cubits in height. This gives the sides a *seked* of 5½ palms and an angle of 51° 40'. Petrie identified the same proportions in the design of the King's Chamber, where the

perimeters of the north and south walls are the length of a circumference formed by the 10 cubit width of the chamber.

Petrie concluded that the use of these circular ratios was deliberate, and a number of Egyptologists and archaeologists have reached a similar conclusion. To these scholars it seems plausible that a culture that used a 7-part measure as its basic standard could have been aware of the relationship that a circle of 7 palms diameter has a circumference of 22 palms, and that they applied these good approximations in their architectural designs.

On the other hand, other Egyptologists and researchers doubt that the ancient Egyptians could have employed the circle ratio Pi. One of the main arguments made by these researchers for excluding the Pi ratio from the mathematical knowledge of the time is that known papyri and ostraca never employ it for calculations of circular areas, and the scribes had apparently

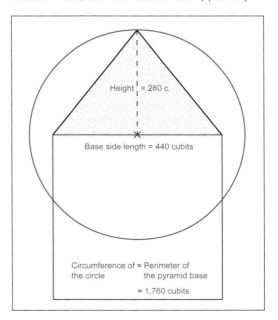

Height = 280 c.

Base side length = 440 cubits

Circumference of ≈ Perimeter of
the circle   the pyramid base

≈ 1,760 cubits

RIGHT Rhind
Mathematical
Papyrus problem
50, demonstrating a
method to calculate
the area of a circle.
(Franck Monnier)

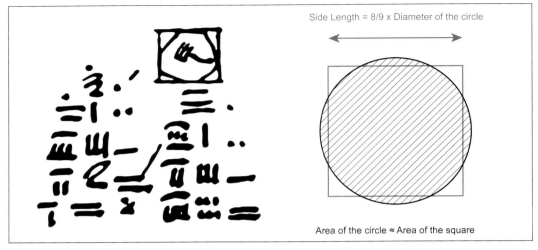

Side Length = 8/9 x Diameter of the circle

Area of the circle ≈ Area of the square

BELOW Limestone
ostracon with a
red ochre painted
diagram, setting out
dimensions for an arch
or vault, from Saqqara
(3rd dynasty).
(Alain Guilleux)

found another practical way of calculating
this property. Problem 50 on the Rhind
Mathematical Papyrus, for example, shows that
the area of a circle is equivalent, or close to,
that of a square with all sides one-ninth shorter
than the diameter of the circle. For comparison,
this algorithm gives the same result as the
conventional method would if an approximate
value for Pi of 3.16 was used.

With respect to the Golden Ratio, which
other researchers have proposed was also
incorporated into the designs, it seems clear that
the proposal should be rejected. The Golden
Ratio would have had no practical value to
the Egyptians whose focus was on functional
systems, and it was also unknown to the Greeks.

It was first identified as a notable ratio during the
Renaissance and has no place in discussions
about ancient Egypt or ancient Greece.

Whatever the means of calculation, the
slope of the Great Pyramid's faces and all of its
casing stones equate to 5½ palms, but most
of the other measurable slopes, such as the
shafts and passages, also appear to have been
defined using whole or half *seked*-like ratio*s*,
suggesting that the *seked* method was used
at Giza, despite the absence of contemporary
texts that explicitly show this.

The only contemporary mathematical
document from the Old Kingdom connected
to a pyramid complex is in fact a geometric
figure sketched out on a limestone ostracon,
discovered at the edge of the northern pavilion
of the Step Pyramid complex of Djoser. Red
ochre painted lines on the ostracon trace
out an arched curve with regularly spaced
ribs. Dimensions in cubits, palms and digits
are written beside the vertical ribs. These
dimensions had been worked out in advance
using some method that remains enigmatic. The
results were written on the limestone fragment
for the workers and craftsmen so that they
could construct a vault, or perhaps an arch-
shaped decoration, with the intended profile.

Astronomy

Even more abstract is the astronomical
knowledge that the ancient Egyptians
associated with the pyramids. Textual evidence
for astronomical concepts is mostly based on
later sources, such as the Pyramid Texts from

the later Old Kingdom, or texts produced after the Second Intermediate Period. During the 4th dynasty, funerary texts were not inscribed on the walls of the pyramids and no detailed plans have been recovered, so any interpretations remain largely hypothetical. Nevertheless, two of the major stars or asterisms mentioned in the Pyramid Texts were known as Sopdet and Sah. Sopdet refers to the brightest star in the sky, which is now known in English as Sirius and is now part of the Canis Major (Great Dog) constellation, while Sah is now known as Orion or Orion's Belt. These stars or asterisms occupied a central place in the funerary beliefs expressed in the Pyramid Texts of the Old Kingdom, and in the Coffin Texts of the Middle Kingdom, and for the ancient Egyptians they represented the gods Isis and Osiris as they travelled across the night sky.

According to the now famous 'Orion Theory' devised by Belgian-Egyptian researcher Robert Bauval, the arrangement of the three great pyramids of Giza was intended to be an intentional topographic representation of the three belt stars of the Orion constellation. The thesis laid the groundwork for a larger hypothesis that tried to incorporate all of the pyramids into a master plan that replicated part of the sky map on the ground. Although it draws on a few hard facts, the theory is not well supported by the wider body of evidence currently available. The theory also proposes the existence of an elaborate master plan that required multi-generational planning, and there is little evidence for this sort of perspective. Each pharaoh built his own pyramid during his own lifetime according to his own design. Only an opportunistic choice made by Menkaure could explain how such a plan could have resulted intentionally, at least in its final phase.

It is clear that the designs for the pyramids usually changed several times, both inside and out, and the choice of a location was most likely not predefined during a previous reign. No plans can realistically be envisaged that reached outside the confines of a single reign. Khufu's immediate successor Djedefre left Giza to install his own complex several kilometres to the north, while his heir travelled further south to Zawiyet el-Aryan. Khafre then returned to Giza, and finally, Menkaure, the builder of the

third pyramid, completed the Giza pharaonic triplet. The final appearance of Giza is therefore only attributable to this last sovereign and his architect, and while the pharaoh would certainly have taken into account the existing heritage to define the position and layout of his funeral complex, there are many factors that could have influenced this choice that were not the result of astronomical concepts, including the limitations of the available landscape.

Other theories put forward to explain the locations include a diagonal alignment that Hans Goedicke suggested was intended to aim towards Heliopolis. He proposed that a connection between the pyramids of Giza and the site of Heliopolis highlighted the growing importance of the solar cult that was based there during the 4th dynasty. Miroslav Verner confirmed this orientation with regard to Khufu

ABOVE The three stars of Orion's Belt showing their visual resemblance to the ground plan of the Giza complex. *(Wikimedia ©Mouser)*

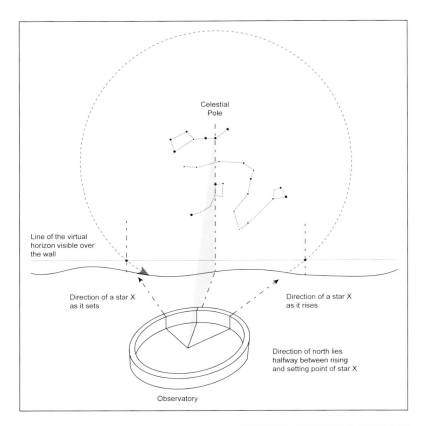

Celestial Pole

Line of the virtual horizon visible over the wall

Direction of a star X as it sets

Direction of a star X as it rises

Direction of north lies halfway between rising and setting point of star X

Observatory

ABOVE The method devised by I. E. S. Edwards to determine true north using the circumpolar stars and a circular wall with a horizontal edge. *(Franck Monnier)*

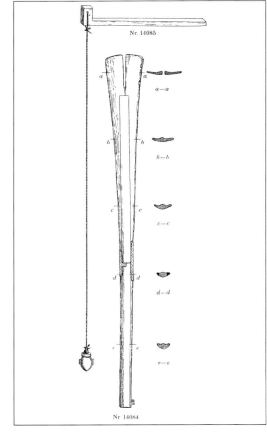

Nr. 14085

a—a

b—b

c—c

d—d

e—e

Nr 14084

RIGHT A 'merkhet' or gnomon stick used to check vertical alignments, including stellar positions, by line of sight. *(Ludwig Borchardt, 1899)*

and Khafre's pyramids, but the south-west corner of Menkaure's pyramid in fact deviates by around 10 m from this line, and so seems to compromise this line of enquiry.

The Heliopolis alignment theory has been enlarged to include other pyramids of the Memphite Necropolis, and in particular those of Abusir, which also seem to orient towards Heliopolis. It seems that the researchers were forced to adapt their theory to find additional justification, but again there is a lack of supporting documentation for the claims made. It is therefore difficult to establish if the alignments were intentional or are a grouping of unrelated data.

There is no doubt, however, that there were conceptual links between the architecture of the pyramids and the skies above, as was already discussed in the opening chapter. The most notable architectural aspect is that during the Old Kingdom the descending passages leading into the majority of the pyramids were oriented back up towards the circumpolar region of the northern hemisphere. Scholars all agree that this part of the sky held religious significance for the ancient Egyptians, who associated one of the constellations there with a bull's thigh called Meskhetiu. The stars that rotated around the celestial North Pole were known as the Imperishables, as they never sink below the horizon although they become obscured during daylight hours. The soul of the pharaoh was thought to join the Imperishable Stars in the afterlife:

> *Serene is the sky, Sopdet lives [shines] for it is Unas indeed who is the living [star], the son of Sothis [Sirius]. The two Enneads have purified themselves for him as Meskhetiu; the Imperishable Stars. The house of Unas which is in the sky will not perish. The throne of Unas which is on earth will not be destroyed.* (Pyramid Texts, Utterance 302, §458).

Texts of later eras describe traditional foundation rituals for monuments in which the cardinal orientation of ground plans for buildings were set out by aligning their axes to the position of the stars in the sky. This ritual is known as the 'stretching of the cord' ceremony, and the practice may have been closely related to the procedure that was used to set out and orient the ground plan of the Great Pyramid to the four cardinal directions with great precision and accuracy. The 4th dynasty technicians achieved extraordinary levels of refinement, which reached a pinnacle with the orientation of Khufu's pyramid, where the offset of the whole building from true north is only 3' 54" (less than one-fifteenth of a single degree).

The Egyptians left little information to show the methods used to achieve this feat, but there are several possible astronomical methods they could have used. Thuban, the star closest to the celestial pole during the Old Kingdom, was too distant from it to offer a satisfactory target to achieve the observed level of accuracy. The pole star at the beginning of the Old Kingdom was not the one that can be seen in the northern skies today (Polaris or Alpha Ursae Minoris), because of the 'precession of the equinoxes', the slight drift of the stars over time as the earth's axis wobbles slowly. In fact, the northern celestial pole was a featureless point in the sky located approximately two degrees from the star Thuban (Alpha Draconis). Researchers who have studied the orientation have nevertheless developed several plausible techniques that could have been used to accurately determine the direction of true north using the naked-eye techniques available at the time.

One of these theories envisaged careful night observation of the position of the circumpolar stars. According to Egyptologist I. E. S. Edwards, the Egyptians would have watched the rise and fall of Thuban, and perhaps other Imperishable Stars nearby, as they rotated around the celestial pole. By watching and marking out two lines of sight to where the stars rose and then set over a horizontal wall, and then bisecting the angle thus formed, they would have been able to determine the direction of true north, which lay precisely on the centre line. To use this method accurately would have required an artificial skyline. Edwards proposed that they used a circular and perfectly horizontal wall, the top of which was equidistant from the observer over its whole surface; however, no structure matching this description has ever been found at Giza or at any other ancient Egyptian site.

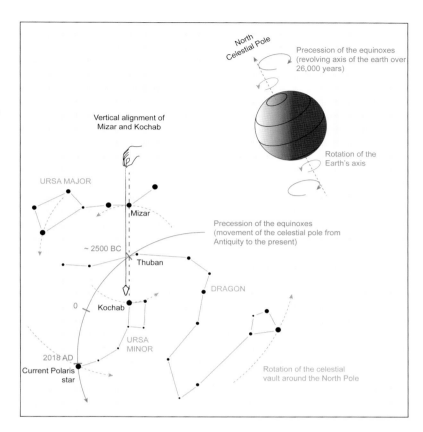

More recently, English Egyptologist Kate Spence proposed that the increasing accuracy of pyramid orientations through the 4th dynasty until the early 5th dynasty demonstrates that the architects had originally established a reference point in the night sky that, due to the precession of the equinox over the decades, first increased in accuracy as the reference point approached the celestial pole, and then began to diverge from it as it passed to the other side. Spence theorised that the surveyors used a plumb line and watched until Mizar (a star of the Big Dipper) and Kochab (a star of the Little Dipper) turned into a position where they were vertically aligned close to the celestial pole. Based on the previous observations, this then became an established convention and they then assumed that this method defied the direction of true north, for evermore. This is now known as the simultaneous transit method. Spence used astronomical calculations to match the stellar positions over time with the measured building orientations on the ground, and there was certainly a degree of correspondence. The progressive shift of the axis of rotation of the earth eventually moved

ABOVE Kate Spence's simultaneous transit method for finding true north, which would have been abandoned due to the precession of the equinoxes. *(Franck Monnier)*

RIGHT Two possible methods of determining true north using the movement of the sun throughout the day. The left side shows the method used on the days of the equinoxes, and the right side shows its use during the days around the summer solstice. *(Glen Dash)*

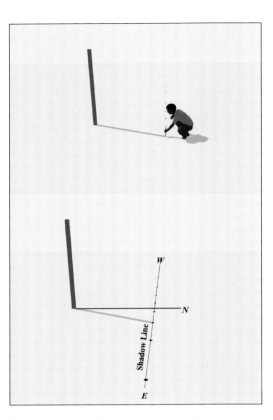

BELOW Diagram showing how closely the main axes of the pyramid are aligned with the cardinal directions. *(Glen Dash)*

the alignment of these two stellar objects so far away from the celestial pole that the increasingly large margin of error on the ground would have become evident. The use of these targets would therefore have been abandoned.

According to pyramid scholars Maragioglio

and Rinaldi, north could have been determined by tracing out the shadow projected by a mast from sunrise to sunset on a completely flat pavement. Finding the mid-point between the ends of the two lines running towards the points on the horizon would have defined a third line running from the base of the mast and aiming at true north.

American scientist Glen Dash developed a similar solar method and was able to produce high precision experimental results. By plotting the point where a shadow fell throughout the day, and linking the points together, he was able to form a curve. By then drawing a sufficiently large circular arc on the ground centred on the mast, two points of intersection between the circle and the curve were obtained. An equilateral triangle can be set out running between these two points and the base of the mast. A fourth line can then be set out that runs precisely through the central axis of the equilateral triangle. This line, starting at the base of the mast and running between the two points on the curves, forms a line oriented straight towards true north. Any or all of these methods may have been known or used by the ancient Egyptians, but it can certainly be said that the

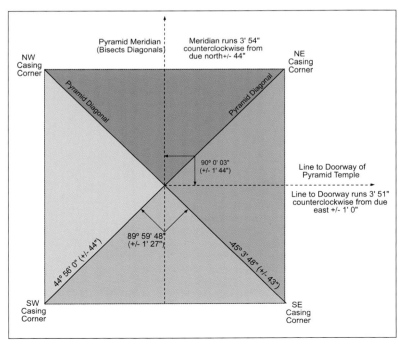

results of their astronomical orientation methods were extremely precise.

Engineering

In addition to establishing the orientation of the Great Pyramid, the preparatory stage of the building works consisted of setting out the four sides, establishing the angles of the corners and levelling the platform on which it was built with respect to the horizontal. Setting out the pavement and the extents of the ground plan was a massive task. The pavement around the pyramid is almost a kilometre in length, but even on such a monumental scale, the Egyptian surveyors were able to demonstrate the quality of their meticulous work, since the corners of the Great Pyramid deviate by less than one-fifteenth of a degree from perfect right angles on average, and the entire base is levelled with a variation of only 2.1 cm.

The horizontal levelling of the pavement around the sides of the base could have been achieved by extrapolating sight lines from accurately levelled reference 'plane tables' located at the four corners of the building. The tables would all have been levelled locally with A-frame plumb levels. Raising or lowering each table compared to the others would have allowed their levels to be synchronised with each other. Once a common level had been established, the rocky soil below would have been cut down or paved over until it formed an almost perfectly flat surface right around the base.

A similar process would have been used to create and harmonise the corner angles. The corners would have been joined to each other by sight lines aimed around the perimeter, one by one around the base, until the last sight-line finally reached back to the original corner. Any errors would then have become evident, adjustments could be made, the procedure could have been repeated and the final results improved. The presence of a bedrock outcrop under the centre of the building made it impossible to verify the squareness of the monument using diagonal sight lines, so the surveyors had to rely on the outer perimeter of the monument to define its base plan before construction of the core of the monument could begin. Levelling could also have been carried out using a system of continuous

water channels dug or built around the perimeter, but while functional water levelling systems have been described, no physical evidence of one has ever been recovered.

Many circular and square holes have been found bored into the pavement around the pyramids of Khufu and Khafre, spaced out by around 3 to 5 m. They may have been used to set out the side lines of the base, but according to Georges Goyon, they may have been used to create perpendicular lines. This was done by planting two stakes, carefully aligned with the sides, then drawing two arcs out on the ground using a cord attached to each stake in turn. Joining the two points where the two arcs intersect defined a line perpendicular to the sides, which could be extended in either direction. This may have been the method used to define the right angles at the corners of the base, or to define perpendicular lines at points

ABOVE Method for creating perpendicular lines with highly precise 90-degree angles between them, using cords and short rods installed in holes in the bedrock.
(Franck Monnier)

along the sides of the building where the casing stones were to be installed.

The Egyptians demonstrated a remarkable ability to build structures combining the strengths of different materials to produce optimum levels of structural stability.

Archaeological analysis of the surviving monuments demonstrates that the ancient architects approached technical problems from very innovative angles. The techniques they developed and their architectural accomplishments inspire admiration, particularly when the rudimentary means at their disposal and the absence of established theoretical knowledge are taken into consideration.

The architects utilised very pragmatic solutions to meet the challenges posed by the pharaoh. They prioritised the development of key building components, which were carefully designed and manufactured before transportation to the site, such as the vault beams over which the mass of the core blocks was destined to rest. Systems were also tested beforehand, as can be seen in the structure of the so-called 'trial passages' built to the east of the Great Pyramid, which probably served as a prototype to test the closing mechanisms designed for the pyramid. When the Egyptians decided to create buildings that reached heights never before attained, they had to develop architectural concepts that had never previously existed.

The pyramid of Djoser was constructed in several steps, but with each layer sloping towards the centre of the structure rather than being built on a horizontal plane. Enveloping buttress walls leaned against the core and acted to support the whole structure. The

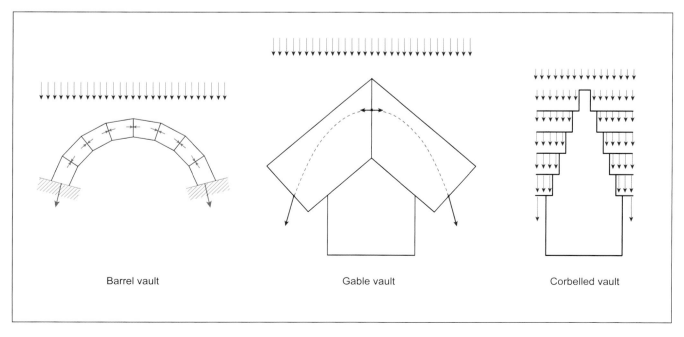

Barrel vault   Gable vault   Corbelled vault

forces created by the stonework were therefore directed towards the centre of the structure, preventing any pieces from sliding towards the exterior. The blocks that constituted the structure were squared, but their courses were not always perfectly laid. Later, when it was decided to arrange the stones in horizontal layers, it became necessary to accurately level the courses to create the most stable structure possible. This was necessary in order to reduce the risk of localised subsidence or collapse in the masonry structure. The Meidum Pyramid illustrates very well this qualitative difference, between the sloped masonry of the internal structure where the levels vary significantly and the horizontal layers of the external envelope, which is levelled with an error of only 8.3 cm.

Close studies of the monuments indicate that the builders learned not to worry excessively about cracks appearing during construction. Fissures in the thick lintels that covered the corridors, for example, evidently did not prevent the Egyptians from using them. They completed the erection of the Bent Pyramid at Dahshur-South despite extensive masonry movements that took place well before the end of the project. It seems then that they were able to judge how serious different structural problems might be and determine the appropriate course of action to be taken, based on the specific circumstances.

LEFT Horizontal passage built with limestone and granite in the pyramid of Teti at Saqqara.
(Franck Monnier)

One of the most significant innovations was the selection of building materials according to their structural strengths. The architects of Khufu's pyramid, for example, clearly preferred red Aswan granite to the fine limestone from Tura when it came to protecting the pharaoh's burial chamber. This approach, where structures were designed based on a consideration of the physical properties of available materials, seems to demonstrate the existence of a scientific mindset that did not really emerge again until Roman times, or perhaps even the Renaissance.

BELOW A completed late Old Kingdom pyramid, with a triple-layered gable roof over the burial chamber, and three sliding granite portcullises to protect the deceased. The corridors are built using Tura limestone ashlars.
(Franck Monnier)

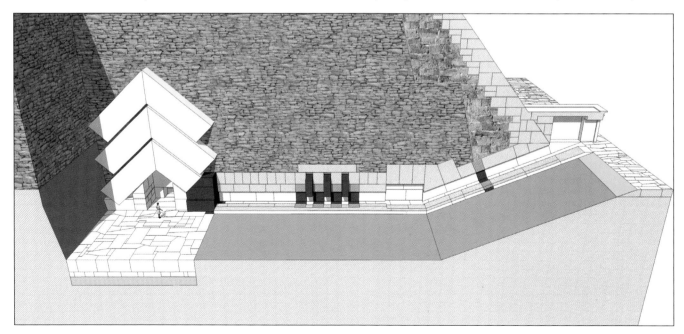

Chapter Four

Exploring the Great Pyramid

The Great Pyramid has stood at Giza through all of recorded history. Many scholars, antiquarians, Egyptologists, scientists and amateurs have studied it and explored it over the centuries, and many recorded what they found there for posterity. The plateau has often attracted the top experts employing the finest instruments of their day, and the story of the study of the Great Pyramid is almost as compelling as the story of how it was built.

OPPOSITE The site of Giza, as seen through the eyes of Renaissance travellers. *(Cornelius de Bruyn, 17th century)*

aware of the true extents of the complex for the first time. The excavators revealed an Egyptian necropolis with a huge field of mastabas stretching out into the western desert; a true city of the dead. The remains of ancient ancillary buildings were also uncovered for the first time.

Since the 1960s, the Great Pyramid has become a testing ground for investigators employing the latest advanced technologies, as scientists with expertise in a range of disciplines try to probe the pyramid's secrets and detect hidden chambers. Now caught between science, the media and the subject of a continuous stream of conflicting new theories, the Great Pyramid nevertheless continues to fascinate the global audience with the questions it raises.

The first archaeologists

The oldest known depiction of the Great Pyramid dates back to the New Kingdom of the pharaonic era. It is a stele attributed to a man called Montuher that includes the first iconographic representation of the monument. The pyramid is shown in perspective, behind the Great Sphinx, and beside the pyramid of Khafre. Historically, however, it provides little information about the state of the building and it is unclear if the pyramid was even accessible at that time.

It is clear, however, that the monuments of Giza were already covered by sand at that time. The Dream Stele, another source of information from the New Kingdom, records that the young Thutmose IV restored the Great Sphinx back to its former splendour by clearing away the sands. According to the text on the stele that recorded this excavation work, it was carried out in response to a dream the pharaoh had. Once the sands were cleared, the Dream Stele was erected between the paws of the sphinx to commemorate the work carried out, and it can still be seen there today. Based on the text on the stele and kings lists located elsewhere in Egypt, it is clear that the names of the pharaohs buried at Giza were still known at that time, but the identity of the pharaoh the sphinx represented, if any, was already forgotten.

In the 19th dynasty, Prince Khaemwaset, son of the illustrious Ramesses II, also restored many Old Kingdom monuments in the Memphite Necropolis. Many of them had suffered from

Archives worldwide contain accounts of voyages to Giza and descriptions of the Great Pyramid. A handful of those records were written by ancient travellers who visited the Great Pyramid, and some reach as far back as ancient Egyptian times. Greek and Roman authors also left reports and descriptions, some of them relatively extensive. Less detailed information is available for the period from Antiquity through the Middle Ages. The majority of those information sources are more like fables or legends, but some of the documents constitute valuable sources of information about the state of the monument over the ages.

Organised exploration of the Great Pyramid and its surroundings can be traced back to the 17th century. More adventurous Europeans would extend their Grand Tours as far as Cairo, and travellers began to record accurate information about their expeditions. Some of these European pioneers took detailed measurements of the architecture for the first time.

The survey organised by Napoléon Bonaparte during his military campaign to Egypt in 1798 heralded the start of the era of truly scientific investigations. The archaeological projects that followed through the 19th century and continued up to the start of World War Two in the 20th century provided reliable and accurate information about the monument to readers around the globe. Scholars became

exploitation of their materials beginning as early as the Middle Kingdom and were already abandoned. Middle Kingdom pharaohs Amenemhat I and Senwosret I reused stone elements from the pyramids of Khufu and Khafre for their own pyramids as a way of bestowing them with the symbolic power of the older monuments. Khaemwaset is often described as the first archaeologist in history and he left many testimonies engraved into the monuments to commemorate his restoration work. This inscription from Saqqara was carved on one of the faces of the Old Kingdom pyramid of Unas:

His Majesty has commissioned the head overseer of craftsmen, the sem priest, prince Khaemwaset to re-establish the name of the King of Upper and Lower Egypt, Unas, because his name was no longer to be found on the face of his pyramid. The sem priest prince Khaemwaset wanted to restore the monuments of the pharaohs of Upper and Lower Egypt because of what they did, and because their strength was being ruined. A decree was established to make his divine offerings.

There is currently no evidence to show that he did the same at Giza. Herodotus described hieroglyphic texts inscribed on the faces of the pyramids at Giza, but they could have been graffiti left behind by travellers or be related to later restorations. All the evidence suggests that the pyramids did not originally carry any external inscriptions when they were built. The Egyptians of the Saïte period (around 660–530 BC) left many traces of renovation works at the pyramids, especially at the Step Pyramid in Saqqara. They copied and revived the ancient

ABOVE Khaemwaset, a son of Ramesses II, restored many monuments and memorialised his work on the pyramid of Unas at Saqqara. *(Franck Monnier)*

BELOW This inscription near the entrance to Menkaure's pyramid at Giza shows that Egyptians from the Saïte period carried out restoration work at Giza. *(Franck Monnier)*

artistic styles they saw there and even reused the complex for their own burials. Similarly, at Giza, a Saïte period inscription was engraved in the granite blocks near the entrance of Menkaure's pyramid testifying to restoration works carried out at that time. It would be surprising if their efforts did not include the Great Pyramid and its subsidiary buildings.

By the end of the dynastic era, the Egyptians had forgotten the details of how the Giza complex was built, but oral tradition remembered Khufu as a tyrannical ruler. In his *Histories* written around 450 BC, Herodotus discussed the legends surrounding the sovereign as well as the methods of construction used, but did not seem to enter the pyramid himself or know reliable details of what was inside. He only briefly recounted that the pharaoh was laid to rest in an underground chamber that contained an island created by diverting the waters of the Nile (Herodotus, *Histories* II, 124). This fable is the first known 'description' of the pyramid's internal spaces. The Greek visitor also paid attention to the causeway leading up to the pyramid, which was apparently still intact and still covered with inscriptions. He wrote that it was so gigantic that the effort required to construct it must have been comparable to that required for the erection of the Great Pyramid itself.

Four centuries later, the Greek geographer Strabo recorded that there was only one access route into the interior of the monument:

On proceeding forty stadia [a unit of measurement] from the city, one comes to a kind of mountain-brow; on it are numerous pyramids, the tombs of kings, of which three are noteworthy; and two of these are even numbered among the Seven Wonders of the World, for they are a stadium in height, are quadrangular in shape, and their height is a little greater than the length of each of the sides; and one of them is only a little larger than the other. High up, approximately midway between the sides, it has a movable stone, and when this is raised up there is a sloping passage to the vault. (Strabo's Geography, *Book XVII*)

Unfortunately, the description of what was behind the entrance was very brief and it is impossible to tell if an access route to the upper chambers was known, inaccessible or not.

In the first century AD, the Roman writer Pliny the Elder wrote that: 'In the interior of the largest pyramid there is a well, eighty-six cubits deep, which communicates with the river, it is thought' (*Natural History* Book 36:17). It is possible that this quote refers to the lower end of the 'service shaft', which was probably visible but blocked by rubble. This evidence may have been combined with the testimony of Herodotus to produce the quotation above. Like Strabo, Pliny does not describe or seem to be aware of any chambers or passages higher up inside the pyramid.

The fall of the Roman Empire and the centuries of trouble marking the beginning of the Christian era meant that any attempts to compile an accurate history of the site were abandoned.

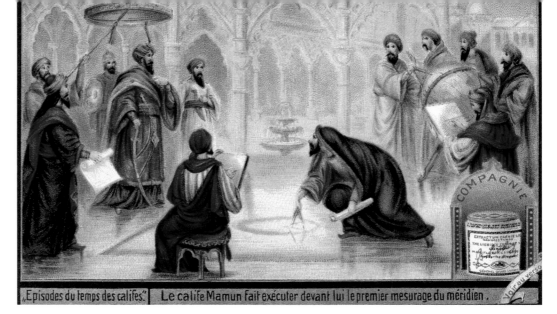

„Épisodes du temps des califes". | Le calife Mamun fait exécuter devant lui le premier mesurage du méridien .

Legends and exploration in the Middle Ages

During the first millennium AD, the idea that the pyramids served as gigantic granaries spread widely. According to the Book of Genesis in the Bible, Joseph son of Jacob was able to interpret a dream that the pharaoh was trying to understand. The prophetic dream announced that Egypt would experience seven years of abundance followed by seven years of famine. Impressed by Joseph's gift of interpretation, the pharaoh retained him as an adviser so that Egypt could avoid any dangers that might be anticipated. According to the later myth, Joseph then built the pyramids as gigantic granaries to store wheat in case of famines.

The connection between this biblical passage and the great pyramids has been around since the 4th century AD. Christian pilgrims who went to Egypt did not question its veracity, and the scene was eventually and magnificently represented in mosaics on one of the cupolas of the Basilica San Marco in Venice, dating to the 13th century AD.

This Christian vision was not shared by the Arabs. At the beginning of the Muslim era they developed their own concepts regarding the pyramids, first on the basis of narratives, then by incorporating them into their hermetic philosophy that was disseminated through the Middle Ages.

In AD 641, Egypt was conquered by Muslim armies and became predominantly Islamic, despite the survival of the Coptic church. Some 760 years later, Egyptian historian Al-Maqrizi compiled a collection of testimonies and stories written during the reign of the various caliphs who had ruled over the intervening period, all relating to the pyramids, and he published this in the 15th century AD. It is now known by its abbreviated title as Al-Khitat, *the survey*. Although it is mainly limited to recording earlier texts, his collection is nevertheless one of the main documentary sources about exploration carried out during the Middle Ages at Giza. Many of the stories are highly fantastic and record improbable events, largely due to the hermetic tradition that had been imposed on texts over the centuries, but they do deserve to be retained and read, if only as a demonstration of the type of folklore that fascinated people during those centuries.

Al-Maqrizi quoted the writer Ibrahim ibn Wasif Shah from the 12th century AD, who in his *History of Egypt and its Wonders* reported that Sourid, one of the pharaohs who ruled Egypt before the flood, ordered the pyramids to be built and canals dug to connect it to the Nile, and to fill reservoirs from which water would flow. He filled the pyramids with talismans, wonders, riches and idols, and had the bodies of pharaohs deposited there, and according to his orders the priests traced out on these monuments all the philosophies of the wise. All the sciences familiar to the Egyptians were written on all possible surfaces. On the walls, on the exteriors of the pyramids, on the ceilings, and on the foundations, the figures of the stars were drawn, and the names of the drugs and their useful and harmful properties were written there. The science of talismans, mathematics, architecture and all the sciences of the world were included, and it was all set out very clearly in this way, to those who knew the script and understood the language.

In the eastern pyramid (the Great Pyramid), rooms were made that contained representations of the sky and the stars, and they were filled with statues of Sourid's ancestors. Perfumes were burned to honour the heavens. The rooms contained books about the planets and tables of the fixed stars, and tables of their revolution through the course of time, and a list of events of past epochs, which were subject to their influences, and the moment when it is necessary to examine them to know the future. They contained texts about all that concerned Egypt until the end of time, and basins containing magic liquids and other similar things were placed there.

In the Painted Pyramid (Khafre's?), they laid the bodies of priests, which were shut up in coffins of black granite. With each priest was a book recording the marvels of the art he had exercised, what had been done in his lifetime, and what had been and what will be from the beginning to the end of time. On each face of the pyramids were depicted Egyptians engaged in all sorts of works and arranged according to their status, and these representations were accompanied by a description of their trades, the tools they needed, and everything else that concerned them. No science was neglected. All were there described and drawn. Treasures offered for the planets were deposited in the pyramid, and those which had been given to the stars, and the treasures for the priests. All this amounted to a huge and incalculable sum of value.

Gold and knowledge are combined in these stories to symbolise all that is desirable. Such stories were able to captivate a large audience, including the court scholars who were particularly prominent at the time. They were also part of the reason that Caliph al-Ma'mun went to Egypt in AD 832, accompanied by Dionysius of Tell Mahre, the archbishop of Antioch, a town now in southern Turkey. The caliph entered the Great Pyramid by force from the exterior, and all tourists today take the tunnel he had excavated. It is said that he spent a fortune in the process and his reputation in Egyptological literature is mostly as a looter in search of wealth. The real reason for his

attraction to Egypt was in fact quite different. Al-Ma'mun took the throne of the caliphate in AD 813 and gained a reputation as a scholar during his lifetime. He travelled extensively, founded universities and had an interest in ancient Greek manuscripts, which he had translated. He encouraged research into the sciences, including astronomy and geography, all of which is far from the image of a ruler eager for gold and wealth. On the political front, he had to deal with conflicts and revolts, and it was an uprising of the Copts, known as the Bashmurian Revolt, that forced him to intervene in Egypt in AD 832.

To help negotiate with the Coptic Christians, he engaged the services of Dionysius of Tell Mahre. The revolt was finally brutally crushed without recourse to diplomacy, and al-Ma'mun's stay in Egypt lasted only 47 days, according to the geographer al-Ya'qubi of the 9th century AD. It therefore appears that the caliph only had a short time to undertake exploration of the Great Pyramid, as a significant part of his time must have been invested in attempts to resolve the conflict.

There is no doubt then that al-Ma'mun visited the pyramids, and it appears likely that he was primarily motivated by scientific interest. The myths surrounding the monument and the wealth of knowledge it reputedly contained, sometimes even described as 'the key to the whole universe', must have attracted the

BELOW The tunnel that tourists use to enter the Great Pyramid today is thought to have been opened by the caliph al-Ma'mun.
(Franck Monnier)

curious caliph. The Egyptian historian al-Idrisi
(AD 1251) recorded that:

> *When he came to Egypt on the date already*
> *mentioned in this book [AD 832], moved by*
> *his lofty ambition and noble spirit to expose*

the secrets concealed by the pyramids, and
to learn their true meaning, he found no one
who could translate for him what he found
there, or render into Arabic the obscurities it
presented, except for one Ayyub b. Maslama,
an old man who had been recommended to
him by the other sages of Egypt because he
could decipher hieroglyphs.

Michael Cooperson, who originally translated
this passage into English, concluded that this
demonstrates an effort to decipher hieroglyphs in
the early Islamic era. Cooperson also translated
an excerpt from Dionysius of Tell Mahre's
Ecclesiastical History where he wrote that:

> *In Egypt we also beheld those edifices*
> *mentioned by the Theologian [Saint Gregory*
> *of Nazianzus] in one of his discourses. They*
> *are not, as some believe, the granaries of*
> *Joseph. Rather, they are marvellous shrines*
> *built over the tombs of ancient kings, and*
> *in any event oblique [consisting of inclined*
> *planes] and solid, not hollow and empty.*
> *They have no interior, and none has a door.*
> *We noticed a fissure in one of them and*
> *ascertained that it is approximately 50 cubits*
> *deep. Evidently the stones [in this place] had*
> *been solidly packed before being broken*
> *by people who wanted to see whether the*
> *pyramids were solid.*

Dionysius's observation that an existing fissure
was found supports the conclusions of the
French orientalist Sylvestre de Sacy in 1801
and German Egyptologist Rainer Stadelmann
in the 1990s, who questioned the conventional
assumption that al-Ma'mun dug the first
entrance into the pyramid, but the truth of the
matter may lie somewhere in between.

Dionysius in fact went to Egypt twice. The
second time was on his mission with the
caliph to quell the Coptic troubles, and he left
Egypt as soon as his diplomatic services were
no longer required. It is possible then that it
was only after Dionysius left that al-Ma'mun
finally managed to enter the Great Pyramid. It
is also possible that al-Ma'mun extended the
existing fissure that the archbishop mentioned,
which already had a length of 24 m, but which
seemed to end in a dead end.

De Sacy quoted from the 'Account of Egypt' written by historian Abd al-Latif al-Baghdadi in the 12th or 13th century AD that demonstrates clearly that the Great Pyramid was fully accessible by that time:

One of these two pyramids is open and has an entrance through which we enter the interior. This opening leads to narrow passages, conduits which extend to a great depth, to wells and to precipices. The people who have the courage to sink … into its deepest cavity finally arrive at a place where it is no longer possible for them to push further. The most frequent passage, which is usually followed, is a glacis [slope] which leads towards the upper part of the pyramid, where there is a square chamber, and in this room a stone sarcophagus. This is the opening through which one now enters the interior of the pyramid. It is not the door that had been created during its construction. It is a hole made with effort and formed at random. It is said that it was the Caliph Al-Ma'mun who opened it.

Al-Idrisi also mentioned the actions of al-Ma'mun by referencing older authors who lived between the 10th and 13th centuries. His works were translated and brought to light in the 1990s. He quoted Abu al-Salt (AD 1134):

When al-Ma'mun came to Egypt he ordered that [the pyramids] be breached. After great efforts and protracted toil, a breach was made in one of the pyramids facing al-Fustat. In it they found passages going up and others going down, all of them frightening and difficult to move through. At the top of them was a cubical room eight by eight cubits in area. In the middle of it was a closed basin of marble. When the cover was removed, it was found to contain nothing but decayed remains. At that point, the caliph called a halt to further exploration. It is said that the breaching of the pyramid was extremely costly and laborious.

And Ibn Mammati (AD 1209):

Among the marvellous tales of the pyramids is that when al-Ma'mun entered Egypt and

saw them, he wanted to demolish one and see what was inside. He was told that this was impossible. He said: 'I must open one of them'. So excavations were carried out, at great expense, on the [existing] breach. Fires were lit and ballistae were used to fire projectiles at it. It was thus discovered that the wall was nearly twenty cubits thick. (Both translations by Michael Cooperson)

This is the only text that mentions the use of a ballista, which is a machine designed to throw rocks, but as many people at the time envisaged the pyramids to be hollow inside, it makes sense that al-Ma'mun tried to punch a hole through the external faces with his military equipment.

All these documents confirm that the caliph did organise an investigation into the pyramid, and it seems likely that he was able to complete the work relatively rapidly because he was extending an existing tunnel, which had already been seen by Dionysius of Tell Mahre.

The main, original entrance to the pyramid, under the apexed vault, seems to have remained invisible until its position was identified from the inside via the descending

ABOVE Folk tales often evoke the enduring attraction of hidden treasure, typified by Ali Baba, the poor woodcutter who discovered the secret to the forty thieves' den, which he entered by using the phrase, 'Open Sesame!' It is likely that historians such as Al-Maqrizi were influenced by similar tales written during the Islamic Golden Age. *(Engraving of the early 20th century)*

passage. This theory is supported by the fact that the graffiti left by travellers on the blocks surrounding the entry vault all dates from later than the 13th century AD.

There is also evidence that the Great Pyramid had already been entered far back in Egyptian history, perhaps as early as the First Intermediate Period, around 2000–2150 BC. The Egyptians of that era may even have remembered details about the pyramid's internal design, but by the first millennium AD this information had long since been forgotten. The Egyptians of the Saïte period (around 660–530 BC) explored the monuments of the Memphite region, restored them and reused parts of some of them for their own burials. As already mentioned, it is possible that their renovation work included the Great Pyramid, and they may even have added the swinging entry door described by Strabo. An existing breach could therefore have been closed off, then reopened later by al-Ma'mun, and this may explain why he was able to penetrate inside so rapidly.

It is impossible to give an accurate date for the first forced entry, but the descriptions left by the Greek and Roman authors only mention that the descending passage and the subterranean chamber were accessible. This most likely means that access was via the original entrance, not the breach that al-Ma'mun worked on later, which accessed the upper chamber system as well. If this was the case, the 'service shaft' whose lower end was visible near the subterranean chamber could have provided access to the Grand Gallery for the most athletic explorers. This in turn explains evidence of an attempt to dismantle the granite plugging blocks from the inside, to try and clear the ascending passage down to connect with the descending passage. The effort to destroy the granite blocks was abandoned, however, and a small passage was created that circumvented them and succeeded in connecting the descending and ascending passages.

If al-Ma'mun or one of his predecessors later attempted to create or extend a separate tunnel, then the original entrance must have been closed off and hidden again after the Greek and Roman authors had written about that access route. Today, the southern end of Al-Ma'mum's tunnel meets the top of the bypass tunnel dug down to connect the ascending passage to the descending passage. Tourists can climb down into the descending passage to look back up the straight shaft to the northern entrance, if they are so permitted.

Once the caliph succeeded in getting inside the monument, what he found fits well with the sequence of events reconstructed above. Like tourists still do today, he climbed up and down the passages. In the highest chamber, described as 'eight by eight cubits', he found a stone sarcophagus, with its lid, containing the deteriorated remains of a mummy. The presence of the sarcophagus shows that the author was describing the King's Chamber, but no traces of furniture or pharaonic documents were mentioned, except objects that were probably fanciful later additions. The pyramid had clearly been robbed of all its valuable content long ago, and the curious caliph left without discovering the wisdom he so desired.

Al-Maqrizi's book included additional quotes containing information about what happened after al-Ma'mun had entered the pyramid. One part of the account says that al-Ma'mun discovered gold in the sarcophagus that precisely equalled the

RIGHT The three pyramids of Giza depicted in the *Cosmographia* of Sebastian Münster, published in 1544. It appears that the entrance vault was visible at that time.

LEFT Giza as depicted in an engraving by George Sandys.
(George Sandys, 1615)

cost of the excavation works, 1,000 dinars, but this may have been a memory of the way he paid his workers rather than historical or archaeological fact regarding what was found there. Another part of the story tells that a green human-shaped sarcophagus containing the body of a man, covered with gold, was found in the pyramid. It was said that the sarcophagus remained on display near the entrance to the caliph's palace in Cairo until AD 1214.

Other parts of this work tell that after al-Ma'mun entered the pyramid, many other attempts were made to follow his example. The explorers would prepare with food, drink, ropes and candles. Some came back safely, but some perished in their efforts to explore the interior, which at that time would not have been cleared of accumulated debris and would not have been fitted out with stairs, lighting, and ventilation, as it is today. Superstitions thus developed, warning others not to follow in their footsteps.

Whether or not the caliph was fully responsible for creating the horizontal entry tunnel that is still used today, it now provides access for thousands of travellers and pilgrims who are still seduced by the extraordinary stories surrounding the Great Pyramid, and its unique and very ancient internal architecture.

There was little else of significance published about the great pyramids during the later Middle Ages. Only a couple of texts describe the external appearance of the monument. During a pilgrimage to the region in AD 1395–96 the Lord of Anglure, from a town now in north-eastern France, noticed that blocks of the pavement around Khufu's pyramid were being removed and reused for construction in Cairo. It was not until the start of the Renaissance that more significant information began making its way into Europe once again.

The Renaissance and the first scientific investigations

The three pyramids were represented in something approaching their current state in an engraving included in a book by Englishman George Sandys, published in AD 1615. Sandys was an explorer and colonist and his travel narrative was published as *The*

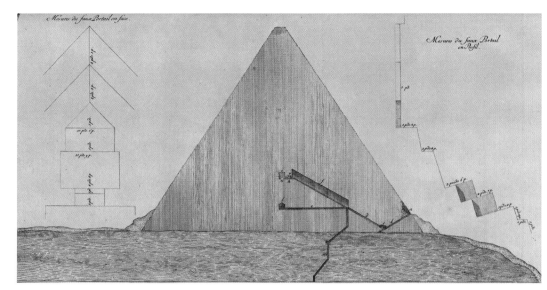

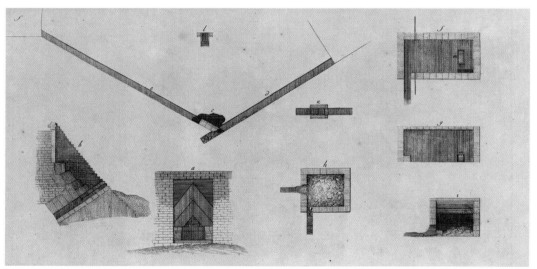

Relation of a Journey begun an. Dom. 1610, in four books (1615). This remained a standard account of the eastern Mediterranean region for many decades in the English-speaking world. He described that he found the underground chamber inaccessible and the Queen's Chamber half-cluttered with rubble. He then ascended the Grand Gallery to find the King's Chamber with its sarcophagus beside which an excavation pit had been dug, which is today closed over. He also noticed the openings to the ventilation/star shafts.

Many other travellers described the chambers within Khufu's pyramid, particularly the King's Chamber in which the empty sarcophagus was located, although the lid disappeared in time. They included the Italian physician and botanist

Prospero Alpini who travelled to Egypt to study the flora in the late 16th century AD.

In the years 1636–40, the English polymath John Greaves travelled to the Levant and to Cairo. He had studied Arabic and Persian languages at Oxford and also taught maths and astronomy there. He wanted to reach Alexandria to measure the latitude of that city so that he could better understand the works of the Greek astronomer Claudius Ptolemy, who worked from Alexandria and whose important work on astronomy, *The Almagest*, had survived from Antiquity. While he was there, Greaves also went to Giza and measured the internal dimensions of the chambers of the pyramids. He reported his investigative work on the pyramids along with the results of extensive research into their origins based on documents from Antiquity. He presented this survey in his great synthetic work *Pyramidography* that was published in 1646. In the introduction he wrote:

I found the Pyramids in the yeares one thousand six hundred thirty-eight ... For I twice went to Grand Cairo from Alexandria, and from thence into the deserts, for the greater certainty, to view them: carrying with me a radius of ten feet most accurately divided, besides some other instruments, for the fuller discovery of the truth. But before I descend to a particular description, I shall make enquiry by whom: at what time: and to what end, these Monuments were erected.

The author described the internal chambers more meticulously than Sandys had. The 'service shaft' was explored for several tens of metres. Its lower section was still blocked with debris below the level of the grotto, but the grotto and the upper parts of the shaft were clearly open by that time. The hole in the niche of the Queen's Chamber had also already been excavated and was described. Around the outside of the pyramid he noted the presence of basalt blocks, which he correctly identified as parts of the old mortuary temple. Based on the information left by the classical authors, Greaves correctly determined that the monument was the tomb of Pharaoh Khufu, and from that time on there could be no doubt that the pyramids were monumental tombs erected for the ancient pharaohs. Greaves' measurements of the interior of the pyramids were so accurate that Isaac Newton, who was himself interested in studying scientific works from Antiquity and who wanted to understand the ancient measurement systems, was able to use them to correctly determine the length of the Egyptian cubit used to construct the King's Chamber. He calculated it to be '1 and 719/1000ths of the English foot', or 52.396 cm, a difference of less than 1 part in 2,000 from the value calculated by Flinders Petrie 250 years later.

On 8 July 1765, the British diplomat Nathaniel Davison discovered the tunnel that opens at the top of the south wall of the Grand Gallery and which leads into the first 'relieving chamber' above the roof of the King's Chamber.

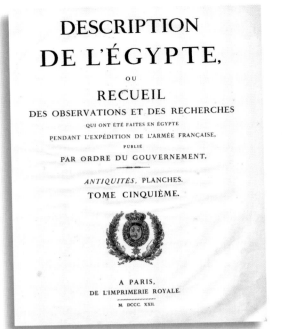

DESCRIPTION
DE L'ÉGYPTE,
OU
RECUEIL
DES OBSERVATIONS ET DES RECHERCHES
QUI ONT ÉTÉ FAITES EN ÉGYPTE
PENDANT L'EXPÉDITION DE L'ARMÉE FRANÇAISE,
PUBLIÉ
PAR ORDRE DU GOUVERNEMENT.

ANTIQUITÉS. PLANCHES.
TOME CINQUIÈME.

A PARIS,
DE L'IMPRIMERIE ROYALE.
M. DCCC. XXII.

LEFT Title page of one of the 23 volumes that made up the *Description de l'Égypte*. This work reported the huge scientific research project carried out by the French savants during Napoléon Bonaparte's military expedition into Egypt.

This lower 'relieving chamber' is referred to in his name up to the present day.

Early modern period

Not until the end of the 18th century was another major intellectual advance made with respect to the Great Pyramid and Giza. At that time, the conflict between England and revolutionary France persuaded the French *Directoire* to send general Napoléon Bonaparte to invade Egypt, primarily to secure a strategic location on the trade route between Europe and India. Napoléon assembled an army of 50,000 men, which included no less than 167 scholars or *savants,* and they invaded Egypt in 1798.

BELOW Napoléon Bonaparte leading the French army at the Battle of the Pyramids. The military campaign was ultimately a failure, but the expedition was a great success from a scientific point of view. *(Abel Hugo, 1835)*

The huge expedition was both scientific and military in nature. Among other concerns, it allowed the French to study the terrain with a view to digging a canal to connect the Mediterranean Sea to the Red Sea, and so the skilled savants, who included engineers, were undoubtedly useful. The scientific study of ancient monuments, however, took up a large proportion of the scholars' attention. The military mission finally proved to be a bitter failure, but the scientists managed to carry out one of the largest and most ambitious scientific studies ever undertaken. After several decades they published the results of their work in the monumental *Description de l'Égypte*. The last volume of the profusely illustrated series was published in 1822.

One Colonel Coutelle and the young engineer Edmé François Jomard, who were both part of the expedition, made progress studying the Great Pyramid in detail. For the first time, the colonel produced a comprehensive scientific description of all of the various passages and chambers, enriched with very precise measurements. He recorded small details, including that the granite beams of the first 'relieving chamber' were cracked, and that the blocks of its walls were breaking up in places. He included an account of his exploration of the 'service shaft', in which he highlighted the extreme difficulty of negotiating its tight twists and turns, something that Petrie also encountered during his exploration work 80 years later. Coutelle could not reach its lower section because it was filled with debris, and he guessed that the rubble was the result of earlier attempts to clear out the grotto. Outside the pyramid, Jomard and Coutelle cleared the base of the north-east corner of the pyramid from under piles of stone debris that had fallen down from its faces over the years, so that precise measurements of the building's original dimensions could be taken. They were also interested in studying the surrounding monuments, including the mastabas. A shaft in one of them was excavated and a granite sarcophagus was extracted, thereby confirming that they were also tombs.

Paradoxically, while the French scientists' expedition marked the arrival of Egyptology as a scientific field of study in its own right, the complex discussions and ideas disseminated to the educated public by Jomard played a role in encouraging a wave of speculation to develop over the course of the 19th century. Writers like John Taylor and, most famously, the Astronomer Royal for Scotland, Charles Piazzi Smyth, produced elaborate theories in their attempts to explain what had been found at Giza. Their knowledge of ancient Egypt was at best limited, and they confounded the scientific data with their own religious, nationalist or mystical ideas. As is discussed below, it was not until the talented young Flinders Petrie arrived on the scene that the threads of these convoluted intellectual discussions, ancient as well as modern, were finally unravelled.

In the meantime, in 1837, Englishmen Colonel Howard Vyse and engineer John Shae Perring began to explore the pyramids of the Memphite region, initially with the Italian Giovanni Battista Caviglia who had been excavating the monuments for several years. Their primary goal was to uncover antiquities, although they did demonstrate some historical curiosity during their investigations. Vyse, for example, took measurements to clarify questions surrounding astronomical alignments that had already been attributed to elements of the Great Pyramid. Between them, they drew up plans and an inventory of the individual monuments that is still used today by those who study this type of architecture.

The most renowned aspect of their mission was, however, their extensive use of large quantities of gunpowder to expedite their excavations. They repeatedly used explosions to create trenches and tunnels in order to confirm or disprove their latest suspicions about what might be hidden. Vyse, for example, was convinced that another burial chamber remained to be discovered in the Great Pyramid.

Their methods would be inconceivable nowadays, but expedited their clearing of the subterranean chamber, the star/ventilation shafts in the King's Chamber and the 'service shaft', which had already progressed significantly thanks to Caviglia. They also discovered and entered the additional 'relieving chambers' above 'Davison's' chamber, and found inscriptions left by the ancient pyramid builders there, irrefutably confirming that the pyramid was indeed a work commissioned by Pharaoh Khufu.

At the same time, these explorers damaged the monument in various places; in the vicinity of the King's and Queen's chambers, in the subterranean chamber and, most significantly, out on the southern face of the pyramid, where they blew an enormous chasm in the core blocks in their attempts to uncover a second entrance located opposite the first. This gash is still clearly visible on the south side of the monument.

They cleared rubble to expose the remaining giant lower layer of casing stones at the foot of the north face, as well as the 'trial passages' to the east, and drew up accurate records of what they discovered. After months of trying to find the 'real' burial chamber, Vyse concluded that the current chambers were the only ones built in the pyramid, that the King's Chamber was certainly

LEFT Portrait of the English engineer John Shae Perring. He joined Howard Vyse in 1837 to explore the pyramids of the Memphite necropolis. *(1842)*

the burial place of the pharaoh and that it was certainly used for that purpose in the distant past. Despite their now dubious methods, some of their discoveries and the advances they made in understanding the Great Pyramid were among the most significant ever made.

In 1842, another scientific mission arrived at Giza with plans almost as ambitious as those of Napoléon's *savants* half a century earlier. The Prussian Egyptologist Karl Richard Lepsius was at the head of a scientific team that

BELOW One of the first photos ever taken of the Great Pyramid. *(Francis Frith, mid-19th century)*

The archaeological era

During the period from 1870 to 1902, Egyptology finally developed into a systematic field of study under the influence of the newly developing science of archaeology. One particular event took place during that time that fundamentally changed the educated public's understanding of the Great Pyramid. In 1880, the English archaeologist William Matthew Flinders Petrie carried out a triangulation survey of the monuments of the Giza Plateau. The survey report he produced resolved many unanswered questions surrounding the pyramids and the monumental architecture of Old Kingdom Egypt.

When Petrie first set up his tripods on the dusty sands in the shadows of the ancient pyramids, he took with him all the religious, academic, nationalist and political concerns that influenced people in AD 1880. The young Flinders Petrie, although he may not have been aware of it at the time, was in many ways acting out the role of a typical colonial European gentleman, and he recreated at Giza, on a small scale, what was happening on a regional and global basis. Colonial survey of new territory was very much in the air when, in 1880, the 27-year-old Flinders Petrie arrived in Egypt, alone, with his father's theodolites. Unlike the well-trained Royal Engineers of the Palestine survey, Petrie never went to school or university but quite independently developed an interest, and eventually an expertise, in surveying and archaeology. Archaeology was emerging at the time from a subject practised by gentlemen scholars into a subject of professional academic study. Most archaeologists were still amateur, so Petrie's lack of formal education was no bar to his acceptance by those who were interested in the field. Egyptology was just as much an amateur field, and Petrie was fortunate to live at the point where the professional excavator was just beginning to emerge and oust the amateur. In fact, in 1880 when Petrie headed out to Egypt, there was no academic department of Egyptology anywhere in Britain. But all that was about to change.

In 1882, the British invaded Egypt by force and remained there as the occupying power until 1936. While this military domination was

carried out research in Egypt and Nubia from 1842–45, culminating with the publication of the immense work *Denkmaeler aus Aegypten und Aethiopien* (Monuments of Egypt and Ethiopia). At Giza, the team concentrated their efforts on the necropolises around the Great Pyramid containing the Old Kingdom mastabas. Forty-five tombs were entered, searched, identified, and their decoration and inscriptions copied for publication. Thirty-seven other burials were also recorded. Hieroglyphs had only recently been deciphered by the Frenchman Jean-François Champollion, and this advance allowed Lepsius to translate and reveal the history of the men and women who lived and worked during the era of the great pyramids, for the first time.

The only other notable new discovery made in the Great Pyramid in the second half of the 19th century was that there are ventilation/star shafts connecting to the Queen's Chamber as well as to the King's Chamber. This discovery was made by the Scottish doctor and antiquarian James Grant Bey, and the shafts were opened by Grant Bey and Waynman Dixon in 1872. The artefacts they discovered in these shafts are now known as the Dixon relics.

very real, Petrie's amateur triangulation survey of Giza and his professional archaeological excavations, which followed all over Egypt, helped to put England in a powerful position with respect to European academic and ideological domination over ancient Egypt and the Middle East. British leadership in these domains lasted into the early 20th century. At a time when Nationalism was an ever-growing force across the world, the achievements of scholars from different countries was of national significance. Although he was initially working alone and was virtually unknown at the time, Petrie's survey became an important event for the advancement of English intellectual ideology outside of the official organisations of the British Empire. The results were published in 1883, one year after the Egyptian Exploration Fund was launched. Almost immediately after the publication of this survey, Petrie became heavily involved with the new organisation. This was in a large part thanks to the wealthy and successful novelist and amateur Egyptologist, Amelia Edwards, who quickly noticed Petrie's

talents, and went on to support him financially and professionally throughout his career.

Petrie's work was also directly linked to some more unusual religious beliefs relating to the Holy Land and the Great Pyramid that were circulating in some European ideological circles at the time, and which today seem rather odd. Since the publication of John Taylor's complex mathematical work entitled *The Great Pyramid: Why was it Built? And Who Built it?* in 1859, many of the technical characteristics of the Great Pyramid had become embroiled in discussions surrounding the new metric system that was being adopted across the globe. Taylor and his followers, who included the Astronomer Royal of Scotland, Charles Piazzi Smyth (1819–1900), supposedly found numerous coincidences between the measurements of the pyramids and the geometry of the earth and the solar system. They also concluded (incorrectly) that the British Imperial system of measures (inches, feet, yards) was derived from a far more ancient and possibly divine system. These types of theories played a significant role in the

BELOW Diagram illustrating the triangulation survey carried out by Flinders Petrie to measure the dimensions and positions of the Giza monuments with great accuracy. *(Flinders Petrie, 1883)*

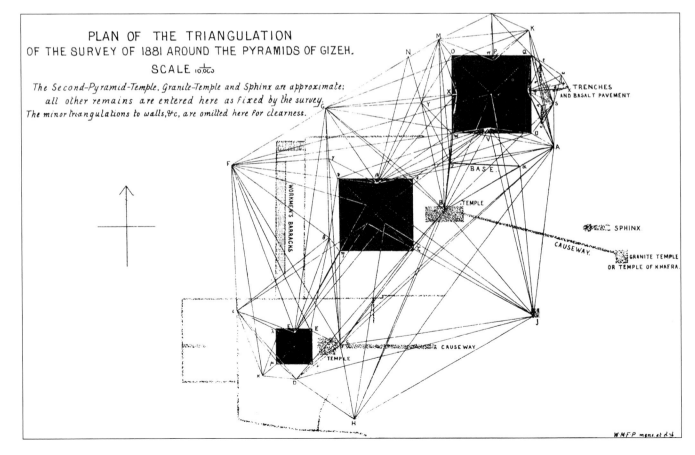

Bonfils

The Great Pyramid during the inundation season, in the late 19th century, before the Aswan dams were built. In the foreground is the Khedive Ismail rest-house, built in 1869 and demolished by King Farouk in 1944. He built his own rest-house at the same location in 1946.
(Félix Bonfils, late 19th century)

BELOW **Alabaster sarcophagus of Khufu's mother, Hetepheres I, found empty and now on display in the Cairo Museum.**
(Franck Monnier)

debates over whether Britain and the United States should adopt the metric system.

Into this intellectual milieu; out onto the dusty hot sand of Giza, stepped Flinders Petrie. Although he was interested in Smyth's theories, and although his father had followed them closely, Petrie's legacy to the study of ancient Egypt turned out to be quite secular in nature, as he drew conclusions that were mostly contrary to those drawn by Smyth and Taylor. Perhaps because he initially worked independently of any official organisation, Petrie was somehow able to stand back from all the ideological issues and produce a remarkably frank, balanced, polished and objective scientific survey report. The publication accurately reflected the archaeological remains at Giza, and accurately discerned the details of the work set in place by the ancient pyramid builders. Petrie measured the pyramids, discovered their true dimensions and properties, disproved most of Smyth and Taylor's theories and established himself as the new authority on ancient Egypt.

Even today, Egyptologists frequently refer to his survey, which remains the authoritative source for the basic measurements of many of the features of the whole funerary complex. To survey the plateau with his theodolites he first set up and accurately measured a survey base line just to the south of the Great Pyramid, and used this as the basis from which to extend a triangulation network that encompassed the whole plateau. This allowed him to accurately

measure it all to within a fraction of an inch. The network consisted of around 14 stations, and theodolite angles were taken between all of these to various key architectural points visible on the pyramids and temples, and also back to the points that had already been geographically fixed, such as the summit of the Great Pyramid.

The sighting stations were generally set up on prominent outcrops to ensure good visibility, such as on the top of the large tomb of Khentkawes and the Mortuary Temple of Khafre's pyramid. Stations to the north of the plateau were established along a straight line running SW to NE that may have been set up deliberately in this way to ensure additional accuracy, due to the ease of establishing station points visually along a straight line. One of the most significant parts of the survey was Petrie's detailed measure of the base of the Great Pyramid. By pinpointing the front edges of the surviving casing stones uncovered by Vyse, he was able to delineate the original side lines of the base, and by extrapolating these he located the intersection points at the corners where large complex foundation stones had originally been located. In this way he was able to determine the original dimensions of the sides. By measuring the casing stone angles and the layer heights he was also able to determine the original height of the monument with a high degree of precision. What he ultimately found was an impressive level of precision achieved by the ancient Egyptian builders themselves. Finally, Petrie even surveyed inside the pyramids by setting up a chain of theodolites, penetrating into the deepest shafts and most distant chambers. The report of all this work was published in 1883. It included a mass of measurement details, an extensive and comprehensive historical analysis of the data and theories, and a detailed retrospective analysis of the precision of the survey.

At the beginning of the 20th century, the concessions to excavate the Giza necropolis were shared among several organisations from several different nations. Over the next 60 years, German, Italian and American teams slowly uncovered the remaining structures on the plateau. George Andrew Reisner led the American team originally called the Hearst Expedition after its sponsor, and then worked

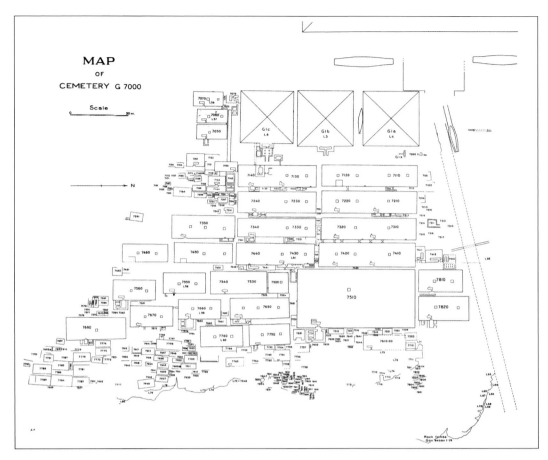

MAP
OF
CEMETERY G 7000

Scale

LEFT Map of the
eastern cemetery that
was excavated during
the first half of the
20th century.
(George Reisner, 1941)

for Harvard University and the Boston Museum of Fine Arts. For 40 years, until his death in 1942, he led a team studying the cemetery west of the Great Pyramid and established the mastaba numbering system still used today. Within the western necropolis, he recognised that an extremely regular grid of avenues had been established during the reign of Khufu, which was then disrupted by additions built during subsequent reigns that did not follow the original plan.

In 1924, Reisner's research extended into the eastern cemetery. In 1925, members of his team discovered cache G7000x, a deep rock-cut chamber located near Khufu's queens' pyramids that contained the magnificent furniture of Queen Hetepheres, mother of Khufu. Finely decorated but unostentatious compared to the gaudy New Kingdom tomb furniture now so familiar to Egyptologists, this cache contained an empty alabaster sarcophagus, an alabaster canopic chest, a curtain box, a canopy frame, wooden chairs, a wooden bed and jewellery boxes containing

bangles inlaid with butterflies made from semi-precious stones.

The largest mastaba of the area, G7510, contained inscriptions bearing the titles of the vizier in charge of constructing the Great Pyramid towards the end of Khufu's reign; Ankhhaf. A fine bust of the vizier was also discovered, which is now on display in the Boston Museum of Fine Arts. Ankhhaf's name was recently found on the papyri recovered from the Red Sea port at the Wadi al-Jarf that recorded work to transport Tura limestone blocks to Giza. Finally, Reisner's team uncovered a group of greywacke statues buried deep within Menkaure's valley temple, which had until then been covered by silt and downwash from the central wadi. These are among the greatest treasures to have been recovered from ancient Egypt. Most of them are now on display in the Cairo Museum or in the Boston MFA.

A German team from the University of Leipzig also excavated the western and southern cemeteries next to the Great Pyramid, from 1903 to 1929. They were led

RIGHT A 'reserve
head' found in a
mastaba of the
necropolis surrounding
the Great Pyramid.
(Cairo Museum, photo:
Franck Monnier)

by Georg Steindorff from 1903 to 1907, and
then by Hermann Junker from 1912 to 1929.
Junker was responsible for the discovery
and excavation of the giant mastaba G4000
that was built for Khufu's nephew Hemiunu.
Hemiunu was probably responsible for the
construction of the Great Pyramid during the
first years of Khufu's reign. He is now a familiar
face to Egyptologists, as the tomb contained
a remarkably lifelike statue of its esteemed and
slightly overweight middle-aged owner, now on
permanent display in the Hildesheim Museum
in Germany.

During the excavations of the 4th dynasty
mastabas, the German and American teams
also brought to light approximately 40 'reserve'
heads. These are lifelike carved limestone
representations of the deceased. The degree
of realism and individuality used to create them
demonstrates that they represent real people.
They were finished with coloured paints, but
they are also stylised representations that were
adorned with formal inscriptions. Their precise
symbolic or funerary function and meaning
remains enigmatic.

The great national excavation campaigns
ended with the Second World War, but study
of the mastaba fields never really stopped.
Additional scientific reports focusing on
particular details of the excavations continue
to be published, supplemented by occasional
reports of newly discovered tombs.

Before the Second World War, an Egyptian
team led by Egyptologist Selim Hassan revealed
the large empty boat pits on the east side of the
pyramid, as well as the remains of the mortuary
temple closer to the pyramid. As a result of their
investigations, they were able to reconstruct
the original ground plan of the dismantled
temple. They also recovered several decorated
relief fragments from the sands around the
causeway, including a fragmented depiction of
Khufu with Horus holding the shen ring flying
above his head.

Post-war and the high-tech era

In 1954, Egyptologist Kamal el-Mallakh
discovered the two sealed boat pits near
the southern face of Khufu's pyramid. The
easternmost pit was carefully opened, revealing
thousands of pieces of a huge cedar boat that
had been dismantled and stored there at the
time of the pharaoh's funeral. The decision
was taken to extract it and reconstruct it as it
had originally appeared. The project was led
by Hag Ahmed Youssef and the reconstruction
work was surely one of the greatest triumphs of
Egyptology. His team began by making miniature
copies of each plank that had been discovered,
and they then practised reconstructing the
original hull form using these pieces. The small
finished model is now on display in the 'solar'
boat museum, alongside the ancient rebuilt
vessel, which is positioned over the now-empty
pit that it was removed from.

Over the next decades, Egyptology
continued under the leadership of smaller
groups of foreign academics and enthusiasts,
self-funded specialists and under the direction
of the Egyptians themselves. During the
1960s, for example, Italian architects Vito
Maragioglio and Celeste Rinaldi undertook
extremely detailed surveys of the pyramids
of the Memphite Necropolis, including the
pyramid of Khufu. They eventually published an
extensive set of volumes, including plans of the
monuments, along with detailed descriptions
of almost every element of the Great Pyramid
complex.

In the 1980s, American Egyptologist Mark Lehner commenced investigations spanning the entire Giza Plateau. When Lehner originally arrived at Giza he was a proponent of some old mystical ideas relating to the Giza Plateau, but gradually developed into an archaeological expert with the support of some notable American backers. His hard work eventually led his team to discover the pyramid builders' town at Heit el-Ghurab on the south-eastern edge of the plateau. Over the years, he has also been able to build up the AERA organisation so that it is now one of the foremost authorities on the Giza Plateau, and which now runs field schools to train the next generation of Egyptologists and archaeologists.

Lehner worked closely with the most famous Egyptologist of recent years, the Egyptian Zahi Hawass. In the 1990s, Hawass became one of Egypt's most prominent international celebrities and eventually served as head of the Supreme Council of Antiquities. At Giza, he led a team that uncovered parts of the causeway, and pieces of the valley temple and the port, buried deep under silt on the Nile floodplain below the plateau. They also discovered fragmented remains of Khufu's satellite pyramid G1D, which had until then evaded detection.

The 1960s signalled the start of a new era in the exploration of the pyramids at Giza. Progressive technologies, including non-destructive scanning and digital surveying equipment, and carbon 14 dating and 3D imaging methods, began to challenge traditional excavation as a way to reveal new data and information about the ancient monuments. Because of the significance of the Giza plateau, it has often been used as a testing ground for new technologies and as a means to demonstrate their effectiveness to the public.

American researcher Luis Walter Alvarez introduced several innovative advanced technologies to the study of the pyramids. The physicist was famous for winning the Nobel Prize for particle physics in 1968, and also for his part in the Manhattan project to develop the first atomic bomb used to end World War Two. Alvarez realised that because cosmic rays can penetrate through structures as massive and as large as the Great Pyramid, then they can be used to produce images of the internal

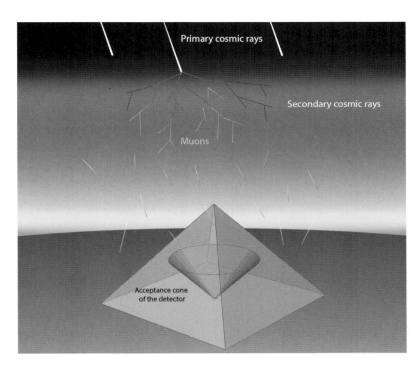

structures of the pyramids. This technique is now known as muography. Alvarez first targeted the pyramid of Khafre, which he thought had an abnormally simple internal arrangement compared to the pyramid of Khufu, and would therefore be more likely to contain hidden compartments. As Khafre's pyramid was built after Khufu's, Alvarez thought that its architects could have found a more effective way to conceal internal chambers, perhaps up in the superstructure of the monument, like the passages and chambers in Khufu's pyramid.

The muons used for these imaging experiments are negatively charged particles created when cosmic radiation hits the atoms of the upper atmosphere. The high-energy particles produced then travel to the surface of the planet and can penetrate far underground, even into some of the deepest mines. The imaging technique consists in measuring a flow of these muons through solid materials. The more solid material they encounter, the more muons are absorbed. They arrive in all directions, but by orienting the detectors, the plates can produce an image rather like an x-ray that represents the inside of the structure in that direction. Variations in the total number of muons collected represent differences in density within natural or artificially built masses. The exposure time, however, is in the order of

ABOVE Illustration showing the phenomenon that generates muons from cosmic rays in the upper atmosphere. Detectors placed inside the monuments have a limited field of view. *(Franck Monnier)*

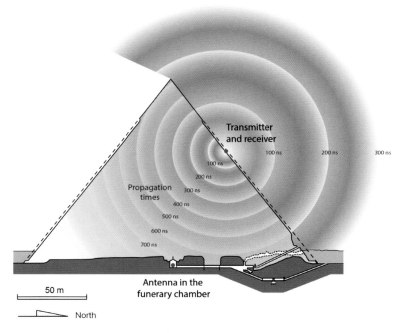

LEFT Illustration of the Ground Penetrating Radar (GPR) technique used in the pyramid of Khafre in 1974. The electromagnetic waves are slowed and attenuated in proportion to the quantity of materials they passed through. *(Franck Monnier)*

several weeks, since the particles arrive at a low rate of only 170 muons per square metre per second, on average at sea level.

To carry out this unique research mission, which they called the Pyramid Project, the Egyptian antiquities service worked with the University of California and the Egyptian University of Ain Shams. An impressive array of electronic machines was installed in Khafre's burial chamber, which was transformed into an experimental physics laboratory for the duration of the experiments.

The experiment's results led to the conclusion that there is no void in the pyramid of Khafre other than the burial chambers already known. The project was subsequently criticised because of the limitations of the results produced by the detection technique, and assumptions made during the analysis of the results. For example, the detectors placed in the burial chamber could only detect muons arriving down a narrow cone covering a 45° angle directly above the burial chamber. This reduced the volume studied to only 19% of the total volume of the pyramid. Anything below or beside the burial chamber did not fit into the 'field of vision' of the measuring instruments. Alvarez's scientific objectivity, however, should be admired, as he did not hesitate to revise an original judgement about what seemed to be the detection of unknown chambers:

Unfortunately, this large and persistent signal, together with a larger signal over a smaller angular range, disappeared as we

RIGHT Outline schematic showing how a gravimeter works. *(Franck Monnier)*

Micrometer screw

Zero-length spring

Pivot point

Weight

0

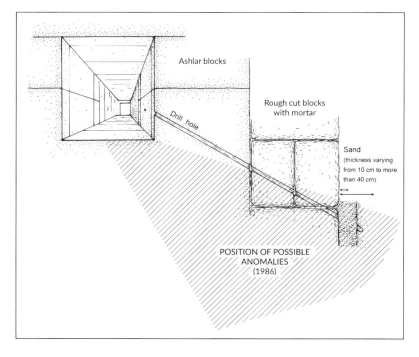

Ashlar blocks

Drill hole

Rough cut blocks with mortar

Sand
(thickness varying from 10 cm to more than 40 cm)

POSITION OF POSSIBLE ANOMALIES
(1986)

LEFT Cross section of the horizontal passage leading to the Queen's Chamber, looking south. The west wall was drilled at three points along the corridor separated by 1.3 m in an attempt to locate a hypothetical void space. The probes did not locate a space but did yield information about the structure of the surrounding masonry. *(Franck Monnier)*

learned more exactly all the dimensions of the apparatus and of the pyramid that were important in the simulation programme. (We had not anticipated the need for such accurate data.) The artefacts we observed are mentioned only to show that far from 'seeing nothing' throughout the analysis period, we had three very exciting signals that disappeared only after the greatest care had been taken to make the simulation programme correspond exactly to the geometry of both the apparatus and the pyramid.

This high-tech mission was closely followed in 1974 by a US-Egyptian team led by the Stanford Research Institute that attempted to use ground penetrating radar (GPR) to detect spaces in the Giza Pyramids. Their first target was the pyramid of Khafre again, whose lack of internal passages and chambers continued to intrigue researchers. A method was developed specifically for the mission. Preliminary tests were performed to validate the method, then a radio transmitter and a receiver were placed on the north face, and another set placed on the south face of Khafre's pyramid. A receiving antenna was then placed in the burial chamber. The principle of the experiment was to send electromagnetic waves into the structure and then capture them in the burial chamber. The speed of radio signals through a solid mass is a function of the mass of material traversed, so significant changes in density could therefore disrupt the basic signal and indicate the presence of a space in the structure, or a change in the material used. Unfortunately, the signal intensity is also weakened by the material though which it propagates (this loss is expressed in dB/m) and by the time it had passed through the mass of the pyramid and arrived at the burial chamber, it was so weak that it could not be usefully discerned from the radio noise caused by power cables and other radio sources. A test in the pyramid of Khufu led to the same conclusion.

Ten years later, French architects Gilles Dormion and Jean-Patrice Goidin led an investigation that took full advantage of the global media to publicise its progress. In 1985, the two independent researchers carried out a visual architectural survey of the internal chambers of the Great Pyramid, concluding that an unknown structure and possibly a hidden room was located north of the King's Chamber. In order to test their conclusions, they applied for financial assistance from the French Ministry of Foreign Affairs and obtained authorisation for a full investigation from the Egyptian authorities. After further study, the Ministry of Foreign Affairs contacted EDF's (Électricité De France) research department, which specialised in advanced scientific research methods. EDF brought in the CPGF (French Geophysical Prospecting Campaign) to participate in the project, and in conjunction with the Egyptian Antiquities Organisation, then headed by Ahmed Kadry, they carried out the first microgravimetry measurement experiment ever attempted at the Giza site.

Gravimetry is based on Newton's law of Universal Gravitation, which expresses the gravitational influence of one mass on another. Gravity (g) is the attractive field that the earth exerts on neighbouring bodies, including ourselves. Its precise value varies according to several factors including altitude, and it also varies slightly if secondary masses are located near a place of measurement. It is possible then to detect minute variations in local gravity by observing variations in the displacement of a weight attached to a lever which is itself attached to a spring. The precision of the method is increased by placing the weighing machine under a vacuum and by electronically amplifying the output. The maximum precision of measurements obtained this way is then in the order of 1 microgal, or one-billionth of the earth's gravity, g.

Measurements were carried out in 1986 and revealed possible mass anomalies in the horizontal corridor, halfway between the landing of the Grand Gallery and the Queen's Chamber, and located below the level of the corridor and offset to the west. These conclusions were taken on face value, and a more 'physical' investigation was immediately planned. They first considered dismantling the blocks of the floor and the west wall of the corridor to access what they interpreted as a corridor or a room. A more economical solution was fortunately used instead. In late 1986, three small holes were

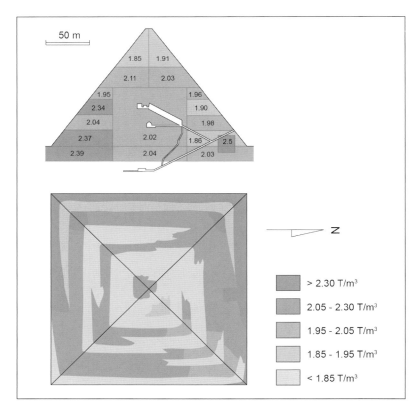

ABOVE The results
of the gravimetry
measurements carried
out by the French
team in 1986 provided
data about the
densities of the stone
used to build the Great
Pyramid.
(Franck Monnier)

boreholes encountered only solid masonry of uneven composition. Scientifically, however, the investigation was useful as it showed that while the blocks of the west wall are finely cut and fitted, they are bound to a coarser layer of blocks behind with a layer of mortar. In addition, at one point the drilling encountered a quantity of sand from 10 cm to more than 40 cm thick, after which the limestone masonry was once again encountered.

A preliminary analysis of the sand indicated that it did not possess the same characteristics as sand from the plateau, and it was possibly brought from a distant region, perhaps the Sinai or from the vicinity of Aswan. It was composed of 99% coarse quartz grains from 100 to 400 microns in size. While this information was an interesting discovery that raised questions still to be resolved, it did not satisfy the expectant public. The disparity between the anticipated discoveries and the actual results of the drilling drew criticism from various quarters, and from then on the Egyptian antiquities department refused all applications to carry out work at the Great Pyramid that involved physical sampling or intrusive probing.

The mission was not, however, limited to this quest for secret rooms. The CPGF team took hundreds of gravimetric measurements and were able to produce an overall density map for the entire monument. Their conclusions were surprising. The mass of the pyramid is lower than previously thought, with an average density of about 2,050 kg/m³, indicating that the large majority of the volume is made from local

drilled through the west wall of the corridor and an endoscopic camera was pushed in to see any voids. The three holes (named S1, S2 and S3) were separated by 1.30 m, were drilled at a height of 30 cm above the floor, and had slope angles that produced 30 to 40 cm drops over a drilling length of approximately 2.55 m.

The operation attracted the attention of the global media who announced that a major discovery in the Great Pyramid was imminent. Hopes were quickly dashed, however, as the

RIGHT Interpretations
of the results obtained
from measurements
carried out in 1986
and 1987 by French
and Japanese teams.
(Franck Monnier)

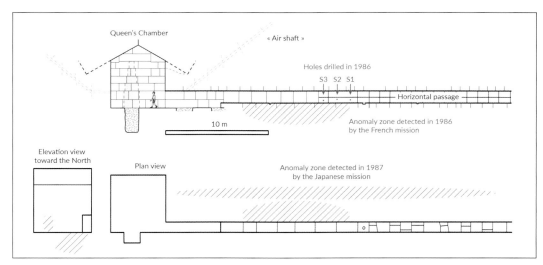

limestone, rubble fill and probably even has some sand-filled voids. The presence of smaller empty voids is also possible. The final mass distribution map indicated that the structure was made up of zones of different densities and it seemed to reveal a stepped internal structure, with a slight spiral formation also suggested.

The following year, a team from Waseda University in Tokyo led by Sakuji Yoshimura was given permission to survey the horizontal corridor leading to the Queen's Chamber in order to verify the results obtained by the French team. The Japanese team used microgravimetry and radar together in order to cross reference the methods and data. Once again, they obtained results that created great media excitement, since they apparently detected a second corridor running parallel to the existing corridor, but further to the west. Permission was, however, never given for any physical probe of the area, as Egyptian officials had been put off by the disappointment and criticism of the previous year.

Gilles Dormion recently stated that a radar survey of the area carried out in 2000 by Jean-Pierre Baron did not support the previous findings. No unknown structure was located near the corridor or the Queen's Chamber. The contradictory sets of results have unfortunately never been analysed together in order to understand what caused them to arrive at false positives, something that could potentially allow future measurements to be calibrated and improved.

Meanwhile, in 1987, outside the main monument, an international team of American and Egyptian scientists conducted an investigation to establish what was in the second boat pit located south of the Great Pyramid. They were able to confirm the presence of a second disassembled boat, similar to the one that had already been rebuilt, and they took measurements of the air quality to evaluate the risk of attempting to extract it. These were the first steps in a project that led to the ship's eventual removal from the pit in 2011, followed by the commencement of its reconstruction in the new laboratories of the Grand Egyptian Museum, north of Giza.

In 1990, the Egyptian antiquities department decided to install a ventilation system in the Great Pyramid because of the growing influx of tourists visiting it. Around the same time, a German engineer called Rudolf Gantenbrink contacted Egyptologist Rainer Stadelmann for help applying to investigate the star/ventilation shafts, which intrigued him. In 1992, Zahi Hawass granted Gantenbrink a permit to carry out investigations, but on the condition that he also helped install ventilation ducts leading to the King's Chamber that were going to utilise the shafts to circulate air into the chambers and passages.

The mission was named the 'Upuaut Project' after the pharaoh's mythical dog who led the way into the afterlife. Gantenbrink developed three different mini-robots between 1992 and 1993 to clear the ducts, measure them accurately and finally determine where the ducts of the Queen's Chamber led. The Upuaut 2 robot, armed with caterpillar tracks and mini-cameras, succeeded in reaching the end of the southern shaft leading from the Queen's Chamber, and revealed to the world that it is closed off by a small limestone slab from which two small copper pins protrude. In the northern shaft, however, the additional twists and turns, as well as the long metal rods left stuck there by the Edgar brothers at the beginning of the 20th century, prevented the robot from progressing more than 20 m. At the time, nobody imagined that discussions of what lay behind this limestone 'door' would continue for almost 20 years, and that a raft of mechanical technologies and extensive media coverage would be employed during the various attempts

BELOW 3D illustration of the Upuaut II robot.
(Franck Monnier)

RIGHT 3D illustration
showing the Upuaut II
robot ascending the
Queen's Chamber's
southern shaft in 1993.
(Franck Monnier)

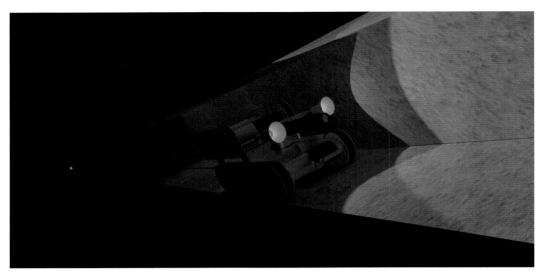

BELOW 3D illustration
showing Upuaut II
reaching the 'door' in
the southern shaft in
1993. (Franck Monnier)

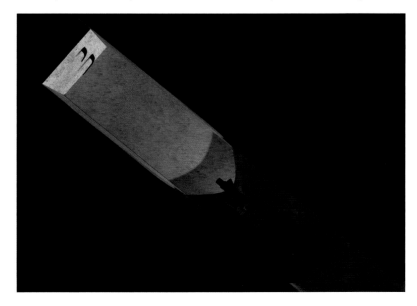

to investigate what was behind it. Zahi Hawass was convinced that a room of some sorts was hidden behind this small slab and called for innovative solutions to penetrate into it, while at the same time minimising the damage to the monument.

A new exploration sponsored by National Geographic was finally carried out in 2002 by Boston's iRobot team. Their robot, the Pyramid Rover, was also fitted with caterpillar tracks, but was additionally armed with a drill to cut through the slab, and a miniature camera that could then be inserted through the hole.

The whole operation was broadcast live over global television networks so that the impact of the expected discovery could be maximised. The robot performed exactly as

designed and reached the end of the duct. It drilled a hole through the limestone slab, which proved to be only 5 cm thick, introduced its camera, and filmed what was on the other side. What it revealed was that the other side was a very small space that was an extension of the existing shaft, barely longer than 19 cm, at the end of which was another limestone block, but this time cut more roughly. The camera could not turn to the sides, so very few details of the small space were actually visible, but everything that could be seen indicated that the shaft did not extend beyond the small space.

The exploration work then continued in the northern shaft. This time the robot was able to negotiate the twists and turns and the objects left behind by previous explorers. Again, the shaft ended with a slab adorned with two copper hooks, located at exactly the same level as the 'door' in the southern shaft.

Far from being discouraged by these results, Zahi Hawass immediately called for the development of another robot that would be able to observe all the details of the space revealed by the Pyramid Rover.

A team from the University of Leeds led by Robert Richardson was eventually given permission to take on the task. The new robot they developed was called the Djedi Rover and it was rather different to the previous machines. It was no longer mounted on tracks, but on wheels. It was equipped with an echo-sounding instrument and had a camera attached to the end of an articulated arm that allowed it to see in all possible directions. This final robotic

expedition into the shafts took place in 2011 and achieved its objectives. It was able to film the whole cavity behind the slab in the southern shaft. It revealed several red-painted construction marks left behind by the ancient pyramid builders, as well as details of the copper fastening system. This mission marked the end of 20 years of robotic exploration into the shafts of the Queen's Chamber.

The investigations served as testing grounds for new technologies and as global media events generating publicity for the Egyptian tourist industry. The media companies involved were able to sell rights to the coverage and produce documentaries that proved to be popular overseas. As the new millennium progressed and the internet developed, this relationship between high-tech research projects and the global audience has only intensified.

One of the major areas where Egyptology has progressed most significantly in recent years is in the fields of imaging, scanning and 3D modelling of the monuments on the plateau. The Giza Mapping Project team led by Mark Lehner pioneered this work at Giza, as they combined high-accuracy survey work with computer modelling software to produce some of the earliest 3D models of the whole plateau. Images of these models were included in Lehner's 1997 publication *The Complete Pyramids*, which became a global bestseller.

The first team to produce high-resolution models using digital laser scanning was from the Vienna Institute for Archaeological Science.

They combined terrestrial laser scanning of the Great Pyramid and the sphinx with high-resolution digital photogrammetry to produce high-resolution, photo-realistic, 3D Digital Terrain Models of the monuments. These were so detailed that they can be used as archaeological documentation and as records of the state of the monument at that time. The project was directed by Professor Manfred Bietak and Dr Wolfgang Neubauer, who acted as field director.

Over the first decade of the new millennium, in order to demonstrate the potential of its 3D simulation software, the French company Dassault Systèmes began working with architect Jean-Pierre Houdin to model his internal spiral ramps theory. Despite the fact

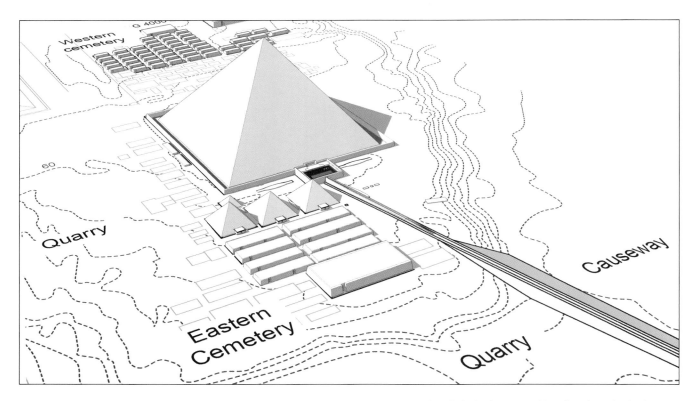

Western cemetery
G 4000
60
Quarry
Eastern Cemetery
Quarry
Causeway

ABOVE 3D modelling of the Great Pyramid complex. Since the late 20th century, 3D tools have become essential for research and publication of scientific works. *(Franck Monnier)*

BELOW Locations of the muons detectors set up by the scientists of the ScanPyramids mission. The white points indicate presumed anomalies. *(Franck Monnier)*

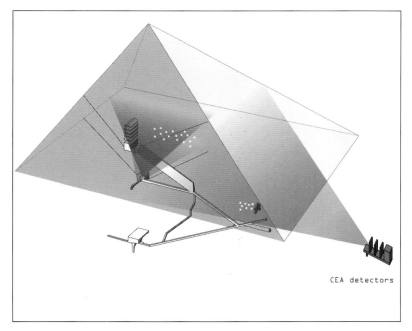

CEA detectors

that little in the way of hard archaeological evidence has ever been found to support the theory, the models they produced took simulations of the Great Pyramid's architecture to new levels. Since then, Dassault Systèmes have gone on to work with Harvard University's Semitic Museum team on the Digital Giza project, making 3D simulations of this type more authentic and accessible to the general public online.

In 2015 Dassault's Mehdi Tayoubi and Professor Hany Helal of the Faculty of Engineering in Cairo established the HIP (Heritage Innovation Preservation) Institute and launched the ScanPyramids mission, in conjunction with several companies and universities. Their aim was to carry out a series of scanning projects to analyse the four greatest pyramids with innovative and non-invasive techniques in order to detect any unknown chambers or internal spaces. They used photogrammetry, laser scanning, thermography and muography to investigate the structures. The Bent Pyramid was the first to be scanned. Scientists from the University of Nagoya carried out the muography in the autumn of 2015 by installing 40 nuclear emulsion detection plates in the lowest chambers, which were set up to receive muon impacts for over 40 days. The laboratories of the Grand Egyptian Museum provided a base to analyse the results. After comparing the data collected with GEANT4 particle simulations, which had modelled the expected results based on the known architecture, the scientists involved concluded that no other chambers existed in the Bent Pyramid apart from those currently known. Following this first experiment, the Scan Pyramids mission at Dahshur was cut short to focus efforts on Khufu's pyramid, in 2016.

The ScanPyramids team had already scanned Khufu's Great Pyramid with infrared thermography, and had already announced to the global media that an important discovery had been made at the foot of the eastern face of the monument. Two blocks apparently generated more heat than the surrounding masonry, possibility indicating that an access tunnel was concealed behind them. This announcement immediately rekindled fantasies of hidden chambers and treasures. The thermal anomaly was eventually explained as being the result of recent renovations to consolidate the building at that point. The existence of a hidden cavity was quickly discarded, as were questions surrounding the interpretation and dissemination of the data collected.

The investigations at Giza continued through 2016 as the University of Nagoya team first moved their muography plates into the upper part of the descending corridor. After several weeks the plates were removed and analysed, and it was announced to the global media that a slight mass deficit had been found behind the entrance vault above the descending corridor. It was interpreted by those in charge of the mission as a

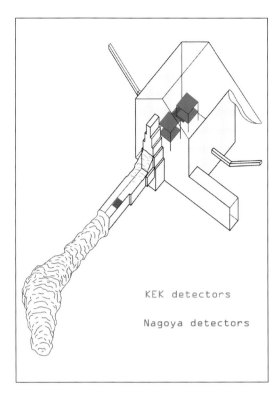

KEK detectors

Nagoya detectors

void possibly indicative of a concealed corridor at that location. Other measurements made in 2017 seemed to confirm the results. During this same period the muography equipment was moved to the Queen's Chamber where two sets of emulsion plates were set up; one set at the west side of the chamber, and another in the tunnel behind the niche that extends into the east wall of the chamber.

The Japanese KEK institute (The High Energy Accelerator Research Organization) also installed muon-detecting 'scintillator hodoscopes' in the same room. Finally, the French research group CEA (Alternative Energies and Atomic Energy Commission) installed a muon telescope

LEFT Location of the muon detectors set up in the Queen's Chamber by the ScanPyramids team. *(Franck Monnier)*

BELOW Illustrations representing the muography results announced by the ScanPyramids team in 2017. On the left is a 3D view of the known structure of the internal spaces in the Great Pyramid, looking upwards from the Queen's Chamber. The central image shows how this known structure would appear on a muon detection plate from that location. The image on the right depicts what was actually detected. A long anomalous void signal can be seen to the right of the Grand Gallery and parallel to it. It is not yet clear how this unexpected feature should be interpreted. *(Michel Michel and Franck Monnier)*

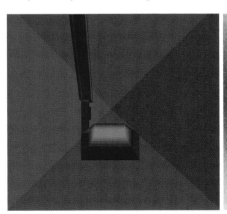

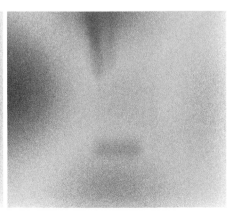

Depth [m]

0.0   1.0   2.0m
S = 1 / 50

outside the entrance to the building, pointing up through the north face, close to the low-density area the team had supposedly identified previously. The results of these measurements were published in a *Nature* journal article in October 2017, and were again presented as another major discovery, although not the same discovery as had been announced previously, which was associated with the entrance vault. The article concluded that the measurements carried out independently by the three teams revealed the existence of a 30 m long (minimum) cavity located about 20 m above the Grand Gallery, which they labelled the Big Void. This was estimated to be located in the same vertical plane as the Grand Gallery, and be just as spacious, and plans were immediately set in motion to build a tiny flying robot to investigate the hidden space.

Many experienced Egyptologists including Zahi Hawass, however, expressed scepticism about the new 'discovery'. Due to the magnitude of the central claim made, the lack of comparable voids in a similar location in any other Egyptian pyramid, and the significant number of recent cases in which archaeological data sets have been misinterpreted or prematurely announced as constituting major

new discoveries, this scepticism seems prudent. Investigations continue and may soon provide clarification, and perhaps indisputable results that will invalidate or confirm the existence of this Big Void. The ScanPyramids project was also expected to test Jean-Pierre Houdin's theory regarding helical internal construction ramps, but to date the muon images produced have shown nothing to indicate that such structures actually exist inside the building.

In parallel with this mission, which has dominated the media and even scientific discussion surrounding the Great Pyramid, other scientists, Egyptologists and independent researchers continue to work to better understand the famous monument. In 2006, Erin Nell and Clive Ruggles of the University of Leicester carried out a week-long total station survey studying the orientation of the Great Pyramid and its subsidiary monuments. The American engineer Glen Dash has also carried out extremely precise new laser survey measurements of the external dimensions and orientations of the faces of the pyramid, and has studied the ancient astronomical methods used to achieve these precise orientations.

Japanese Egyptologist Yukinori Kawae has produced a new photogrammetric survey of

the notch on the north-eastern edge of the pyramid. This method allows photographs taken from different angles to be reconstructed into a 3D building model, supposedly with millimetre precision. It has made it possible to systematically document complex and difficult-to-access structures like the notch for the first time. Kawae has also recently carried out a photogrammetry scan of the entire outer surface of the monument and the results are soon to be published.

Away from the Giza Plateau and the latest high-tech machines, academic Egyptologists and archaeologists following a more traditional methodology continue to make significant progress uncovering information relating to the great pyramids. Leg work, trowel work, desk work and international academic collaboration still rule the roost on projects like the Hierakonpolis excavation project, led initially by Michael Hoffmann and Barbara Adams, and latterly by Renée Friedman. For the last quarter of a century, they have gradually revealed the early history of the proto-pharaonic dynasty of Hierakonpolis, or the people that Hoffman referred to as 'the First Egyptians'.

The most brilliant discovery relating to the Great Pyramid in recent years, however, was undoubtedly made during the archaeological excavations of the Old Kingdom port at Wadi al-Jarf on the west coast of the Red Sea, which is being uncovered by the team led by Pierre Tallet of the University of Paris IV-La Sorbonne and Gregory Marouard of the Oriental Institute of Chicago. The papyri containing the Journal of Merer that they found there are surely the most spectacular finds of recent years, and the texts they contained have thrown a bright splash of light on the construction activities that created the Great Pyramid. Excavations of the rock-cut warehouses and other structures at the site also continue to add new information to our understanding of the Old Kingdom during the reign of Pharaoh Khufu.

All of these historians, Egyptologists, archaeologists, scientists and digital technologists described above deserve our gratitude, because thanks to them we are able to consult rigorous data sets, detailed and descriptive records and images, and deeply meaningful interpretations, all of which help us better understand this monumental world heritage site; the last remaining Great Wonder of the Ancient World.

BELOW Inside of the 'notch' located on the north-eastern corner of the Great Pyramid.
(PEAKIT image created by LANG CO. LTD/ Giza 3D Survey/TV Man Union))

Appendix One

Chronology of Egyptian history

Extract from Hornung, Krauss and Warburton, *Ancient Egyptian Chronology*, 2006. More recent C14 dating of artefacts from the Old Kingdom indicate that these dates should be slightly revised. Khufu's accession to the throne could have occurred somewhat earlier than the dates shown in this table, between 2629 and 2558 BC (See Ramsey *et al.*, *Science* 328 (2010), p. 1556). All dates are BC.

EARLY DYNASTIC PERIOD		2900–2545
Dyn. 1		
	Narmer	2900–?
	Aha	?–2870
	Djer	2870–2823
	'Serpent'	2822–2815
	Den	2814–2772
	Adjib	2771–2764
	Semerkhet	2763–2756
	Qaa	2755–2732
Dyn. 2		
	Hetepsekhemwy	2730–?
	Raneb	?–2700
	Nynetjer	2700–2660
	Peribsen	2660–2650
	Sekhemib	2650–?
	Sened	?–2610
	Khasekhemwy	2610–2593
Dyn. 3		
	Djoser (Netjerykhet)	2592–2566
	Sekhemkhet	2565–2559
	Khaba (?)	2559–?
	Sanakht (?)	?–?
	Huni	?–2544
OLD KINGDOM		2543–2120
Dyn. 4		
	Snefru	2543–2510
	Khufu	**2509–2483**
	Redjedef	2482–2475
	Baka (?)	2474–2473
	Khafre	2472–2448
	Menkaure	2447–2442
	Shepseskaf	2441–2436

Dyn. 5		
	Userkaf	2435–2429
	Sahure	2428–2416
	Neferirkare Kakai	2415–2405
	Neferefre	2404
	Shepseskare	2403
	Neuserre	2402–2374
	Menkauhor	2373–2366
	Djedkare Isesi	2365–2322
	Unas	2321–2306
Dyn. 6		
	Teti	2305–2279
	Userkare	?–?
	Pepy 1	2276–2228
	Merenre	2227–2217
	Pepy 2	2216–2153
FIRST INTERMEDIATE PERIOD		**2152–1980**
(dyn. 7?, 8–dyn. 10)		
MIDDLE KINGDOM		**1980–1760**
(dyn. 11–dyn. 12)		
Dyn. 12		
	Amenemhet 1	1939–1910
	Senwosret 1	1920–1875
	Amenemhet 2	1878–1843
	Senwosret 2	1845–1837
	Senwosret 3	1837–1819
	Amenemhet 3	1818–1773
(dyn. 13–dyn. 17)		
NEW KINGDOM		**1539–1077**
(dyn. 18–dyn. 20)		
Dyn. 18		
	Ahmose	1539–1515
	Amenhotep 1	1514–1494
	Thutmose 1	1493–1483
	Thutmose 2	1482–1480
	Thutmose 3	1479–1425
	Hatshepsut	1479–1458
	Amenhotep 2	1425–1400
	Thutmose 4	1400–1390
	Amenhotep 3	1390–1353
	Amenhotep 4/Akhenaten	1353–1336
	Tutankhamun	?–1324
	Itnetjer Aya	1323–1320
	Haremhab	1319–1292
Dyn. 19		
	Ramesses 1	1292–1291
	Sety 1	1290–1279
	Ramesses 2	1279–1213
	Merneptah	1213–1203
THIRD INTERMEDIATE PERIOD		**1076–723**
(dyn. 21–dyn. 24)		
LATE PERIOD		**722–332**
(dyn. 25–dyn. 30)		

Language and script of the pyramid builders

𓅃	A
𓂝	'A
𓃀	B
𓂧	D
𓇋	i
𓆑	F
𓎼	G
𓉔	H
𓎛	H
𓐍	KH
𓄡	KH
𓆓	J/DJ
𓎡	K
�	K/Q
𓅓	M
𓈖	N
𓍯	O/UA
𓊪	P
𓂋	R
𓃭	R/L/RW
𓋴	S
𓏏	T
𓅱	U or W
�936	SH
𓏤	Z
𓏭	Y

𓉴	Mr - Pyramid
𓊹	Netjer - A God
𓄤	Nefer - Beautiful pure / zero
𓌞	Shemsu Hor Followers of Horus
�	Seqed/seked - slope
𓋹	Ankhhaf - life surrounds him
𓈌	Akhet - Horizon
𓆣	Akh - light
𓊖	Niwt - city/town
𓇳	Re - the sun god
𓇓	Nsw - royal
𓍷	Shenu - cartouche
𓏞	Hemiunu - priest of Iunu
𓂓	Ka - soul / life force
𓏜	Sesh - scribe
𓋓	Hedjet - white crown of Upper Egypt
𓋔	Desheret - red crown of Lower Egypt
𓋖	Sekhemty Double crown of all Egypt
𓋹	Ankh - life
𓌀	Was - power
𓊽	Djed - stability
𓊨	Apr - signifies the name of the crew
𓊵	Hotep - peace/offering
𓅃	Horus - the falcon god
𓇓𓏏	MH nswt - royal or official cubit
𓊤	Ma' kheru - true of voice

Egyptian is the original language of Egypt. It belongs to the language family known as Afroasiatic and is related to North African languages, such as Berber, and Asiatic/Semitic languages, such as Arabic and Hebrew. It first appeared as writing between 3200 and 3300 BC. Old Egyptian is the name given to the earliest known phase of the language and it was used by the 4th dynasty pyramid builders.

The writing system consisted of around 500 common signs now known as hieroglyphs. Hieroglyphs first appeared as a complete and independent script in Egypt during the Predynastic Period, but extensive texts only appeared during the Old Kingdom. Hieroglyphs could be written on pottery, carved on stone walls and ivory, and written on paper made from flattened papyrus stems.

Reading and writing were specialised skills mastered by a few trained scribes and administrators. The Journal of Merer, found in 2013 at Wadi al-Jarf, is the earliest known example of an extensive text written on papyrus paper. The ability to read hieroglyphs was lost at the end of Antiquity. Concerted efforts helped French scholar Jean-François Champollion decode the system by 1824.

Hieroglyphs are made up of ideograms, phonograms and determinatives. Ideograms directly represent the item they refer to. Phonograms represent a sound or sounds that can be grouped with other sounds to make up a word. Determinatives are used after groups of phonograms to indicate what type of word is being signified, such as a town. Texts can be written in any direction, but glyphs typically 'look' towards the start of the sentence. A basic alphabet, on the left, is made up from unilateral phonogram signs representing single spoken syllables. The columns on the right include bilaterals, trilaterals, and examples of names and symbols used during the Old Kingdom.

Bibliography

Dieter Arnold, *Building in Egypt. Pharaonic Stone Masonry*, (Oxford University Press: New York/Oxford, 1991).

Iorwerth Eiddon Stephen Edwards, *The Pyramids of Egypt*, Revised edition, (Penguin: 1986).

Ahmed Fakhry, *The Pyramids*, (University of Chicago Press: Chicago, 1961).

Selim Hassan, *The Great Pyramid of Khufu and its Mortuary Chapel, Excavations at Gîza, Season 1938–39*, vol. X, (Government Press: Cairo, 1960).

Dietrich Klemm and Rosemarie Klemm, *The Stones of the Pyramids. Provenance of the Building Stones of the Old Kingdom Pyramids of Egypt*, (De Gruyter: Berlin/New York, 2010).

Mark Lehner, *The Complete Pyramids*, (Thames & Hudson: London, 1997).

Mark Lehner and Zahi Hawass, *Giza and the Pyramids*, (The American University in Cairo Press: Cairo/New York, 2017).

Vito Maragioglio and Celeste Rinaldi, *L'Architettura delle piramidi Menfite. Parte IV, La Grande piramide di Cheope*, (Rapallo, 1965) (Italian text and English translation).

William Matthew Flinders Petrie, *The Pyramids and Temples of Gizeh – 2nd Edition from 1885 Republished in a New and Revised Edition with an Update by Zahi Hawass*, (Histories and Mysteries of Man Ltd: London, 1990).

George Andrew Reisner, *A History of the Giza Necropolis*, I, (Harvard University Press: Cambridge, 1942).

Denys A. Stock, *Experiments in Egyptian Archaeology. Stoneworking Technology in Ancient Egypt*, (Routledge: London/New York, 2003).

Nigel C. Strudwick, *Texts from the Pyramid Age,* (Society of Biblical Literature: Atlanta, 2005).

Miroslav Verner, *The Pyramids. The Mystery, Culture, and Science of Egypt's Great Monuments*, (Grove Press: New York, 2001).

Richard William Howard Vyse, *Operations Carried on at the Pyramids of Gizeh in 1837: with an account of a voyage into Upper Egypt, and an Appendix*, I and II, (James Fraser: London, 1840).

Richard William Howard Vyse, *Operations carried on at the Pyramids of Gizeh in 1837: with an account of a voyage into Upper Egypt, and an Appendix*, III, *Appendix containing a Survey by J. S. Perring of the Pyramids at Abou Roash, and to the southward, including those in the Faiyoum*, (James Fraser: London, 1842).

Christiane Ziegler, Dorothea Arnold and Krzysztof Grzymski (eds.), *Egyptian Art in the Time of the Pyramids*, (Paris/New York/Toronto, 1999).

WEBSITES

AERA: http://www.aeraweb.org/
Giza Archive Project: http://www.gizapyramids.org/
The Upuaut Project: http://cheops.org/

Index

Abu (Elephantine) – see Aswan
Abusir 50, 133, 137-138, 142, 156
Abydos 15-17, 20, 22-23, 124, 134, 151
AERA organisation 185
Alexander the Great 9, 26
Antropogenez.ru Project 129
Architects and builders 38, 55, 65, 81-82,
    85, 98, 110, 112, 114, 119-120, 152,
    157, 160, 185
    Ankhhaf, vizier 76, 120-121, 133, 183
    Hemiunu, Master of Works 77, 121,
        184
    Imhotep, high priest 30, 35, 51, 120
    Ineni 134
    Kha 153
    language and script 198
    Merer, Inspector 124, 133
    Nefermaat, vizier 121
    Senedjemib Inti, vizier 132-133
        Senedjemib Mehi, son 132
Architecture 9, 11-12, 23, 56, 107, 156
    drawings 120
    funerary complexes 27, 32, 53, 116
    principles 153
    royal tombs 54
Astronomy 102, 154-158, 194
    constellations 156
    Imperishable Stars 116, 156-157
    Orion's Belt 103, 155
    precession of the equinoxes 157
    stellar positions 156
    stellar theories 103, 156, 177
    stars 155-157
    Thuban star 157
Aswan (Abu/Elephantine) 124, 127, 131
Aswan dams 12, 182

Basilica San Marco, Venice 166, 168
Bashmurian Revolt (Copts uprising)
    169
Battle of the Pyramids 175
Bedouins 126
Berlin Museum 26, 32
Bible, The 168
Bonaparte, Napoléon 9, 164, 175, 177
Boston Museum of Fine Arts (MFA) 57, 59,
    76, 120, 183
British Museum 100

Caesar, Julius 9
Cairo 66, 174
Cairo Museum 72-74, 124, 126-127, 136,
    150, 182-183

CEA (Alternative Energies and Atomic
    Energy Commission) 193
Churchill, Winston 9
Cleopatra 9
Climate 12-13
Construction methods 8, 32, 37-38, 42,
    44, 46-47, 75, 84-85, 93-94, 101, 105,
    114, 116, 119-
    calculating slopes of faces (seked) 152
    casing stones 32, 47, 74-75, 81-82,
        123, 130, 133, 140-147, 152, 154,
        160, 177, 182
    gable roofs 110-111, 148
    gaps between blocks 82
    gypsum mortar 82
    levers 126, 144
    lifting blocks 140
    masonry joints 91, 130-131
    mortar 43, 125, 131
    quantities of stone used 51, 85, 108,
        125
    ramps 140, 145, 147-150
    scaffolding 126
    step construction 142-143
    stone working 128-130
        Antopogenex.ru Project 129
        cutting and polishing 130
        ISIDA Project 129
        tools 125-129
        architects' 153
        dolerite balls 127-128
        tubular 128-130
Construction workers and craftsmen
    120-122, 125-126, 154
    quarrymen and stonemasons 126
    sculptors 127
    transport 126, 131-150
CPGF (French Geophysical Prospecting
    Campaign) 187-188
Crowns 19, 34
    sekhmenti double crown 19

Dahshur North and South 36, 40-41, 75,
    95, 136, 142-143, 193
Dassault Systèmes 191-192\
Desheret (crown of Lower Egypt) 19, 198
Djedi the magician 27
Dream Stele 164

EDF (Électricité De France) 187
Egyptian Antiquities Organisation 187-189
Egyptian Exploration Fund 179
Egyptian language 198

Egyptian Ministry of State for Antiquities
    9, 123
Egyptian unification 19-20, 22-23, 33-35,
    58
Egyptologists, archaeologists and explorers
    Abd al-Latif al-Baghdadi 171
    Abu al-Salt 171
    Adams, Barbara 15, 195
    Agnew, H.C. 153
    Al-Idrisi 171
    al-Ma'mun, Caliph 88-89, 168-172
    Al-Maqrizi 168
        Al-Khitat, the survey 168, 172
    Alpini, Prospero 174
    Alvarez, Luis Walter 185-186
    al-Ya'qubi 169
    Androsov, Valery Senmuth 129
    Anglure, Lord of 173
    Badawy, Alexander 100, 103
    Baraize, Emile 79
    Baron, Jean-Pierre 189
    Batrawi, Ahmen 49
    Bauval, Robert 103, 155
    Bietak, Manfred 191
    Borchardt, Ludwig 38, 90, 93, 114, 145
    Carter, Howard 17
    Caviglia, Giovanni Battista 88-89, 177
    Champollion, Jean-François 178, 198
    Chevrier, Henri 137
    Choisy, Auguste 142
    Churchward, Albert 103
    Clarke, Somers 127
    Cooperson, Michael 170-171
    Coutelle, Col 176
    Dash, Glen 158, 194-195
    Davison, Nathaniel 112, 175
    Delvaux, Simon 136
    de Sacy, Sylvestre 170-171
    Deslandes, Bruno 33
    Diodorus of Sicily 145
    Dionysius of Tell Mahre 169-171
    Dixon, Waynman 99-100, 152, 178
    Dormion, Gilles 41, 91, 93-95, 104,
        113, 187, 189
    Dunham, Dows 147
    Edgar brothers 189
    Edwards, Amelia 179
    Edwards, I.E.S. 89, 156-157
    el-Mallakh, Kamai 69, 184
    El-Maqrizi 171
    Engelbach, Reginald 127
    Friedman, Florence 33-34
    Friedman, Renée 15, 195

Gantenbrink, Rudolf 100, 103, 189
Goedicke, Hans 155
Goidin, Jean-Patrice 95, 113, 187
Goyon, Georges 29, 66, 68, 93-94, 105, 147, 150, 159
Grant Bey, James 99-100, 152, 178
Greaves, John 174-175
Harrell, James 92
Hassan, Selim 29, 57, 66, 69, 76, 184
Hawass, Zahi 66, 75, 89, 99-100, 185, 189-190, 194
Helal, Hany 192
Hoffman, Michael 15, 195
Houdin, Jean-Pierre 150, 191, 194
Ibn Mammati 171
Ibrahim ibn Wasif Shah 168
Jomard, Edmé François 176
Junker, Hermann 76, 184
Kadry, Ahmed 187
Kawae, Yukinori 194-195
Kérisel, Jean 113
Klemm, Dietrich and Rosemarie 39, 123, 150
Kruglyakov, Oleg 129
Lauer, Jean-Philippe 93-94, 145
Legrain, Georges 149
Lehner, Mark 69, 81, 89, 93-94, 99, 122, 147, 185, 191
    The Complete Pyramids book 191
Lepsius, Karl Richard 32, 65, 86, 142, 177-178
Lightbody, David 59, 78
Maragioglio, Vito 90, 93, 158, 184
Mariette, Auguste 74
Marouard, Gregory 195
Mathieson, Ian 23
Monnier, Franck 46, 78, 96, 99, 110, 148
Münster, Sebastian 172
    Cosmographia 172
Nell, Erin 194
Neubauer, Wolfgang 191
Norden, Frederic Louis 89, 174
O'Connor, David 22
Perring, John Shae 28, 65, 88-89, 100, 108, 112, 176-177
Petrie, William Matthew Flinders 24, 37-38, 41, 77, 82, 84, 96, 100, 111, 113-114, 129, 153, 175-176, 178-179, 182
Puchkov, Alexander 46
Reisner, George Andrew 73, 76, 147, 182-183
Richardson, Robert 190
Rinaldi, Celeste 90, 93, 158, 184
Ruggles, Clive 194
Salt, Henri 89
Sandys, Georges 173, 175
Smyth, Charles Piazzi 99, 153, 176, 179, 182
Sokolov, Alexander 129
Spence, Kate 157
Stadelmann, Rainer 80, 114, 170, 189

Steindorff, Georg 184
Stocks, Denys A. 130
Tallet, Pierre 133, 195
Taylor, John 153, 176, 179, 182
Tayoubi, Mehdi 192
Vasiutin, Nikolai 129
Verd'hurt, Jean-Yves 41
Verner, Miroslav 155
Vyse, Col Howard 28, 65, 77, 88, 96, 100, 108, 112, 176-177, 182
Wheeler, Noel F. 146
Wilkinson, Toby 58
Yoshimura, Sakuji 189
Youssef, Hag Ahmed 69, 184
Elephantine – see Aswan
El-Markha fortifications 126
Engineering 159-161
    creating perpendicular lines 159
    levelling 159
    open spaces in stone structures 160
Excavations 15, 37, 49, 69, 73, 75-76, 82, 88-90, 104, 122, 127-128, 164, 169, 175, 177, 179, 182-185, 195

Faculty of Engineering, Cairo 192
French Ministry of Foreign Affairs 187

Gisr el-Mudir 23
Giza – throughout
    Digital Giza project 192
    triangulation survey 1881 178-179
Giza Mapping Project 122, 191
Giza necropolises 76, 122, 178, 182
Giza Plateau 81, 123, 147, 163, 178, 182, 185, 195
Gods and goddesses
    Geb 34
    Horus the falcon 8, 16-20, 23, 27, 29, 37, 42, 50-51, 57, 184
    Isis 155
    Ma'at 120
    Meskhetiu 156
    Nekhbet the vulture 19, 28
    Nut 34
    Osiris 58, 75, 155
    Re 27, 50-51, 69, 132
    Re-Horakhty 8
    zoomorphic 17
Golden Ratio 153-154
Grand Egyptian Museum 189, 193
Great Pyramid (Akhet Khufu) 28, 48, 57, 59, 61-195
    Boat Museum 69, 71, 136, 184, 189
    boat pits 68-69, 71-73, 136, 148, 184-185, 189
    causeway 64-66, 68, 143, 166, 184
    chambers and passages 85, 88-117, 172, 176, 185, 187, 189
        Campbell's Chamber 109-110, 112
        Davison's Chamber 109, 177
        funerary chambers 82, 89, 135, 182
        hidden chambers 92, 164, 193

        Lady Arbuthnot's Chamber 109
        Nelson's Chamber 109
        Wellington's Chamber 109
    cemeteries 76-77, 183
    corners 82, 85, 159, 182, 194-195
    dimensions and measurements 64-65, 74, 81-82, 84-88, 90, 92, 96, 101, 103, 106, 108, 153, 175-177, 182, 188-189, 194
    entrances 85-87, 116, 166, 172
        tunnel 169-171
    furniture and artefacts 72-73, 183
        Dixon artefacts 99, 178
    graffiti 109, 165, 172
    Grand Gallery 77-78, 87, 89, 91-96, 103-104, 106-107, 110, 112, 170, 172, 174-176, 187, 193-194
    grotto 103-106, 175-176
    inclination of faces (seked) 82, 153-154
    King's Chamber 28, 82, 85, 87-88, 91, 93-95, 99-101, 103, 105-109, 111-113, 135, 153, 170, 174-175, 177-178, 187-189
        antechamber 106-107
        sarcophagus 88, 108, 111-112, 116, 130, 171-174
        structural failure 113-114
    lower internal arrangement 87-89
    main axes 158
    main proportions 153
    mass and density 188
    mortuary temple 62, 64-65, 77, 79-80, 148, 175 , 184
    orientation 156-159
    pavement around 159
    Queen's Chamber 28, 82, 85, 91, 95-101, 103, 107-108, 111, 116, 174-175, 177-178, 186-187, 189-191, 193
    relieving chambers 109-112, 175-177
    sectional view 117
    service shaft 89, 91, 104-106, 114, 166, 172, 175-177
    star/airshafts 59, 99-103, 114, 127, 174, 177-178, 189-190
    subsidiary pyramids 69-75
        queens' pyramids 71, 74-76, 82, 140, 143, 183
    subterranean chamber 88-89, 104, 106, 116, 172
    surveys 81, 84, 142, 173-195
        internal 187
        scientific 173-175, 179, 182, 185-195
        voids 188, 192-194
    tomb of Hetepheres 72-73
    trial passages 75, 77-78, 160, 177
Greek scholars
    Herodotus 27, 57, 65-66, 73-74, 88, 143-145, 165, 166
    Manetho 20, 23, 26
    Ptolemy, Claudia 174
    Strabo 166, 172
Greco-Roman Period 26

Harper's Weekly journal 100
Harvard University 183
  Semitic Museum team 192
Hearst Expedition 182
Hedjet (crown of Upper Egypt) 19, 198
Heit el-Ghurab workers' town 122, 185
Heliopolis temple 27, 35, 50-51, 120, 128,
  155-156
Hellenistic/Ptolemaic Period 26
Hierakonpolis 15-20, 22, 195
Hieroglyphs 17-19, 29, 66, 80, 86, 101,
  109, 124, 150, 165, 170, 178, 198
  deciphering 170, 198
Hildesheim Museum 77, 121, 184
HIP (Heritage Innovation Preservation)
  Institute 192
Hori the scribe 135
Human sacrifice 16

Iconography 19, 23, 42, 140, 164
ISIDA Project 129

Journal of Merer 28, 124, 133, 195, 198

KEK institute (High Energy Accelerator
  Research Organization) 193
King Farouk 182

Levant 13, 18, 174
Looters and robbers 44, 49, 82, 88-89, 97,
  104, 106-107, 112, 169

Marischal Museum, Aberdeen 99
Mastaba tombs 22-23, 30, 76, 120, 132,
  138, 142, 147, 164, 176, 178, 184
  Ankhhaf 76, 183
  Djedhefhor 76
  Hemiunu 77, 184
  Hetepheres II 184
  Hetepherakhti 135
  Horbaef 76
  Idu, Giza 135
  Kawab 76
  Khnumhotep 135
  Khufukhaf 76
  Meresankh II 76
  Neferetkau 76
  Niankhkhnum 135
  numbering system 183
  Ptahhotep, Saqqara 134
  Wepemnefret 76
Materials 122-130, 161
  alabaster 73, 79, 124-125, 182-183
  basalt 64, 66, 125, 130, 138-139, 175
  copper 27, 125, 127-130
  granodiorite 124, 127
  gypsum 82, 125
  limestone 39, 46, 79, 82, 123, 130-131,
    135, 146, 161, 183, 189
  nummulitic limestone 82
  processing 126-131
  quartzite 106-108, 127
  red Aswan granite 30, 82, 112,
    124, 127, 130-132, 147, 161

sandstone 127
  sources 123-126
  structural strengths 161
  wood 126
Mathematics 150-154
  base ten number system 150
  linear measurement system 151-152
  numeracy 151
  365-day calendar 151
Measurements
  British Imperial system 179
  metric system 179, 182
Memphis (White Walls) 20, 22-23, 29,
  34-35, 58, 144
Memphite Necropolis 9, 16, 22, 124, 127,
  156, 164, 177, 184
Middle Ages explorations 168-173
Moscow Mathematical Papyrus 152

Napoleonic Egyptian expedition 85, 164,
  175-177
  Description de l'Égypte 175-176
Naqada I period 15
Naquada (Nubt) 16
Narmer Palette 18-20
National Geographic TV channel 100, 190
National Museum of Scotland 23
Nazlet el-Semman 65-66
Nekhen 15, 17
Neolithic Subpluvial period 12-13
Newton, Isaac 175
Nile rivers and Delta 12-13, 18-19, 36, 59,
  131, 133, 139
  Aswan Dam 12, 182
  floodplain 12, 22, 38, 47, 65-66, 122,
    151, 185
  silt 37, 66, 137, 183, 185
Nile Valley 11-15. 35, 65, 132
Nubian and Sudanese cultures 59

Obama, Barack 9
Obelisks 127-128, 134-136, 149
  unfinished 127-128
Oriental Institute of Chicago 195

Palermo Stone 33-34, 52, 58, 126, 151
Papyrus Anastasi I 135-136, 145
Pharaohs 196-197
  Amenemhat I 29, 66, 138, 165
  Amenhotep II 80
  Den 20
  Djedefre 52, 66, 69, 81, 155
  Djer 33, 58
  Djet 17, 19
  Djoser 11, 20, 23, 29, 32-36, 50, 52,
    58, 82, 99, 114, 120-121, 124, 127,
    129, 142, 154, 160
  Hatshepsut 128, 134
  Hotepsekhemwy 52
  Khafre 20, 52, 55, 57, 64, 78-81, 85,
    114, 122, 124, 130, 146-147, 155-
    156, 159-160, 169, 182, 185-187
  Khasekhemwy 22
  Khufu (Cheops) 19, 20, 23, 26-29, 52,

    55, 57, 59, 62 et seq.
    family members 76
  Menes 18
  Menkaure 20, 51-52, 57, 121-122,
    127, 131, 142, 147, 155-156,
    165-166, 183
  Merenre 124
  Narmer 18
  Neferefre 50, 142
  Ninetjer 52
  Niuserre 20, 57
  Pepi II 55, 57, 114
  Ramesses II 164
  Sahure 57, 137-138
  Sekhemkhet 32, 52, 125, 142
  Senwosret I 29, 138, 165
  Senwosret II 138
  Senwosret III 136
  Shepseskaf 51
  Snefru 20, 26, 35-49, 51-52, 57, 91,
    116, 120-121, 123, 126, 142, 153
  Sourid 168-169
  Teti 59, 161
  Thutmose I 134
  Thutmose IV 80, 164
  Unas 58-59, 124, 131-132, 156, 165
Pharaohs' funerals 22, 69, 184
  rituals 20, 59
Pharaonic culture and system 9, 11-12,
  15-19
  administration and economy 22-23
  ceremonial names 27-28
  facemasks 17
  rituals 17, 23, 33-34, 58
    heb sed ceremony 20, 22, 29, 33-34,
    42, 55, 57-59
    serekh 17-18, 20, 27-28, 41
  symbols and emblems 19-20
    falcon 17-18, 20, 27
    meanings 50-52,
    sema-tawi 19, 57-58
Pharaonic dynasties and regimes 8,
  23, 26
  chronology and dating 23-26
  dynasty '0' Protodynastic period 18, 20,
    24,195
  Early Dynastic Period 18, 20, 23, 25, 50,
    52, 58, 114, 124, 129, 196
  First Intermediate Period 23, 172, 197
  Late Period 26, 197
  Middle Kingdom 23, 26, 42-43, 57, 107,
    127, 138, 152, 165, 197
  New Kingdom 23, 43, 59, 120,
    134-135, 145, 164, 183, 197
  Old Kingdom 16, 20, 23, 26, 28, 37-38,
    41, 49-50, 56, 58-59, 73, 76, 81, 87,
    107, 120-121, 128, 132-134,
    136-138, 146, 150-151, 153-157,
    161, 164-165, 178, 195-196
  Predynastic Period 15-18, 23,
    129, 198
  Second Intermediate Period 23, 155
  Third Intermediate Period 23, 26, 197
  1st dynasty 15, 16-20, 22, 33

2nd dynasty 22-23, 52
3rd dynasty 20, 30, 36, 38, 51-52, 121, 140, 142, 146, 154
4th dynasty 35-36, 50-52, 55, 57, 61, 76, 110, 116, 121, 127, 134, 138, 142-143, 152, 155, 157, 184, 198
5th dynasty 51-52, 57-58, 76, 107-108, 110, 116, 124, 131-132, 134-135, 137-138, 142-143, 151, 157
6th dynasty 56-57, 76, 107-108, 116, 124, 128, 130, 134, 142
12th dynasty 29, 66, 138
18th dynasty 43, 127-128, 134-135, 145, 153
19th dynasty 135, 164
26th dynasty 74
Polish Archaeological Expedition 18
Prince Hardedef 26-27
Prince Khaemwaset 164-165
Princess Henutsen 74
Pyramid Project 186
Pyramid Texts 50-52, 55, 58-59, 103, 111, 154-156
Pyramids – see also Great Pyramid
    Abu Rawash 66, 123
    Bent Pyramid, Dahshur-South (Snefru's) 36-37, 40-46, 49, 57, 94-95, 146, 152, 161, 192-193
    development 29-36
    El-Sinki 146
    Khafre's pyramid 79-81, 85, 119, 123, 125, 130, 146-147, 156, 159, 164, 169, 182, 185-187
    Lisht complex 28, 138
    Meidum Pyramid (False/Collapsed) (Snefru's) 36-43, 47, 49, 82, 91, 94, 140, 142, 145-146, 153, 161
    Menkaure's pyramid, Giza 51-52, 127, 142, 147, 155-156, 165-166, 183
    Merenre's pyramid 124
    Neferirkare's pyramid, Abusir 142
    Niuserre pyramid, Abusir 142
    Red (Northern) Pyramid, Dahshur-North (Snefru's) 36, 42, 46-49, 55, 138
    Sahure's pyramid, Abusir 57, 137-138
    Sekhemkhet pyramid, Saqqara 32, 142
    Senwosret I pyramid, Lisht 138
    Senwosret II pyramid, Lahun 138, 140
    Senwosret III pyramid, Dahshur 136
    Step Pyramid, Saqqara (Djoser's) 11, 20, 29-36, 50, 52, 55, 82, 99, 122, 127, 129, 142, 154, 160
    Teti's pyramid 59, 161
    Unas's pyramid complex, Saqqara 59, 124, 131-132, 165
    unfinished
        Neferefre's Abusir 50, 142
        Zawiyet el-Aryan 'Great Pit' 140, 142-143
        Zawiyet el-Aryan 'layered' 32, 140, 142
Quarries and mines 27, 81, 84, 119, 123, 126, 147-148
    Aswan 27, 108, 124, 127-128, 131-132, 134, 138, 151, 161

Gebel el-Asr 27, 125, 138-139
Hatnub 19, 27, 124-125, 137-138
Maasara 39, 123, 135
Mokattam East 123
Serabit el-Khadim 125-126
Sinai 125, 188
Tura limestone 47, 69, 75, 82, 123-124, 131-133, 135, 146, 161, 183
Umm el-Sawwan 125
Wadi Hammamat 137
Wadi el-Maghara 27
Widan el-Faras (Gebel Qatrani) 64, 125, 138, 151
Queen Hetepheres I 57, 71-73, 125, 182-183
Queen Meritites I 72, 74
    Kawab, son 72, 76

Ramesseum 135
Reconstructions 16, 22-23, 30-31, 34, 41, 46, 56, 62, 64, 93-94, 111, 148-149
Renaissance 120, 154, 161, 163, 173-175
Rhind Mathematical Papyrus 152, 154
Roman Empire 166
Roman scholars
    Pliny the Elder 135, 166
Ruddedet 27

Sahara Desert 12-13, 36
Saïte period 165-166, 172
Saqqara 11, 20, 23, 32, 34, 51, 55, 82, 114, 134-135, 138, 142, 154, 165
Second World War 184
ScanPyramids mission 84, 87, 150, 192-194
Shunet ez-Zebib 20, 22
Slaves 52
Sphinxes 78, 127, 191
    beard 81
    temple 79-81
Stanford Research Institute 187
Statues 20, 26, 34-35, 42, 56-57, 59, 77, 80, 99, 119, 127, 130, 137, 150, 169, 184
Stele of Montuher 164
Stele of Neferperet 135
Stonehenge 8
Supreme Council of Antiquities 185
Surveying techniques and equipment
    carbon 14 dating 25-26, 185
    digital 185
    endoscopic camera 188
    gravimeter 186-188
    ground penetrating radar (GPR) 186-187
    microgravimetric 142
    muography 185, 192-194
    photogrammetry 191-192, 194-195
    radar 189
    robots 100-101, 189-191
        Djedi Rover 101, 190-191
        flying 194
        irobot 190
        Pyramid Rover 100, 190
        Upuaut II 100, 111, 189-190

terrestrial laser scanning 191-192, 194-195
thermography 192-193
3D imaging and models 62, 64, 93, 185, 191-192, 195
Symbolism 50-59, 142, 184, 198

Temple of Deir el-Bahari (Hatshepsut's) 134
Temple of Edfu 121
Temple of Karnak 128, 134, 137
    Great Hypostyle Hall 149
Temple of Ramesses II, Thebes 135
Theban necropolis (El Qurn) 59
Thinis 20
Tomb of Djehutyhotep, Der el-Bersheh 137
Tomb of Ibi, Deir el Gebrawy 130
Tomb of Khentkawes 182
Tomb of Sabn, Qubbet el-Hawa 128
Tomb of vizier Rekhmire 126-127, 145
Tomb of Weni the Elder, Abydos 134
Tourism 65, 169, 172, 189
    Grand Tours 164
Transport of materials 108, 122, 124, 131, 150, 183
    boats/by water 124-126, 128, 131-135,139
    monoliths 113, 134
    muscle power (human and animal) 135-137
    overland 135-140
        lubrication of tracks 137
        sleds 135-140
        slipways 138-139
        wheels 136, 140
    workers employed 122
True north 156-158
Turin Museum 153

UNESCO world heritage sites 9
University of Ain Shams 186
University of California 186
University of Leeds 101, 190
University of Leicester 194
University of Leipzig 183
University of Nagoya 192-193
University of Paris IV-La Sorbonne 195
Upuaut Project 100, 189

Valley of the Kings 59
Vienna Institute for Archaeological Sciences 191

Wadi al-Jarf 123, 126, 139, 195
    papyrus 76, 121, 123-124, 133, 183, 195, 198
Waseda University, Tokyo 189
Wepemnefret, master of the scribes 76
Westcar papyrus 26-27, 101
Wonders of the Ancient World 9, 114, 195
Writing with ink on paper /papyrus 150, 198
    phonetic writing 20, 198

Egyptian people on top of the small pyramid G1c at Giza.
(Franck Monnier)